THE DEATH OF EXPERTISE

PRAISE FOR THE FIRST EDITION OF
THE DEATH OF EXPERTISE

"A highly researched and impassioned book . . . will have many political and news junkies nodding their heads in agreement."

—*Publishers Weekly*

"Tom Nichols is fighting a rear-guard action on behalf of those dangerous people who actually know what they are talking about. In a compelling, and often witty, polemic, he explores why experts are routinely disregarded and what might be done to get authoritative knowledge taken more seriously."

—Sir Lawrence Freedman, Emeritus Professor of War Studies, King's College London, and author of *Strategy*

"We live in a post-fact age, one that's dangerous for a whole host of reasons. Here is a book that not only acknowledges this reality, but takes it head on. Persuasive and well-written, *The Death of Expertise* is exactly the book needed for our times."

—Ian Bremmer, President and Founder, Eurasia Group

"Americans are indifferent to real journalism in forming their opinions, hoaxes prove harder to kill than a slasher-flick monster, and the word 'academic' is often hurled like a nasty epithet. Tom Nichols has put his finger on what binds these trends together: positive hostility to established knowledge. *The Death of Expertise* is trying to turn back this tide."

—Dan Murphy, former Middle East and Southeast Asia Bureau Chief, *The Christian Science Monitor*

"Tom Nichols has written a brilliant, timely, and very original book. He shows how the digital revolution, social media, and the internet have helped to foster a cult of ignorance. Nichols makes a compelling case for reason and rationality in our public and political discourse."
—Robert J. Lieber, Georgetown University, and author of *Retreat and Its Consequences*

"A genial guide through the wilderness of ignorance."
—*Kirkus Reviews*

"Nichols is a forceful and sometimes mordant commentator, with an eye for the apt analogy."
—*Inside Higher Education*

Amazon Best Nonfiction of 2017

THE DEATH OF EXPERTISE

The Campaign against Established
Knowledge and Why It Matters

Second Edition

Tom Nichols

OXFORD
UNIVERSITY PRESS

Oxford University Press is a department of the University of Oxford. It furthers
the University's objective of excellence in research, scholarship, and education
by publishing worldwide. Oxford is a registered trade mark of Oxford University
Press in the UK and certain other countries.

Published in the United States of America by Oxford University Press
198 Madison Avenue, New York, NY 10016, United States of America.

Library of Congress Cataloging-in-Publication Data
Names: Nichols, Thomas M., 1960– author.
Title: The death of expertise : the campaign against established knowledge
and why it matters / Tom Nichols.
Description: Second edition, Updated and expanded edition. |
New York : Oxford University Press, [2024] |
Previous edition published in 2017.
Identifiers: LCCN 2023049382 (print) | LCCN 2023049383 (ebook) |
ISBN 9780197763827 (hb) | ISBN 9780197763834 (pb) | ISBN 9780197763858 (epub)
Subjects: LCSH: Information society—Political aspects. | Knowledge,
Theory of—Political aspects. | Knowledge, Sociology of. | Expertise—Political
aspects. | Education, Higher—Political aspects. | Internet—Political aspects.
Classification: LCC HM851 .N54 2024 (print) | LCC HM851 (ebook) |
DDC 303.48/33—dc23/eng/20231204
LC record available at https://lccn.loc.gov/2023049382
LC ebook record available at https://lccn.loc.gov/2023049383

DOI: 10.1093/oso/9780197763827.001.0001

Paperback printed by Sheridan Books, Inc., United States of America
Hardback printed by Bridgeport National Bindery, Inc., United States of America

For
Lynn Marie Nichols
and
Hope Virginia Nichols
Expert wife and peerless daughter

CONTENTS

PREFACE TO THE UPDATED AND
EXPANDED EDITION

Authors usually prize the opportunity to release another edition of their work. Much like teachers updating a syllabus, as I did when I was still a professor, we take such opportunities to freshen up some of our old stories and introduce a new group of readers to our ideas. (We also get a chance to tidy up some of our errors.) I feel some of that enthusiasm offering this edition of *The Death of Expertise* to you now, whether you are encountering the book for the first time or revisiting it after reading the first edition.

But I also felt some unease in reopening *The Death of Expertise*, because I realize that as dark a picture as I painted several years ago, I underestimated the intensity and breadth of the many assaults on knowledge. (Although I am reluctant to admit it, I am at heart an optimist.) I was far too trusting about whether a crisis might bring those attacks to an end: When I wrote the first edition, and then when I would go on the road to discuss the book, I made clear that I believed that a war, an economic downturn—or even, yes, a pandemic—might be the moment that snaps the public back to its senses.

I was distinctly wrong on all three of these possibilities.

We have now suffered through a pandemic that was brought under control with vaccines developed in record time. In Europe, the largest war since the Nazis went on the march in the early twentieth century continues, as of this writing, without respite or mercy; so far, however, adept international diplomacy has prevented the disaster of a global conflict. The economic collapse that so many feared would follow the pandemic did not come to pass; the United States is (at least for now) experiencing a period of relative economic stability, with slow growth but both inflation and unemployment mostly under control. And yet, ordinary citizens refuse to believe that experts and sensible policymakers had much of a hand in any of these remarkable outcomes. Indeed, they refuse to believe that such outcomes have even happened at all: Many citizens think the vaccines are dangerous, that Russia's invasion of Ukraine is the West's fault, and that the economy is (as always) terrible. The twenty-first-century crisis around expertise, which should have been alleviated by these trials, has somehow gotten *worse.*

The sour distrust of almost everyone and everything around us is rooted in the same sullen narcissism, the same willful rejection of any reality that conflicts with our deeply held beliefs, that underlies the continuing attacks on knowledge. The first version of *The Death of Expertise* came from a blog post and then an article I wrote in late 2013. Even a decade ago, however, I suspected that I was writing about something else, in addition to the problem of knowledge: The attacks on expertise were really the first indications of a global, anti-democratic, populist movement built on rejection of *all* institutions and the dreaded "elites" who ostensibly run them. And because those institutions are the guardrails around classical liberal ideas—rationality, tolerance, informed debate, and cooperation, among others—those ideas fell under the same attack.

I explored the problem of illiberal populism in more detail in a subsequent book, *Our Own Worst Enemy*, in which I tried to illuminate how this know-nothing populism was part of a much larger problem that continues to threaten democracy itself. That work informed some of the rethinking I've done in this new edition of *The Death of Expertise*. I still tie attacks on knowledge to some basic causes, including how our brains work, the commodification of education, the pernicious influence of the Internet, and the erosion of traditional journalism. But after years of additional research, I now give more weight to the influences of narcissism, existential levels of ennui and boredom, and high living standards, all of which contribute to a panoply of deeply mistaken beliefs held by many citizens that experts should be pushed aside and that almost any challenge, from running a lab to running a country, is relatively easy and that almost anyone can do it if they watch enough YouTube videos.

I've therefore returned to *The Death of Expertise* with the even stronger conviction that the defense of knowledge is integral to the defense of democracy. After the COVID-19 pandemic, however, I also felt a responsibility to examine why I was wrong: I never expected that people would reject vaccines—literally choosing to die rather than let go of their tribal affiliations—or that prominent scientists would not only be attacked for their views but would have to travel with armed security guards. A decade ago, I wrote with concern, but also with a certain amount of bemusement at flat-earther foolishness. I am far more alarmed today.

I've retained many of the anecdotes and stories from the first edition, as a reminder that the foundations for the death of expertise were set long ago. In the years since the book first appeared, I've accumulated many more such stories, some of them heartbreaking: A pediatric surgeon in the Midwest, for example, told me of a family who demanded that he perform a risky operation on a small child. When he refused to take a scalpel to a toddler on demand, the parents informed him that they had "done their own research," that they were clients engaging him for a specific service, and that they did not need his advice. When he demurred, they went to another surgeon who agreed to do the job. The child, in the end, was gravely injured.

I have resisted the temptation to bombard you with too many more of these kinds of stories, but I have added some new material, and a new chapter on the COVID crisis. Nonetheless, I think it's important to remember that the problems we face now have been with us for some time, and they certainly predate the maelstrom of anti-expert hostility that arose during Donald Trump's presidential campaign and the subsequent battle to contain the pandemic. (Indeed, the death of expertise created the environment in which politicians such as Trump could flourish.) Although I have made some exceptions for notable new participants in the attacks on knowledge—people such as Elon Musk and Robert F. Kennedy, Jr., to name but two— the general danger we face today stems from trends that have been steadily poisoning public life in the United States and other nations for decades.

I am grateful to Oxford University Press and to my editor, David McBride, for the invitation to update and expand *The Death of Expertise*, and I wish to thank my editors at *The Atlantic* (and especially Isabel Fattal) for their understanding as I completed this new edition. Many of the people who helped me organize and think about the book a decade ago (including Dave) returned over the past few years to help me think about the book anew, but I am very grateful to the readers who gave the work such impact in the United States and around the world. (As of 2023, *The Death of Expertise* has been translated into fourteen languages.) Your many questions and comments were not only thought-provoking and helpful, but were part of the inspiration to issue a new edition.

To new readers, welcome. And to returning readers, I can only say that I wish I had better news. The campaign against established knowledge is stronger than ever. Facts and reason are under siege on multiple fronts. The democratic stability that relies on a thoughtful and informed public is dissolving before our eyes; the dismissal of learning and expertise is now an ingrained habit of mind that is crippling the ability of millions of citizens in democratic nations to exercise even basic civic and social responsibilities in their communities. I only hope that this book remains useful for anyone trying to find their footing in the ongoing blizzard of irrationality, misinformation, and outright lies that still surround us.

Tom Nichols
Autumn 2023

PREFACE TO THE 2017 EDITION

"The death of expertise" is one of those phrases that grandly announces its own self-importance. It's a title that risks alienating a lot of people before they even open the book, almost daring the reader to find a mistake in it somewhere just to take the author down a peg. I understand that reaction, because I feel much the same way about such sweeping pronouncements. Our cultural and literary life is full of premature burials of everything: shame, common sense, manliness, femininity, childhood, good taste, literacy, the Oxford comma, and so on. The last thing we all need is one more encomium for something we know isn't quite dead.

While expertise isn't dead, however, it's in trouble. Something is going terribly wrong. The United States is now a country obsessed with the worship of its own ignorance. It's not just that people don't know a lot about science or politics or geography; they don't, but that's an old problem. And really, it's not even a problem, insofar as we live in a society that works because of a division of labor, a system designed to relieve each of us of having to know about everything. Pilots fly airplanes, lawyers file lawsuits, doctors prescribe medication. None of us is a Da Vinci, painting the *Mona Lisa* in the morning and designing helicopters at night. That's as it should be.

No, the bigger problem is that we're *proud* of not knowing things. Americans have reached a point where ignorance, especially of anything related to public policy, is an actual virtue. To reject the advice of experts is to assert autonomy, a way for Americans to insulate their increasingly fragile egos from ever being told they're wrong about anything. It is a new Declaration of Independence: no longer do we hold *these* truths to be self-evident, we hold *all* truths to be self-evident, even the ones that aren't true. All things are knowable and every opinion on any subject is as good as any other.

This isn't the same thing as the traditional American distaste for intellectuals and know-it-alls. I'm a professor, and I get it: most people don't like professors. When I began my teaching career nearly three decades ago, it was at a college not far from my hometown, and so I would drop in now and then to say hello and visit a small tavern owned by my brother. One evening, after I left, a patron turned to my brother and said, "He's a professor, huh? Well, he seems like a good guy anyway." If you're in my profession, you get used to that.

But that's not why I wrote this book. Intellectuals who get outraged over zingers about the uselessness of intellectuals should find a different line of work. I've been a teacher, a political adviser, a subject-matter expert for both government and private industry, and a commenter on various media. I'm used to people disagreeing with me; in fact, I encourage it. Principled, informed arguments are a sign of intellectual health and vitality in a democracy.

Rather, I wrote this because I'm worried. We no longer have those principled and informed arguments. The foundational knowledge of the average American is now so low that it has crashed through the floor of "uninformed," passed "misinformed" on the way down, and is now plummeting to "aggressively wrong." People don't just believe dumb things; they actively resist further learning rather than let go of those beliefs. I was not alive in the Middle Ages, so I cannot say it is unprecedented, but within my living memory I've never seen anything like it.

That's not to say that this is the first time I've ever thought about this subject. Back in the late 1980s, when I was working in Washington, D.C., I learned how quickly people in even casual conversation would immediately instruct me in what needed to be done in any number of areas, especially in my own areas of arms control and foreign policy. (As usual, it was what "they" should do, as in "they ought to. . . .") I was young and not yet a seasoned expert, but I was astonished at the way people who did not have the first clue about those subjects would confidently direct me on how best to make peace between Moscow and Washington.

To some extent, this was understandable. Politics invites discussion. And especially during the Cold War, when the stakes were global annihilation, people wanted to be heard. I accepted that this was just part of the cost of doing business in the public policy world. Over time, I found that other specialists in various policy areas had the same experiences, with laypeople subjecting them to ill-informed disquisitions on taxes, budgets, immigration, the environment, and many other subjects. If you're a policy expert, it goes with the job.

In later years, however, I started hearing the same stories from doctors. And from lawyers. And from teachers. And, as it turns out, from many other professionals whose advice is usually not contradicted easily. These stories astonished me: they were not about patients or clients asking sensible questions, but about those same patients and clients actively telling professionals why their advice was wrong. In every case, the idea that the expert knew what he or she was doing was dismissed almost out of hand.

Worse, what I find so striking today is not that people dismiss expertise, but that they do so with such frequency, on so many issues, and with such *anger*. Again, it may be that attacks on expertise are more obvious due to the ubiquity of the Internet, the undisciplined nature of conversation on social media, or the demands of the twenty-four-hour news cycle. But there is a self-righteousness and fury to this new rejection of expertise that suggest, at least to me, that this isn't just mistrust or questioning or the pursuit of alternatives: it is narcissism, coupled to a disdain for expertise as some sort of exercise in self-actualization.

This makes it all the harder for experts to push back and to insist that people come to their senses. No matter what the subject, the argument always goes down the drain of an enraged ego and ends with minds unchanged, sometimes with professional relationships or even friendships damaged. Instead of arguing, experts today are supposed to accept such disagreements as, at worst, an honest difference of opinion. We are supposed to "agree to disagree," a phrase now used indiscriminately as little more than a conversational fire extinguisher. And if we insist that not everything is a matter of opinion, that some things are right and others are wrong . . . well, then we're just being jerks, apparently.

It's possible, I suppose, that I am merely a symptom of generational change. I grew up in the 1960s and 1970s, an era when perhaps too much deference was paid to experts. These were the heady days when America was at the forefront of not only science but also international leadership. My parents were knowledgeable but uneducated people who, like most Americans, assumed that the same people who put a man on the moon were probably right about most other important things. I was not raised in an environment of utter obedience to authority, but in general, my family was typical in trusting that the people who worked in specialized fields, from podiatry to politics, knew what they were doing.

As critics of expertise rightly point out, in those days we were trusting the people who landed Neil Armstrong in the Sea of Tranquility, but who also landed a lot of less famous American men in places like Khe Sanh and the Ia Drang Valley in Vietnam. The public's trust, both in experts and political leaders, was not only misplaced but abused.

Now, however, we've gone in the other direction. We do not have a healthy skepticism about experts: instead, we actively resent them, with many people assuming that experts are wrong simply by virtue of being experts. We hiss at the "eggheads"—a pejorative coming back into vogue—while instructing our doctors about which medications we need or while insisting to teachers that our children's answers on a test are right even if they're wrong. Not only is everyone as smart as everyone else, but we all think we're the smartest people ever.

And we couldn't be more wrong.

I have many people to thank for their assistance with this book, and many more to absolve from any association with its views or conclusions.

I first wrote a post called "The Death of Expertise" for my personal blog, *The War Room*, back in 2013. It was reproduced at an online magazine called *The Federalist*, and shortly thereafter David McBride at Oxford University Press saw the article and contacted me about turning its main thesis into a book. His editorial guidance and advice were key to fleshing out the argument at greater length, and I am grateful to him and to Oxford, as well as to the anonymous reviewers of the proposal, for bringing the book to fruition.

I am fortunate to work at the US Naval War College, and many of my colleagues there, including David Burbach, David Cooper, Steve Knott, Derek Reveron, and Paul Smith, among others, provided comments and material. But the opinions and conclusions in this book are mine: they do not in any way represent the views of any other institution, nor of any agency of the US government.

Several friends and correspondents in various professions were kind enough to provide comments, read chapters, or to provide answers to a variety of questions outside my area of expertise, including Andrew Facini, Ron Granieri, Tom Hengeveld, Dan Kaszeta, Kevin Kruse, Rob Mickey, Linda Nichols, Brendan Nyhan, Will Saletan, Larry Sanger, John Schindler, Josh Sheehan, Robert Trobich, Michael Weiss, Salena Zito, and especially Dan Murphy and Joel Engel. I owe special thanks to David Becker, Nick Gvosdev, and Paul Midura for their comments on several drafts of the manuscript.

I am very grateful to the Harvard Extension School, for not only the opportunity to teach in the program, but also the many excellent student research assistants that Extension provides to its faculty. Kate Arline was an invaluable assistant on this project: she fielded even some of the oddest queries quickly and with aplomb. (Want to know how many fast-food joints have opened in America since 1959? Kate can find out.) Any of the factual errors or misinterpretations in this book, however, are mine and mine alone.

Writing a book can be a wonderful and engaging experience for the author, but less so for the people around him. My wife, Lynn, and my daughter, Hope, were as patient as ever with me while I worked on this volume, and I owe them a significant debt of gratitude for putting up with me while I was writing. This book is dedicated to both of them, with love.

Finally, I must thank the people who assisted me with this book but who, for obvious reasons, wish to remain anonymous. I am grateful to the many medical professionals, journalists, lawyers, educators, policy analysts, scientists, scholars, military experts, and others who shared their experiences and contributed their stories to this book. I could not have written it without them.

I hope in some way this book helps them and other experts in their work. But in the end, the clients of all professionals are the people of the society in which they live, and so I especially hope this book helps my fellow citizens in better using and understanding the experts on whom we all rely. More than anything, I hope this work contributes to bridging the rift between experts and laypeople that in the long run threatens not only the well-being of millions of Americans, but also the survival of our democratic experiment.

Tom Nichols
Winter 2016

Introduction

The Death of Expertise

There is a cult of ignorance in the United States, and there always has been. The strain of anti-intellectualism has been a constant thread winding its way through our political and cultural life, nurtured by the false notion that democracy means that "my ignorance is just as good as your knowledge."

Isaac Asimov

In the early 1990s, a small group of "AIDS denialists," including a University of California professor named Peter Duesberg, argued against virtually the entire medical establishment's consensus that the human immunodeficiency virus (HIV) was the cause of Acquired Immune Deficiency Syndrome. Science thrives on such counterintuitive challenges, but there was no evidence for Duesberg's beliefs, which turned out to be baseless. Once researchers found HIV, doctors and public health officials were able to save countless lives through measures aimed at preventing its transmission.

The Duesberg business might have ended as just another quirky theory defeated by research. The history of science is littered with such dead ends. In this case, however, a discredited idea nonetheless managed to capture the attention of a national leader, with deadly results. Thabo Mbeki, then the president of South Africa, seized on the idea that AIDS was caused not by a virus but by other factors, such as malnourishment and poor health, and so he rejected offers of drugs and other forms of assistance to combat HIV infection in South Africa.

Mbeki relented before he left office in 2008, but not before his fixation on AIDS denialism ended up costing, by the estimates of doctors at the Harvard School of Public Health, well over three hundred thousand lives and the births of some thirty-five thousand HIV-positive children whose infections could have been avoided.[1] Mbeki, to this day, thinks he was on to something.

Many Americans might scoff at this kind of ignorance, but they shouldn't be too confident in their own abilities. In 2014, the *Washington Post* polled Americans about whether the United States should engage in military intervention in the wake of the first Russian invasion of Ukraine in 2014. The United States and Russia are former Cold War adversaries, each armed with hundreds of long-range nuclear weapons. A military conflict in the center of Europe, right on the Russian border, carries a risk of igniting World War III, with potentially catastrophic consequences. And yet only one in six Americans—and fewer than one in four college graduates—could identify Ukraine on a map. Ukraine is the largest country entirely in Europe, but the median respondent was still off by about 1,800 miles. In 2022, Russia launched a much larger invasion and tried to capture all of Ukraine—a nation that borders four members of NATO—sparking the largest war in Europe since 1939. And yet only a third of Americans today know where "Ukraine" is located.[2]

Map tests are easy to fail. Far more unsettling is that this lack of knowledge did not stop respondents from expressing fairly pointed views about the matter. Actually, this is an understatement: the public not only expressed strong views, but respondents showed special enthusiasm for military intervention in Ukraine *in direct proportion to their lack of knowledge about Ukraine*. Put another way, people who thought Ukraine was located in Latin America or Australia were the most enthusiastic about the use of US military force.[3]

These are dangerous times. Never have so many people had so much access to so much knowledge and yet have been so resistant to learning anything. In the United States and other developed nations, otherwise intelligent people denigrate intellectual achievement and reject the advice of experts. Not only do increasing numbers of laypeople lack basic knowledge, they reject fundamental rules of evidence and refuse to learn how to make a logical argument. In doing so, they risk throwing away centuries of accumulated knowledge and undermining the practices and habits that allow us to develop new knowledge.

This is more than a natural skepticism toward experts. I fear we are witnessing the *death of the ideal of expertise* itself, a Google-fueled, Wikipedia-based, blog-sodden collapse of any division between professionals and laypeople, students and teachers, knowers and wonderers—in other words, between those of any achievement in an area and those with none at all.

Attacks on established knowledge and the subsequent rash of poor information in the general public are occasionally amusing. Sometimes they're even hilarious. Late-night comedians have made a cottage industry of asking people questions that reveal their ignorance about their own strongly held ideas, their attachment to fads, and their unwillingness to admit their own cluelessness about current events. It's mostly harmless when people emphatically say, for example, that they're avoiding gluten and then admit that they have no idea what gluten is. And let's face it: watching people confidently improvise opinions about ludicrous scenarios like whether "Margaret Thatcher's absence at Coachella is beneficial in terms of North Korea's decision to launch a nuclear weapon" never gets old.

When life and death are involved, however, it's a lot less funny. The clownish antics of antivaccine entertainers such as Jenny McCarthy or Nicki Minaj undeniably make for great television or for a fun afternoon of reading on social media. (In a strange mini-drama in 2021, Minaj claimed that she had a cousin in Trinidad whose friend received the COVID vaccine and then suffered from swollen testicles and impotence.) [4] The price of AIDS denialism and COVID vaccine hesitation have already been immense, but the continued activism of uninformed celebrities and other public figures spreading myths and misinformation about vaccines is an ongoing danger to millions of people, and especially children, who could suffer preventable afflictions like measles and whooping cough.

The growth of such stubborn ignorance in the midst of the Information Age cannot be explained away as merely the result of poor education or a lack of access to sources of reliable news. Many of the people who campaign against established knowledge are otherwise adept and successful in their daily lives. In some ways, it is all *worse* than ignorance: it is unfounded arrogance, the outrage of an increasingly narcissistic culture that cannot endure even the slightest hint of inequality of any kind.

By the "death of expertise," I do not mean the death of actual expert abilities, the knowledge of specific things that sets some people apart from others in various areas. There will always be doctors and diplomats, lawyers and engineers, and many other specialists in various fields. On a day-to-day basis, the world cannot function without them. If we break a bone or get arrested, we call a doctor or a lawyer. When we travel, we take it for granted that the pilot knows how airplanes work. If we run into trouble overseas, we call a consular official who we assume will know what to do.

These concessions to the need for specialized assistance, however, only represent a reliance on experts as technicians. They are not part of a *dialogue* between experts and the larger community, but the use of established knowledge as an off-the-shelf convenience as needed and only so far as desired. Stitch this cut in my leg, but don't lecture me about my diet. (More than two-thirds of Americans are overweight.) Help me beat this tax problem, but don't remind me that I should have a will. (Roughly half of Americans with children haven't bothered to write one.) Keep my country safe, but don't confuse me with the costs and calculations of national security. (Most US citizens do not have even a remote idea of how much the United States spends on its armed forces.)

Such choices, from a nutritious diet to national defense, require a conversation between citizens and experts, but citizens are deeply resistant to having that conversation. They'd rather believe they've gained enough information to make all of their decisions on their own, and in some cases, when it comes to national policy, they seem uninterested in making any decisions at all.

On the other hand, many experts, and particularly those in the academy, have abandoned their duty to engage with the public. They have retreated into jargon and irrelevance, preferring to interact only with each other. Meanwhile, the people holding the middle ground to whom we often refer as "public intellectuals"—I'd like to think I'm one of them—are becoming as frustrated and polarized as the rest of society.

The death of expertise is not just a rejection of existing knowledge. It is fundamentally a rejection of science and dispassionate rationality, which are the foundations of modern civilization. It is a sign, as the art critic Robert Hughes once described late twentieth-century America, of "a polity obsessed with therapies and filled with distrust of formal politics," chronically "skeptical of authority" and "prey to superstition." We have come full circle from a premodern age, in which folk wisdom filled unavoidable gaps in human knowledge, through a period of rapid development based heavily on specialization and expertise, and now to a postindustrial, information-oriented world where all citizens believe themselves to be experts on everything.

Any assertion of expertise from an actual expert, meanwhile, produces an explosion of anger from certain quarters of the American public, who immediately complain that such claims are nothing more than fallacious "appeals to authority," sure signs of dreadful "elitism," and an obvious effort to use credentials to stifle the dialogue required by a "real" democracy. Americans now believe that having equal rights in a political system also means that each person's opinion about anything must be accepted as equal to anyone else's. This is the credo of a fair number of people despite being obvious nonsense. It is a flat assertion of actual equality that is always illogical, sometimes funny, and often dangerous. This book, then, is about expertise. Or, more accurately, it is about the relationship between experts and citizens in a democracy, why that relationship is collapsing, and what all of us, citizens and experts, might do about it.

The immediate response from most people when confronted with the death of expertise is to blame the Internet. Professionals, especially, tend to point to the Internet as the culprit when faced with clients and customers who think they know better. As we'll see, that's not entirely wrong, but it is also too simple an explanation. Attacks on established knowledge have a long pedigree, and the Internet is only the most recent tool in a recurring problem that in the past misused television, radio, the printing press, and other innovations the same way.

So why all the fuss? What exactly has changed so dramatically for me to have written this book and for you to be reading it? Is this really the "death of expertise," or is this nothing more than the usual complaints from intellectuals that no one listens to them despite their self-anointed status as the smartest people in the room? Maybe it's nothing more than the anxiety about the masses that arises among professionals after each cycle of social or technological change. Or maybe it's just a typical expression of the outraged vanity of overeducated, elitist professors like me.

Indeed, maybe the death of expertise is a sign of progress. Educated professionals, after all, no longer have a stranglehold on knowledge. The secrets of life are no longer hidden in giant marble mausoleums, the great libraries of the world whose halls are intimidating even to the relatively few people who can visit them. Under such conditions in the past, there was less stress between experts and laypeople, but only because citizens were simply unable to challenge experts in any substantive way. Moreover, there were few public venues in which to mount such challenges in the era before mass communications.

Participation in political, intellectual, and scientific life until the early twentieth century was far more circumscribed, with debates about science, philosophy, and public policy all conducted by a small circle of educated males with pen and ink. Those were not exactly the Good Old Days, and they weren't that long ago. The time when most people didn't finish high school, when very few went to college, and when only a tiny fraction of the population entered professions is still within living memory of many Americans.

Social changes only in the past half century finally broke down old barriers of race, class, and sex not only between Americans in general but also between uneducated citizens and elite experts. A wider circle of debate meant more knowledge but more social friction. Universal education, the greater empowerment of women and minorities, the growth of a middle class, and increased social mobility all threw a minority of experts and the majority of citizens into direct contact, after nearly two centuries in which they rarely had to interact with each other.

And yet the result has not been a greater respect for knowledge, but the growth of an irrational conviction among Americans that everyone is as smart as everyone else. This is the opposite of education, which should aim to make people, no matter how smart or accomplished they are, learners for the rest of their lives. Rather, we now live in a society where the acquisition of even a little learning is the endpoint, rather than the beginning, of education. And this is a dangerous thing.

WHAT'S AHEAD

In the chapters that follow, I'll suggest several sources of this problem, some of which are rooted in human nature, others that are unique to America, and some that are the unavoidable product of modernity and affluence.

In the next chapter, I'll discuss the notion of an "expert" and whether conflict between experts and laypeople is all that new. What does it even mean to be an expert? When faced with a tough decision on a subject outside of your own background or experience, whom would you ask for advice? (If you don't think you need any advice but your own, you're likely one of the people who inspired me to write this book.)

In chapter 2, I'll explore why conversation in America has become so exhausting not just between experts and ordinary citizens, but among everyone. If we're honest, we all would admit that any of us can be annoying, even infuriating, when we talk about things that mean a great deal to us, especially regarding beliefs and ideas to which we're firmly attached. Many of the obstacles to the working relationship between experts and their clients in society rest in basic human weaknesses, and in this chapter we'll start by considering the natural barriers to better understanding.

We all suffer from problems, for example, like "confirmation bias," the natural tendency to accept only evidence that confirms what we already believe. Personal experiences, prejudices, fears, and even phobias—all of them prevent us from accepting expert advice. If we think a certain number is lucky, no mathematician can tell us otherwise; if we believe flying is dangerous, even reassurance from an astronaut or a fighter pilot will not allay our fears. And some of us, as indelicate as it might be to say it, are not intelligent enough to know when we're wrong, no matter how good our intentions. Just as we are not all equally able to carry a tune or draw a straight line, many people simply cannot recognize the gaps in their own knowledge or understand their own inability to construct a logical argument.

Education is supposed to help us to recognize problems like "confirmation bias" and to overcome the gaps in our knowledge so that we can be better citizens. Unfortunately, the modern American university, and the way students and their parents treat it as a generic commodity, is now part of the problem. In chapter 3 I'll discuss why the broad availability of a college education—paradoxically—is making many people think they've become smarter when in fact they've gained only an illusory intelligence bolstered by a degree of dubious worth. When students become valued clients instead of learners, they gain a great deal of self-esteem, but precious little knowledge; worse, they do not develop the habits of critical thinking that would allow them to continue to learn and to evaluate the kinds of complex issues on which they will have to deliberate and vote as citizens.

The modern era of technology and communications is empowering great leaps in knowledge, but it's also enabling and reinforcing our human failings. While the Internet doesn't explain everything about the death of expertise, it explains quite a lot of it, at least in the twenty-first century. In chapter 4, I'll examine how the greatest source of knowledge in human history since Gutenberg stained his fingers has become as much a platform for attacks on established knowledge as a defense against them. The Internet is a magnificent repository of knowledge, and yet it's also the source and enabler of a spreading epidemic of misinformation. Not only is the Internet making many of us dumber, it's making us meaner: alone behind their keyboards, people argue rather than discuss, and insult rather than listen.

In a free society, journalists are, or should be, among the most important referees in the great scrum between ignorance and learning. And what happens when citizens demand to be entertained instead of informed? We'll look at these unsettling questions in chapter 5.

We count on the media to keep us informed, to separate fact from fiction, and to make complicated matters comprehensible to people who do not have endless amounts of time and energy to keep up with every development in a busy world. Professional journalists, however, face new challenges in the Information Age. In an earlier time, even a half-century ago, journalists and editors had to make hard choices about what should claim inches on a newspaper page and minutes of broadcast time on radio and television. Today, cable and broadband provide virtually bandwidth space for news, but consumers expect all of that space to be filled instantaneously, to be updated continuously, and to be entertaining—despite the reality that there are not enough hours in the day for them to process all of it.

In this hypercompetitive media environment, editors and producers no longer have the patience—or the financial luxury—to allow journalists to develop their own expertise or deep knowledge of a subject. Nor is there any evidence that most news consumers want such detail. Experts are often reduced to sound bites or "pull quotes," if they are consulted at all. And everyone involved in the news industry knows that if the reports aren't pretty or glossy or entertaining enough, the fickle viewing public can find other, less taxing alternatives with the click of a mouse or the press of a button on a television remote.

Experts are not infallible. They have made terrible mistakes, with ghastly consequences. To defend the role of expertise in modern America is to invite a litany of these disasters and errors: thalidomide, Vietnam, the *Challenger* space shuttle disaster, the dire warnings about the dietary hazards of eggs. (Go ahead and enjoy them again. They're off the list of things that are bad for you.) Experts, understandably, retort that this is the equivalent of remembering one plane crash and ignoring billions of safely traveled air miles. This rejoinder may be true, but sometimes airplanes *do* crash, and sometimes they crash because an expert screwed up.

In chapter 6, I'll consider what happens when experts are wrong. Experts can be wrong in many ways, from outright fraud to well-intentioned but arrogant overconfidence in their own abilities. And sometimes, like other human beings, they just make mistakes. It is important for laypeople to understand, however, how and why experts can err, not only to make citizens better consumers of expert advice but also to reassure the public about the ways in which experts try and police themselves and their work. Otherwise, expert errors become fodder for ill-informed arguments that leave specialists resentful of attacks on their profession and laypeople fearful that the experts have no idea what they're doing.

When I wrote the first edition of *The Death of Expertise*, I was confident that a major crisis would remind people how much they rely on experts. After all, in the aftermath of two world wars, experts rebuilt the planetary economy, conquered a slew of diseases, beat back global poverty, and raised living standards faster and higher than any time in human history. And when a once-in-a-lifetime pandemic arrived, scientists and governments managed to produce a vaccine and avert more death (and a possible global economic meltdown) within a few years.

And yet, the COVID pandemic served only to deepen distrust between experts, policymakers, and ordinary citizens. In chapter 7, we will consider the failures and mistakes from government and expert communities, and how they combined with the preexisting suspicion of expertise to overshadow the successes of the global response to COVID.

Finally, in the conclusion I'll raise the most dangerous aspect of the death of expertise: how the narcissistic rejection of established knowledge and the collapse of critical thinking has undermined American democracy. The United States is a republic, in which the people designate others to make decisions on their behalf. Those elected representatives cannot master every issue, and they rely on experts and professionals to help them. Despite what many people think, experts and policymakers are not the same people, and to confuse the two, as Americans often do, corrodes trust among experts, citizens, and political leaders, all of whom must cooperate to make democracy work

Experts advise. Elected leaders decide. If they are to judge the performance of the experts and the decisions of their representatives, laypeople must familiarize themselves with the issues at hand. This does not mean that every American must engage in deep study of policy, but if citizens do not bother to gain basic literacy in the issues that affect their lives, they abdicate control over those issues whether they intended to or not. And when voters lose control of these important decisions, they risk not only the sudden hijacking of their democracy by ignorant demagogues, but the more quiet and gradual decay of their democratic institutions into authoritarian technocracy.

Experts, too, have important responsibilities in a democracy, and they've been shirking those duties in recent decades. Where public intellectuals (often in tandem with journalists) once strove to make important issues understandable to laypeople, educated elites now increasingly speak only to each other. Citizens, to be sure, reinforce this reticence by *arguing* rather than *questioning*—an important difference—but that does not relieve experts of their duty to serve society and to think of their fellow citizens as their clients rather than as annoyances.

Experts have a responsibility to educate. Voters have a responsibility to learn. In the end, regardless of how much advice the professionals might provide, only the public can decide the direction of the important policy choices facing their nation. Only voters can resolve among the choices that affect their families and their country, and only they bear the ultimate responsibility for those decisions.

But the experts have an obligation to help. That's why I wrote this book.

Chapter 1

Experts and Citizens

WASHINGTON, DC—Citing years of frustration over their advice being misunderstood, misrepresented or simply ignored, America's foremost experts in every field collectively tendered their resignation Monday.

The Onion

A NATION OF EXPLAINERS

We've all met them. They're our coworkers, our friends, our family members. They are young and old, rich and poor, some with education, others armed only with a laptop or a library card. But they all have one thing in common: they are ordinary people who believe they are actually troves of knowledge. Convinced that they are more informed than the experts, more broadly knowledgeable than the professors, and more insightful than the gullible masses, they are the explainers who are more than happy to enlighten the rest of us about everything from the history of imperialism to the dangers of vaccines.

We accept such people and put up with them not least because we know that deep down, they usually mean well. We even have a certain affection for them. The 1980s television sitcom *Cheers*, for example, immortalized the character of Cliff Clavin, the Boston mailman and barfly who was an expert on everything. Cliff, like his real-life counterparts, prefaced every statement with "studies have shown" or "it's a known fact." Viewers loved Cliff because everyone knew someone like him: the cranky uncle at a holiday dinner, the young student home from that crucial first year of college.

We could find such people endearing because they were quirky exceptions in a country that otherwise respected and relied on the views of experts. But something has changed over the past few decades. The public space is increasingly dominated by a loose assortment of poorly informed people, many of them autodidacts who are disdainful of formal education and dismissive of experience. "If experience is necessary for being president," the cartoonist and author Scott Adams tweeted during the 2016 election, "name a political topic I can't master in one hour under the tutelage of top experts," as though a discussion with an expert is like copying information from one computer drive to another. A kind of intellectual Gresham's Law is gathering momentum: where once the rule was "bad money drives out good," we now live in an age where misinformation pushes aside knowledge.

This is a very bad thing for not only the well-being of billions of people but also the stability of democratic governments. A modern society cannot function without a social division of labor and a reliance on experts, professionals, and intellectuals. (For the moment, I will use these three words interchangeably.) No one is an expert on everything. No matter what our aspirations, we are bound by the reality of time and the undeniable limits of our talent. We prosper because we specialize, and because we develop mechanisms, practices, and institutions that allow us to trust each other in those specializations.

In the early 1970s, the science fiction writer Robert Heinlein issued a dictum, often quoted since, that "specialization is for insects." Truly capable human beings, he wrote, should be able to do almost anything from changing a diaper to commanding a warship. It is a noble sentiment that celebrates human adaptability and resilience, but it's wrong. There's a reason we don't do things that way anymore. While there was once a time when every homesteader lumbered his own trees and built his own house, this was not only was inefficient, but produced only rudimentary housing. When we build skyscrapers, we do not expect the metallurgist who knows what goes into a girder, the architect who designs the building, and the glazier who installs the windows to be the same person. That's why we can enjoy the view from a hundred floors above a city: each expert, although possessing some overlapping knowledge, respects the professional abilities of many others and concentrates on doing what he or she knows best. Their trust and cooperation lead to a final product greater than anything they could have produced alone.

The fact of the matter is that we cannot function without admitting the limits of our knowledge and trusting in the expertise of others. We sometimes resist this conclusion because it undermines our sense of independence and autonomy. We want to believe we are capable of making all kinds of decisions, and we chafe at the person who corrects us, or tells us we're wrong, or instructs us in things we don't understand. This natural human reaction among individuals is dangerous when it becomes a shared characteristic among entire societies.

IS THIS NEW?

Is knowledge in more danger, and are conversation and debate really all that more difficult today than they were fifty or a hundred years ago? Intellectuals are always complaining about the denseness of their fellow citizens, and laypeople have always distrusted the pointy-heads and experts. How new is this problem, and how seriously should we take it?

Some of this conflict in the public square is just so much predictable noise, now amplified by the Internet and social media. The Internet gathers factoids and half-baked ideas, and it then splays all that bad information and poor reasoning all over the electronic world. (Imagine what the 1920s would have sounded like if every crank in every small town had his own radio station.) Maybe it's not that people are any dumber or any less willing to listen to experts than they were a hundred years ago: it's just that we can hear them all now.

Besides, a certain amount of conflict between people who know some things and people who know other things is inevitable. There were probably arguments between the first hunters and gatherers over what to have for dinner. As various areas of human achievement became the province of professionals, disagreements were bound to grow and to become sharper. And as the distance between experts and the rest of the citizenry grew, so did the social gulf and the mistrust between them. All societies, no matter how advanced, have an undercurrent of resentment against educated elites, as well as persistent cultural attachments to folk wisdom, urban legends, and other irrational but normal human reactions to the complexity and confusion of modern life.

Democracies, with their noisy public spaces, have always been especially prone to challenges to established knowledge. Indeed, they're more prone to challenges to established *anything*: it's one of the characteristics that makes them "democratic." Even in the ancient world, democracies were known for their fascination with change and progress. Thucydides, for example, described the democratic Athenians of the fifth century BCE as a restless people "addicted to innovation," and centuries later, St. Paul found that the Athenians "spent their time doing nothing but talking about and listening to the latest ideas." This kind of restless questioning of orthodoxy is celebrated and protected in a democratic culture.

The United States, with its intense focus on the liberties of the individual, enshrines this resistance to intellectual authority even more than other democracies. Of course, no discussion about "how Americans think" is complete without an obligatory nod to Alexis de Tocqueville, the French observer who noted in 1835 that the denizens of the new United States were not exactly enamored of experts or their smarts. "In most of the operations of the mind," he wrote, "each American appeals only to the individual effort of his own understanding." This distrust of intellectual authority was rooted, Tocqueville theorized, in the nature of American democracy. When "citizens, placed on an equal footing, are all closely seen by one another," he wrote, they "are constantly brought back to their own reason as the most obvious and proximate source of truth. It is not only confidence in this or that man which is destroyed, but the disposition to trust the authority of any man whatsoever."

Such observations have not been limited to early America. Teachers, experts, and professional "knowers" have been venting about a lack of deference from their societies since Socrates was forced to drink his hemlock. In more modern times, the Spanish philosopher José Ortega y Gasset in 1930 decried the "revolt of the masses" and the unfounded intellectual arrogance that characterized it:

> Thus, in the intellectual life, which of its essence requires and presupposes qualification, one can note the progressive triumph of the pseudo-intellectual, unqualified, unqualifiable, and, by their very mental texture, disqualified.
>
> I may be mistaken, but the present-day writer, when he takes his pen in hand to treat a subject which he has studied deeply, has to bear in mind that the average reader, who has never concerned himself with this subject, if he reads does so with the view, not of learning something from the writer, but rather, of pronouncing judgment on him when he is not in agreement with the commonplaces that the said reader carries in his head.[1]

In terms that would not sound out of place in our current era, Ortega y Gasset attributed the rise of an increasingly powerful but increasingly ignorant public to many factors, including material affluence, prosperity, and scientific achievements.

The American attachment to intellectual self-reliance described by Tocqueville survived for nearly a century before falling under a series of assaults from both within and without. Technology, universal secondary education, the proliferation of specialized expertise, and the emergence of the United States as a global power in the mid-twentieth century all undermined the idea—or, more accurately, the myth—that the average American was adequately equipped either for the challenges of daily life or for running the affairs of a large country.

Over a half century ago, the political scientist Richard Hofstadter wrote that "the complexity of modern life has steadily whittled away the functions the ordinary citizen can intelligently and competently perform for himself."

> In the original American populistic dream, the omnicompetence of the common man was fundamental and indispensable. It was believed that he could, without much special preparation, pursue the professions and run the government.
>
> Today, he knows that he cannot even make his breakfast without using devices, more or less mysterious to him, which expertise has put at his disposal; and when he sits down to breakfast and looks at his morning newspaper, he reads about a whole range of issues and acknowledges, if he is candid with himself, that he has not acquired competence to judge most of them.[2]

Hofstadter argued—and this was back in 1963—that this overwhelming complexity produced feelings of helplessness and anger among a citizenry that knew itself increasingly to be at the mercy of smarter elites. "What used to be a jocular and usually benign ridicule of intellect and formal training has turned into a malign resentment of the intellectual in his capacity as expert," Hofstadter warned. "Once the intellectual was gently ridiculed because he was not needed; now he is fiercely resented because he is needed too much."

Fifty years later, the law professor Ilya Somin pointedly described how little had changed. Like Hofstadter before him, Somin wrote in 2015 that the "size and complexity of government" have made it "more difficult for voters with limited knowledge to monitor and evaluate the government's many activities. The result is a polity in which the people often cannot exercise their sovereignty responsibly and effectively." More disturbing is that Americans have done little in those intervening decades to remedy the gap between their own knowledge and the level of information required to participate in an advanced democracy. "The low level of political knowledge in the American electorate," Somin correctly notes, "is still one of the best-established findings in social science."[3]

SO IT'S NOT NEW. IS IT EVEN A PROBLEM?

People who specialize in particular subjects are prone to think that others should be as interested in it as they are. But really, who *needs* to know all this stuff? Most experts in international affairs would have difficulty passing a map test outside of their area of specialization, so what's the harm if the average person has no idea how to nail the exact location of Kazakhstan? After all, when the Rwandan genocide broke out in 1994, future secretary of state Warren Christopher had to be shown the location of Rwanda. So why should the rest of us walk around carrying that kind of trivia in our heads?

No one can master that much information. We do our best, and when we need to find something out, we consult the best sources we can find. I remember asking my high school chemistry teacher (a man I was certain knew everything) for the atomic number of a certain element off the top of his head, in part to challenge him but mostly because I was too lazy to look it up myself. He raised an eyebrow and said that he didn't know. He then gestured over his shoulder at the periodic table of elements posted on the wall and said, "This is why scientists use charts, Tom."

Without doubt, some of these expert complaints about laypeople are unfair. Even the most attentive parent, the most informed shopper, or the most civic-minded voter cannot keep up with the flood of news about everything from childhood nutrition to product safety to trade policy. If ordinary citizens could absorb all of that information, they wouldn't need experts in the first place.

The death of expertise, however, is a different problem than the historical fact of low levels of information among laypeople. The issue is not indifference to established knowledge; it's the emergence of a positive *hostility* to such knowledge. This is new in American culture, and it represents the aggressive replacement of expert views or established knowledge with the insistence that every opinion on any matter is as good as every other. This is a remarkable change in our public discourse.

This change is not only unprecedented but dangerous. Distrust of expertise is no longer a charming idiosyncrasy. In the twenty-first century, attacks on experts have become part of a global crisis of trust and social stability, in which anger at "elites"—meaning almost anyone, but especially those with definitive knowledge in particular fields—has become fused to the rise of authoritarian attitudes among populists of the extreme right. These attitudes predate the great pandemic that began in late 2019, but they intensified after the outbreak of COVID, especially in the United States (which we will discuss in chapter 7). As the journalist John Hendrickson wrote in 2023:

Large numbers of Americans don't merely scoff at experts and institutions; they loathe them. Falling down conspiratorial internet rabbit holes has become an entirely normal pastime. Study after study confirms a very real "epidemic of loneliness." Scores of people are bored and depressed and searching for narratives to help explain their anxiety and isolation. Scroll through social media and count how many times you see the phrase *Burn it down*.[4]

The public's ignorance is no longer only a function of the availability of public education or access to information, both of which surround the modern citizen in abundance. The distrust of experts and the more general anti-intellectual attitudes that go with it are problems that should be getting better, but instead are getting worse. Professor Somin and others may note that the public's ignorance is no worse than it was a half century ago, but holding the line isn't good enough. In fact, the line may not be holding at all; the death of expertise threatens to *reverse* the gains of years of knowledge among people who now assume they know more than they actually do.

It would be easy and reassuring to dismiss a distrust of established knowledge by attributing it to the stereotype of suspicious, uneducated yokels rejecting the big-city ways of the mysterious eggheads. But the reality is far more unsettling: campaigns against established knowledge are being led by people who should know better. The death of expertise represents not only a stubborn refusal to accept and process facts and new information, it is a threat to the material and civic well-being of millions of people around the world, but especially in democracies that rely on informed citizens to guide their own governments.

The rejection of expert advice crosses political and cultural lines. After the partisan wars over measures to stem the COVID pandemic, for example, vaccine rejection is now a hallmark of the American right; even former President Donald Trump was booed in public for telling his supporters to get vaccinated. Years earlier, however, vaccine skepticism was prevalent in places such as the liberal suburbs of San Francisco, as well as among African Americans, who had good historical reasons to distrust medical institutions. (Rural, less educated, and less affluent parents may have had similar feelings in the past, but they had to accept vaccines as a requirement of public education.) Today, opposition to vaccines represents a bizarre confederation of right-wing Republicans and ostensibly more left-leaning figures who have joined with the right in a kind of "horseshoe" of extremism, where the far right and far left meet and share the same points in their paranoia.

Long before COVID, however, ignorance had already become hip, with some Americans wearing their rejection of expert advice as a badge of cultural sophistication. Consider, for example, the raw milk movement, a fad among gourmands over the past decade who advocated for the right to ingest untreated dairy products. In 2012, the *New Yorker* reported on this trend, noting that "raw milk stirs the hedonism of food lovers in a special way" because it is not only "richer and sweeter," but because it retains "a whiff of the farm—the slightly discomfiting flavor known to connoisseurs as 'cow butt.'" Pasteurization, according to Daniel Patterson, a chef who used raw milk at Coi, his two-Michelin-star restaurant in San Francisco, "strips away layers of complexity, layers of aromatics."[5] Chef Patterson is an expert in the preparation of food, and there's no arguing with his, or anyone else's, palate. But while pasteurization may affect the taste of milk, it also strips away pathogens that can kill human beings. (Coi closed during the COVID pandemic and did not reopen.)

The raw milk movement was not some on-the-edge experience plumped by a few exotic chefs. Raw milk adherents argued not only that untreated dairy products taste good, but also that they are healthier and better for human beings. After all, raw grains and vegetables are often better for us—so why not raw everything? Why not eat the way nature intended us to and go back to a purer, simpler time?

It may have been a simpler time, but it was also a time when people routinely died of food-borne diseases. Still, it's a free country, and if fully informed adult gastronomes want to risk a trip to the hospital for the scent of a cow's nether regions in their coffee, that's their choice. I'm not one to judge this too harshly, since my favorite dishes include raw shellfish and steak tartare, items whose menu disclaimers always make me feel as if I'm ordering contraband. Still, while raw meat and raw shellfish carry risks, they are not dietary staples, and especially not for children, for whom raw milk is outright hazardous.

In short order, doctors at the Centers for Disease Control (CDC) tried to get involved, to no avail. The CDC issued a report in 2012 that noted that raw dairy products were 150 times more likely than pasteurized products to cause food-borne illness. A Food and Drug Administration expert put it as bluntly as possible, calling the consumption of raw dairy the food equivalent of Russian roulette. None of this has swayed people who not only continue to ingest untreated products but who insist on giving it to the consumers who have no choice or ability to understand the debate: their children.

Other fads make the raw milk movement seem relatively benign by comparison. In 2017, stories emerged (and I am sorry even to know about this) about the existence of a "poop cult," invented by a woman in Ohio who claimed that all diseases are due to a fungus in the human gut and could be battled, according to one report, by drinking a "fermented slurry of salted cabbage that produces 'waterfalls' of diarrhea."[6] While this might seem worth a brief laugh, it turns out that tens of thousands of people, including some with late-stage cancer, were taken in by this nonsense.

Why listen to doctors about raw milk or cabbage purges or anything else? After all, they've gotten other things wrong. When it comes to food, for example, Americans for decades have been told to limit their consumption of eggs and certain kinds of fats. Government experts told people to limit their intake of red meat, increase the role of grains in their diet, and in general to stay away from anything that tastes good. (That last one, I admit, is how I interpreted those recommendations.) Years later, it turned out that not only are eggs harmless, but they might even be good for you. Margarine is probably worse for us than butter. And a few glasses of wine each week might be better than teetotaling.

So there it is: the doctors were wrong. Is it time to break out the bacon cheeseburgers and pour another martini?

Not quite. The debate about eggs isn't over, but to focus on one aspect of the American diet is to miss the point. The doctors may have been mistaken about the specific impact of eggs, but they're not wrong that a steady diet of fast food, washed down with a sugary soda or a six-pack of beer, isn't good for you. Some folks seized on the news about eggs (much as they did on a bogus story about chocolate being a healthy snack that made the rounds earlier) to rationalize *never* listening to doctors, who clearly have a better track record than the average overweight American at keeping people alive with healthier diets.

At the root of all this is an inability among laypeople to understand that experts being wrong on occasion about certain issues is not the same thing as experts being wrong consistently on everything. The fact of the matter is that experts are more often right than wrong, especially on essential matters of fact. And yet the public constantly searches for loopholes in expert knowledge that will allow them to disregard all expert advice they don't like.

In part, this is because human nature, as we'll see, tends to search for those loopholes in *anything* that contradicts our wishes or preexisting beliefs. But we also hedge against expert advice because when experts and professionals are wrong, the consequences can be catastrophic. Raise the issue of medical advice, for example, and you will almost certainly find someone who will throw out the word "thalidomide" as though it is a self-explanatory rejoinder. It's been more than sixty years since the introduction of thalidomide, a drug once thought safe that was given to pregnant women as a sedative. No one realized at the time that thalidomide also caused horrendous birth defects, and pictures of children with missing or deformed limbs haunted the public imagination for many years afterward. The drug's name has become synonymous with expert failure to this day.

No one is arguing, however, that experts can't be wrong (a subject we'll discuss in this book). Rather, the point is that they are less likely to be wrong than nonexperts. The same people who anxiously point back in history to the thalidomide disaster routinely pop dozens of drugs into their mouths, from aspirin to antihistamines, which are among the thousands and thousands of medications shown to be safe by decades of trials and tests conducted by experts. It rarely occurs to the skeptics that for every terrible mistake, there are countless successes that prolong their lives.

Sometimes, second-guessing the professionals can turn into an obsession, with tragic results. In 2015, a Massachusetts accountant named Stephen Pasceri lost his seventy-eight-year-old mother to cardiovascular disease. Mrs. Pasceri had a long history of health trouble, including emphysema, and died after an operation to repair a heart valve. Pasceri, however, was convinced that one of his mother's doctors, Michael Davidson—the director of endovascular cardiac surgery at a top Boston hospital and a professor at Harvard Medical School—had ignored warnings about a particular drug given to Pasceri's mother. In a literal case of the death of expertise, the accountant showed up at the hospital and shot the doctor to death. He then killed himself after leaving behind a flash drive with his "research" about the drug.

Obviously, Stephen Pasceri was a disturbed man, unhinged by the death of his mother. But a few minutes of conversations with professionals in any field will yield similar, if less dramatic, stories. Doctors routinely tussle with patients over drugs. Lawyers will describe clients losing money, and sometimes their freedom, because of unheeded advice. Teachers will relate stories of parents insisting that their children's exam answers are right even when they're demonstrably wrong. Realtors tell of clients who bought houses against their experienced advice and ended up trapped in a money pit.

No area of American life is immune to the death of expertise. The American public's declining capabilities in science and mathematics are enabling multiple public health crises from obesity to childhood diseases. Meanwhile, in the worlds of politics and public policy—where at least some familiarity with history, civics, and geography is crucial to informed debate—attacks on established knowledge have reached frightening proportions.

THE RISE OF THE LOW-INFORMATION VOTER

Political debate and the making of public policy are not science. They are rooted in conflict, sometimes conducted as respectful disagreement but more often as a hockey game with no referees and a standing invitation for spectators to rush onto the ice. In modern America, policy debates sound increasingly like fights between groups of ill-informed people who all manage to be wrong at the same time. Those political leaders who manage to be smarter than the public (and there seem to be fewer of those lately) wade into these donnybrooks and contradict their constituents at their own peril.

There are many examples of these brawls among what pundits and analysts gently refer to now as "low-information voters." Whether about science or policy, however, they all share the same disturbing characteristic: a solipsistic and thin-skinned insistence that every opinion be treated as truth. Americans no longer distinguish the phrase "you're wrong" from the phrase "you're stupid." To disagree is to disrespect. To correct another is to insult. And to refuse to acknowledge all views as worthy of consideration, no matter how fantastic or inane they are, is to be closed-minded.

The epidemic of ignorance in public policy debates has real consequences for the quality of life and well-being of every American. During the debate in 2009 over the Affordable Care Act, for example, at least half of all Americans believed claims by opponents like former Republican vice presidential nominee Sarah Palin that the legislation included "death panels" that would decide who gets health care based on a bureaucratic decision about a patient's worthiness to live. (Four years later, almost a third of surgeons apparently continued to believe this, and the term has had remarkable staying power in American discourse.)[7] Nearly half of Americans also thought the ACA established a uniform government health plan. Love it or hate it, the program does none of these things.

Legislation is complicated, and it is perhaps unreasonable to ask Americans to grasp the details of a bill their own representatives seemed unable to understand. Then-House Speaker Nancy Pelosi, wilting under a barrage of perfectly reasonable questions in 2011, finally said in exasperation that the debate was simply too complicated and too riven by conflict, and therefore Congress would have to first pass the bill "so that you can find out what is in it, away from the fog of the controversy," a remarkable suggestion that the public should allow a proposal to become law before digesting its full contents.

Taxes are another good example of how public ignorance influences national debates. Everybody hates taxes. Everybody complains about them. And every spring, the hideous complexity of the US tax code produces a fair amount of anxiety among honest citizens who, at best, end up guessing at the right answers when trying to pay their levy.

The sad reality, however, is that the average American has no real idea how his or her money is spent. Polls upon polls show not only that Americans generally feel government spends too much, and taxes them too highly, but also that they are consistently wrong about who pays taxes, how much they pay, and where the money goes. This, despite the fact that information about the budget of the United States is more accessible than the days when the government would have to mail a document the size of a cinder block to the few voters who wanted to see it.

Or consider foreign aid, a hot-button issue among some Americans who deride foreign aid as wasted money. Americans routinely believe, on average, that more than 25 percent of the national budget is given away as largesse in the form of foreign aid. In reality, that guess is not only wrong, but wildly wrong: foreign aid is a small fraction of the budget, less than three-quarters of 1 percent of the total expenditures of the United States of America.

Only 5 percent of Americans know this. One in ten Americans, meanwhile, think that more than *half* of the US budget—that is, several trillion dollars—is given away annually to other countries.[8] Most think that no matter how much it is, it's given as a check worth cold cash. That's also wrong. Foreign aid, in fact, might even qualify as a jobs program, since much of it is given in the form of products, from food to military aircraft, purchased by the government from Americans and then sent to other nations.

To argue that foreign aid is a waste of money is a comprehensible political position. I and other experts might say that such a blanket objection is unwise, but it is at least a position rooted in principle rather than based on an error of fact. To object to foreign aid because of a mistaken belief that it constitutes a quarter of the US budget, however, almost immediately defeats any sensible discussion right at the outset.

This level of ignorance can get pretty expensive. Americans have long supported national missile defenses against nuclear attack, for example, in part because many believe the United States already has them. (This is a public misconception going back decades, long before the United States fielded the small number of interceptors now operational in Alaska.) Whether such systems will work or whether they should be built are now largely irrelevant questions. What began as a highly controversial program aimed at the Soviet Union during the Cold War in the 1980s is now enshrined in the popular imagination and supported by both Republicans and Democrats to the tune of billions of dollars.

The overall problem here isn't among people who have genuine concerns about possible side effects from vaccines, or who might be conflicted about whether to build defenses against nuclear attack. Reasoned skepticism is essential not only to science but also to a healthy democracy. Instead, the death of expertise is more like a national bout of ill temper, a childish rejection of authority in all its forms coupled to an insistence that strongly held opinions are indistinguishable from facts.

Experts are supposed to clear up this kind of confusion or at least to serve as guides through the thicket of confusion issues. But who are the real "experts"? Before we move on to discuss the sources of the campaign against established knowledge, and why we're in such a pickle at a time when citizens should be more informed and engaged than ever before, we need to think about how we divide "experts" or "intellectuals" from the rest of the population.

"Expert" is an overused label, of course: every business proclaims itself "the yard care experts" or the "carpet cleaning experts," and while that has some meaning, surgeons and carpet cleaners are not the same kind of expert. "Intellectual" and "academic" are, more than ever, terms of derision in America. Let's untangle some of this before we proceed.

EXPERTS AND CITIZENS

So who's an expert? What constitutes "expertise"?

A lot of people declare that they're experts or intellectuals, and sometimes they are. On the other hand, self-identification can be worse than misleading. People who claim to be experts are sometimes only about as self-aware as people who think they're good kissers.

Dictionaries aren't much help here. Most define experts in a rather circular way, as people who have "comprehensive" and "authoritative" knowledge, which is another way of describing people whose command of a subject means that the information they provide the rest of us is true and can be trusted. (How do we know it can be trusted? Because experts tell us so.) As Justice Potter Stewart once said of pornography, expertise is one of those things that's difficult to define, but we usually know it when we see it.

There are lots of experts in the world. Some are easy to spot: medical doctors, engineers, and airline pilots are experts, as are film directors and concert pianists. Athletes and their coaches are experts. But so are plumbers, police officers, and carpenters. For that matter, your local mail carrier is an expert, at least in his own field; if you need a blood test interpreted, you should ask a doctor or a nurse, but if you'd like to know exactly how a letter from your friend in Brazil got to your door in Michigan, you might ask someone who's been handling that responsibility for years.

Specialized knowledge is inherent in every occupation, and so here I will use the words "professionals," "intellectuals," and "experts" interchangeably, in the broader sense of people who have mastered particular skills or bodies of knowledge and who practice those skills or use that knowledge as their main occupation in life. This helps us to distinguish the "professional pilot" from the weekend flyer, or even a "professional gambler" from the hapless mark who occasionally hands money to a casino.

Put another way, experts are the people who know considerably more on a subject than the rest of us and are those to whom we turn when we need advice, education, or solutions in a particular area of human knowledge. Note that this does not mean that experts know all there is to know about something. Rather, it means that experts in any given subject are, by their nature, a minority whose views are more likely to be "authoritative"—that is, correct or accurate—than anyone else's.

And even among experts, there are experts. A doctor with a newly minted MD is far more qualified than any layperson to diagnose and treat a disease, but when faced by a puzzling case he or she may in turn defer to a specialist. A practicing attorney and a Supreme Court justice are both lawyers, but the one in the black robes in Washington is more likely to be an expert on constitutional issues than the one handling wills and divorces for a small community. Of course, experience counts, too. In 2009, when a USAir flight in New York City was crippled on takeoff by striking a flock of birds, there were two pilots in the cockpit, but the more expert captain, with many more hours of flying time, said "my aircraft" and guided the jet to a water ditching in the Hudson River. Everyone aboard survived.

One reason claims of expertise grate on people in a democracy is that specialization is necessarily exclusive. When we study a certain area of knowledge or spend our lives in a particular occupation, we not only forego expertise in other jobs or subjects, but also trust that other people in the community know what they're doing in their area as surely as we do in our own. As much as we might want to go up to the cockpit after the engine flames out to give the pilots some helpful tips, we assume—in part, because we have no other choice—that they're better able to cope with the problem than we are. Otherwise, our highly evolved society breaks down into islands of incoherence, where we spend our time in poorly informed second-guessing instead of trusting each other.

So how do we distinguish these experts among us, and how do we identify them? True expertise, the kind of knowledge on which others rely, is an intangible but recognizable combination of education, talent, experience, and peer affirmation. Each of these is a mark of expertise, but most people would rightly judge how all of them are combined in a given subject or professional field when deciding whose advice to trust.

Formal training or education is the most obvious mark of expert status, and the easiest to identify, but it is only a start. For many professions, credentials are necessary for entry into a field: teachers, nurses, and plumbers all have to have certification of some kind to exercise their skills, as a signal to others that their abilities have been reviewed by their peers and meet a basic standard of competence. While some of the most determined opponents of established knowledge deride this as mere "credentialism," these degrees and licenses are tangible signs of achievement and important markers that help the rest of us separate hobbyists (or charlatans) from true experts.

To be fair, some of these credentials are new inventions, and some of them might not matter very much. In some cases, credentials are made up by states and localities as revenue gimmicks, while others affirm no skill other than passing a test once and then never again. Lawyers in modern America complete a law degree, but in earlier times young men merely "read law" and then had to pass admittance to their state's bar. While this less formal system produced men of greatness like Abraham Lincoln—who became a well-regarded and competent attorney—it also produced lesser lights such as Henry Billings Brown, the Supreme Court justice who wrote the majority opinion in the "separate but equal" *Plessy v. Ferguson* decision.

(Brown attended courses in law at both Harvard and Yale but did not graduate from either of them.)

Still, credentials are a start. They carry the imprimatur of the institutions that bestow them, and they are a signal of quality, just as consumer brands tend to promote (and, hopefully, protect) the quality of their products. Look carefully at an actual college degree and note what most of them actually say: that the bearer has been examined by the faculty and admitted to the degree, which in turn is backed by a committee of schools in that region or a body representing a particular profession. Those faculties, and the associations who accredit their courses of study, are in effect vouching for the graduate's knowledge of a particular subject. The name of the school or institution, no less than the degree holder, is on the line, at least as an initial affirmation of capability.

There is no denying that good colleges have graduated a lot of people without a lick of common sense. Lesser institutions have likewise produced geniuses. But as the saying goes, while the race may not always be to the swift, that's the way to bet. The track record for genius production from MIT or Georgia Tech is demonstrably higher than for less competitive schools or self-educated inventors. Still, MIT has also produced people who not only can't balance a checkbook, but who aren't very good engineers. What makes the experts, especially the prominent leaders in their specialization, stand apart from others with similar credentials?

One difference is aptitude or natural talent. Talent is indispensable to an expert. (As Ernest Hemingway once said about writing, "Real seriousness in regard to writing is one of two absolute necessities. The other, unfortunately, is talent.") The person who studied Chaucer in college is going to know more than most other people about English literature, in some purely factual way. But the scholar who has a real talent for the study of medieval literature not only knows more, but can also explain it coherently and perhaps even generate new knowledge on the subject.

Talent separates those who have gained a credential from people who have a deeper feel or understanding of their area of expertise. Every field has maze-bright achievers who, as it turns out, are not good at their jobs. There are brilliant law students who freeze in front of a jury. Some of the high scorers on a police examination have no street smarts and will never develop them. A fair number of new holders of doctorates from top universities will never write another thing of consequence after laboring through a dissertation. These people may have cleared the wickets of entry to a profession, but they're not very good at it, and their expertise will likely never exceed the natural limitation of their own abilities.

This is where experience helps to separate the credentialed from the incompetent. Sometimes, markets themselves winnow out untalented or unskilled would-be experts. While professional stockbrokers make mistakes, for example, most manage to make a living. Amateur day-traders, however, almost never make money. *Business Insider* CEO and former Wall Street analyst Henry Blodgett once called amateur day-trading "the dumbest job there is" and that most people who engage in it "would make more money working at Burger King."[9] Eventually, they run out of cash. Likewise, bad teachers over time will tend to get bad evaluations, lousy lawyers will lose clients, and untalented athletes will fail to make the cut.

Every field has its trials by fire, and not everyone survives them, which is why experience and longevity in a particular area or profession are also reasonable markers of expertise. Indeed, asking about "experience" is another way of asking the age-old question: "What have you done *lately*?" Experts stay engaged in their field, continually improve their skills, learn from their mistakes, and have visible track records. Over the span of their career, they get better, or at least maintain their high level of competence, and couple it to the wisdom—again, an intangible—that comes from time.

There are many examples of the role of experience in expertise. Experienced law enforcement officers often have an instinct for trouble that their younger colleagues miss, an intuition they can explain only as a sense that something "isn't right." Doctors or pilots who've experienced and survived multiple crises in the operating theater or the cockpit are less likely to be panicked by adversity than their newer colleagues. Veteran teachers are less intimidated by challenging or difficult students. Stand-up comedians who've done a lot of gigs on the road do not fear hecklers, and even know how to use them as raw material for more laughs.

These are not always quantifiable skills. Here's an example from my own education and field of study.

After college, I went on to the Harriman Institute at Columbia University for further study in the politics of the Soviet Union. This was part of my own credentialing: I wanted to teach and work in Soviet affairs, and Columbia was one of the best schools in that field at the time. The director of the institute was a professor named Marshall Shulman, a well-known Sovietologist who had also served in Jimmy Carter's White House as an advisor on Soviet matters.

Like all Sovietologists, Shulman studied the Soviet press very carefully for indications of policy positions within the Kremlin. This process was an almost Talmudic exercise in textual analysis, and it was a mystery to those of us who had never done it. How, we students asked him, did he make sense of any of the stilted prose of Soviet newspapers, or divine any meaning from such turgid passages? How could a thousand formulaic stories on the heroic struggles of collective farms illuminate the secrets of one of the most closed systems on earth? Shulman shrugged and said, "I can't really explain it. I just read *Pravda* until my nose twitches."

At the time, I thought that this was one of the stupidest things I'd ever heard. I even started to wonder if I'd made a poor life choice investing in further education. What Shulman meant, however, is that he'd spent years reading Soviet periodicals, and thus he had become so attuned to their method of communication that he could spot changes or irregularities when they passed before his trained and experienced eye.

Although skeptical, I did the same throughout my schooling and into the early years of my career. I read Soviet materials almost daily and tried to see the patterns in them that were previously invisible to me. Eventually, I came to understand what Shulman meant. I can't say that my nose ever twitched or my ears wiggled, but I realized that reading things from a foreign country in a foreign language was a specific kind of expertise. It could not be distilled into a course or a test. There was no quick means to develop it as a skill: it took time, practice, and advice from more experienced experts in the same field.

Another mark of true experts is their acceptance of evaluation and correction by other experts. Every professional group and expert community has its watchdogs, boards, accreditors, and certification authorities whose job is to police its own members and to ensure not only that they live up to the standards of their own specialty, but also that their arts are practiced only by people who actually know what they're doing.

This self-policing is central to the concept of professionalism and is another way we can identify experts. Every specialized group creates barriers to entry into their profession. Some of these barriers are more reasonable and honest than others, but usually they are grounded in the need to ensure that the name of the profession isn't devalued by incompetence or fraud. I could gather a handful of colleagues, hang a shingle outside my home, and call it the "Tom Nichols Institute of High-Energy Physics," but the fact of the matter is that I don't know a thing about high-energy physics. That's why my notional institute would never be accredited by real physicists, who would not take kindly to me printing up phony degrees and who in short order would seek to close me down to protect the meaning of the word "physicist."

Expert communities rely on these peer-run institutions to maintain standards and to enhance social trust. Mechanisms such as peer review, board certification, professional associations, and other organizations and professions help to protect quality and to assure society—that is, the expert's clients—that they're safe in accepting expert claims of competence. When you take an elevator to the top floor of a tall building, the certificate in the elevator does not say "good luck up there"; it says that a civic authority, relying on engineers educated and examined by other engineers, have looked at that box and know, with as much certainty as anyone can, that you'll be safe.

Experience and professional affirmation matter, but it's also true that there is considerable wisdom in the old Chinese warning to beware a craftsman who claims twenty years of experience when in reality he's only had one year of experience twenty times. There are bad dentists who were lousy at pulling teeth when they graduated from dentistry school and who do not get much better at it before retirement. There are teachers who induce narcolepsy in their students on the first day of their class just as they do on their last. But we should remember two important things about experts, even ones who might not be the best in their field.

First, while our clumsy dentist might not be the best tooth puller in town, he or she is better at it than *you*. We don't all need the dean of the dentistry school for a crown or a simple cavity. You might be able to get lucky once and pull a tooth, but you're not educated or experienced enough to do it without a great deal of risk. Most people won't even cut their own hair. (Beauticians, after all, handle all kinds of chemicals and sharp objects, and they are another group that requires training and licensing.) Few of us are going to risk taking out our own teeth or those of our loved ones.

Second, and related to this point about relative skill, experts will make mistakes, but they are far less likely to make mistakes than a layperson. This is a crucial distinction between experts and everyone else, in that experts know better than anyone the pitfalls of their own profession. As the renowned physicist Werner Heisenberg once put it, an expert "is someone who knows some of the worst mistakes that can be made in his subject and how to avoid them." His fellow physicist Niels Bohr had a similar take: "An expert is someone who has made all the mistakes which can be made in a very narrow field."

Both points should help us to understand why the pernicious idea that "everyone can be an expert" is so dangerous. It's true in a relative sense that almost anyone with particular skills can develop specialized knowledge to which others, in most circumstances, must defer. Trouble, however, rears its head when people start to believe that knowing a little bit about something means "expertise." It's a thin line between the hobbyist who knows a lot about destroyers and submarines from reading *Jane's Fighting Ships* and an actual expert on the capabilities of the world's naval vessels, but that line nonetheless exists.

Knowing things is not the same as understanding them. Comprehension is not the same thing as analysis. Expertise is a not a parlor game played with factoids.

And while there are self-trained experts, they are rare exceptions. More common are the people seeking quick entry into complicated fields but who have no idea how poor their efforts are. They are like the moderately entertaining karaoke singers who think they have a chance to become the next winner of *American Idol*, or the scratch golfers who think they might take a shot at going pro. Doing something well is not the same thing as becoming a trusted source of advice or learning about a subject. (Notice that the same people who think they can become singers never think they can become voice coaches.)

This lack of self-awareness and intellectual limits can produce some awkward interactions between experts and laypeople. Some years ago, for example, when I was still teaching at the Naval War College, I had a call from a gentleman who insisted that he had some important work that might be of use in our curriculum. He'd been referred to me by a former student at another school, and he very much wanted me to read an important article about the Middle East. I asked who wrote the piece. Well, he answered, he did. He was a businessman, and he'd "read a lot." I asked if he'd had any training in the subject, visited the region, or read any of the languages of the Middle East. He had no such background, he admitted, and then said, "But after all, you can become an expert reading a book a month, right?"

Wrong.

American culture, steeped in a tradition of egalitarianism, fuels these kinds of romantic notions about the wisdom of the common person or the gumption of the self-educated genius. Such images empower a certain kind of satisfying social fantasy, in which ordinary people out-perform the stuffy professor or the nerdy scientist through sheer grit and ingenuity.

There are plenty of examples of this in American popular culture, especially in films that depict remarkably bright young people outsmarting businesses, universities, and even governments. One of the most famous examples in cinema takes place in the 1997 film *Good Will Hunting*, scripted by Ben Affleck and Matt Damon, about a janitor who turns out to be a secret prodigy. In what is now an iconic scene, Damon growls out a chowdery Boston working-man's accent and faces down an effete, ponytailed Ivy League graduate student in a bar:

> You're a first-year grad student; you just got finished reading some Marxian historian, Pete Garrison probably. You're gonna

be convinced of that 'til next month when you get to James Lemon. Then you're going to be talking about how the economies of Virginia and Pennsylvania were entrepreneurial and capitalist way back in 1740.

That's gonna last until next year. You're gonna be in here regurgitating Gordon Wood, talkin' about, you know, the pre-revolutionary utopia and the capital-forming effects of military mobilization. . . . You got that from Vickers, "Work in Essex County," page 98, right? Yeah, I read that too. Were you gonna plagiarize the whole thing for us? Do you have any thoughts of your own on this matter?

You dropped 150 grand on a fuckin' education you could have got for a dollar fifty in late charges at the public library.

Later, the young man fences with his psychotherapist about the works of Howard Zinn and Noam Chomsky. Stilted and silly, these moments nonetheless resonated with moviegoers at the time. Damon and Affleck went home with Oscars for the screenplay, and no doubt they encouraged at least some viewers to believe that reading enough books is almost like going to school.

In the end, expertise is difficult to define, and experts are sometimes hard to tell from dilettantes. Still, we should be able to distinguish between people who have a passing acquaintance with a subject and people whose knowledge is definitive. No one's knowledge is complete, and experts realize this better than anyone. But education, training, practice, experience, and affirmation by others in the same field should provide us with at least a rough guide to dividing experts from the rest of society.

One of the most basic reasons experts and laypeople have always driven each other crazy is because they're all human beings. That is, they all share similar problems in the way they absorb and interpret information. Even the most educated people can make elementary mistakes in reasoning, while less intelligent people are prone to overlook the limitations in their own abilities. Expert or layperson, our brains work (or sometimes don't) in similar ways: we hear things the way we want to hear them, and we reject facts we don't like. Those problems are the subject of the next chapter.

Chapter 2

How Conversation
Became Exhausting

A few centuries earlier . . . humans still knew pretty well when a thing was proved and when it was not; and if it was proved they really believed it.

C. S. Lewis, *The Screwtape Letters*

Yeah, well, you know, that's just, like, your opinion, man.

"The Dude," *The Big Lebowski*

I'D LIKE AN ARGUMENT, PLEASE

Conversation in the twenty-first century is sometimes exhausting and often maddening, not only between experts and laypeople, but among everyone else, too. If in a previous era too much deference was paid to experts, today there is little deference paid to anyone at all. Even among laypeople in their daily interactions, disagreement and debate have devolved into grueling exchanges of contradiction, random factoids, and shaky sources few of the participants themselves understand. Years of better education, increased access to data, the explosion of social media, and lowered barriers to entry into the public arena were supposed to improve our abilities to deliberate and decide. Instead, these advances seem to have made all of this worse rather than better.

Public debate over almost everything devolves into trench warfare, in which the most important goal is to establish that the other person is wrong. Sensible differences of opinion deteriorate into a bad high school debate in which the objective is to win and facts are deployed like checkers on a board—none of this rises to the level of chess—mostly to knock out other facts. Like the customer in Monty Python's legendary "Argument Clinic" sketch, we find ourselves merely gainsaying whatever the other person said last. ("This isn't an argument," the angry customer tells the professional arguer. "Yes, it is," he responds. "No, it isn't! It's just contradiction!" "No, it isn't." "Yes, it is!")

Here, we need to start with the obvious and universal problem: you and me. Or more accurately, the way you and I think. From biology to social psychology, we fight an uphill battle in trying to understand each other.

We all have an inherent and natural tendency to search for evidence that already meshes with our beliefs. Our brains are wired to work this way, which is why we argue even when we shouldn't. And if we feel socially or personally threatened, we will argue until we're blue in the face. (Perhaps in the Internet age, the expression on social media should be "until our fingers are numb.") Experts are no exception here; like everyone else, we want to believe what we want to believe.

In our personal lives, we tend to be a bit more forgiving, because we are social animals who want acceptance and affection from those closest to us. In our intimate social circles, most of us think we're competent and trustworthy, and we want others to see us that way, too. We all want to be taken seriously and to be respected. In practice, this means we don't want anyone to think we're dumb, and so we pretend to be smarter than we are. Over time, we even come to believe it.

Of course, there's also the basic problem that some people just aren't very bright. And as we'll see, the people who are the most certain about being right tend to be the people with the least reason to have such self-confidence. But it is too facile simply to dismiss the exasperating nature of modern discussion as only a function of the stupidity of others. (That's not to say it isn't sometimes true.) Most people simply are not that intellectually limited, at least not if measured by basic indicators such as rates of literacy or completion of high school.

The fact of the matter is that the pitfalls of discussion and debate aren't limited to mistakes made by the least intelligent among us. We all fall prey to a series of problems, including the way we all try to resolve problems and questions in ways that make us feel better about ourselves and our friends. The many influences on the death of expertise, including higher education, the media, and the Internet, are all enablers of these basic human traits. All of these challenges to better communication between experts and citizens can be overcome with education, rigor, and honesty, but only if we know how they're plaguing us in the first place.

MAYBE WE'RE ALL JUST DUMB

Let's confront the most painful possibility first. Perhaps experts and laypeople have problems talking with each other because the ordinary citizen is just unintelligent. Maybe the intellectual gulf between the educated elites and the masses is now so large that they simply cannot talk to each other, except to exchange expressions of mutual contempt. Maybe conversations and arguments fail because one—or both—of the parties is just stupid.

These are fighting words. No one likes to be called stupid: it's a judgmental, harsh word that implies not only a lack of intelligence, but a willful ignorance almost to the point of moral failure. (I use it, more than I should. So do you, most likely.) You can call people with whom you disagree misinformed, mistaken, incorrect, or almost anything else. But don't call them stupid.

Fortunately, the use of "stupid" is not only rude, it's mostly inaccurate. By any measure Americans are smarter, or at least no less intelligent, than they were several decades ago. Nor was the early twentieth century a Periclean Age of culture and learning. In 1943, incoming college freshmen—only 6 percent of whom could list the original thirteen colonies—named Abraham Lincoln as the first president and the one who "emaciated [sic] the slaves." The New York Times saw those results and took a moment from reporting on World War II to lament the nation's "appallingly ignorant" youth.[1]

Whether people in the twenty-first century can keep up with the gap between their education and the speed of change in the world is another matter entirely. Grade-school students in 1910 and 2010 both had to learn how to calculate the sides of a triangle, but today's students must use that knowledge to comprehend the existence of a permanent international space station, whereas their great-great-grandparents likely had never seen a car, much less an airplane. And nothing can prevent willful detachment, in any era. No amount of education can teach someone the name of their member of Congress if they don't care in the first place.

With that said, there's still the problem of at least some people thinking they're bright when in fact they're not very bright at all. We've all been trapped at a party or a dinner when the least-informed person in the room holds court, never doubting his or her own intelligence and confidently lecturing the rest of us with a cascade of mistakes and misinformation. It's not your imagination: people spooling off on subjects about which they know very little and with completely unfounded confidence really happens, and science has finally figured it out.

This phenomenon is called "the Dunning-Kruger Effect," named for David Dunning and Justin Kruger, the research psychologists at Cornell University who identified it in a landmark 1999 study. The

Dunning-Kruger Effect, in sum, means that the dumber you are, the more confident you are that you're not dumb. Dunning and Kruger more gently label such people as "unskilled" or "incompetent." But that doesn't change their central finding: "Not only do they reach erroneous conclusions and make unfortunate choices, but their incompetence robs them of the ability to realize it."[2]

In fairness to the "unskilled," we all tend to overestimate ourselves. Ask people where they think they rate on any number of talents, and you will encounter the "above average effect," in which everyone thinks they're—well, above average. This, as Dunning and Kruger dryly note, is "a result that defies the logic of descriptive statistics." It is nonetheless so recognizable a human failing that the humorist Garrison Keillor, in his radio show *A Prairie Home Companion*, famously created an entire town dedicated to this principle, the mythical Lake Wobegon, where "all the children are above average."

As Dunning later explained, we all overestimate ourselves, but the less competent do it more than the rest of us.

A whole battery of studies conducted by myself and others have confirmed that people who don't know much about a given set of cognitive, technical, or social skills tend to grossly overestimate their prowess and performance, whether it's grammar, emotional intelligence, logical reasoning, firearm care and safety, debating, or financial knowledge. College students who hand in exams that will earn them Ds and Fs tend to think their efforts will be worthy of far higher grades; low-performing chess players, bridge players, and medical students, and elderly people applying for a renewed driver's license, similarly overestimate their competence by a long shot.[3]

Students who study for a test, older people trying to maintain their independence, and medical students looking forward to their careers would rather be optimistic than underestimate themselves. Other than in fields like athletic competition, where incompetence is manifest and undeniable, it's normal for people to avoid saying they're bad at something.

As it turns out, however, the more specific reason that unskilled or incompetent people overestimate their abilities far more than others is because they lack a key skill called "metacognition." This is the ability to know when you're not good at something by stepping back, looking at what you're doing, and then realizing that you're doing it wrong. Good singers know when they've hit a sour note; good directors know when a scene in a play isn't working; good marketers know when an ad campaign is going to be a flop. Their less competent counterparts, by comparison, have no such ability. They think they're doing a great job.

Pair such people with experts, and predictably enough, misery results. The lack of metacognition sets up a vicious loop, in which people who don't know much about a subject do not know when they're in over their head talking with an expert on that subject. An argument ensues, but people who have no idea how to make a logical argument (or who do not have enough foundational knowledge in the subject being debated) cannot realize when they're failing to offer a coherent response. In short order, the expert is frustrated and the layperson is insulted. Everyone walks away angry.

Even more exasperating is that there is no way to educate or inform people who, when in doubt, will make stuff up. Dunning described the research done at Cornell as something like "a less flamboyant version of Jimmy Kimmel's bit," and it proved the comedian's point that when people have no idea what they're talking about, it does not deter them from talking anyway.

In our work, we ask survey respondents if they are familiar with certain technical concepts from physics, biology, politics, and geography. A fair number claim familiarity with genuine terms like *centripetal force* and *photon*. But interestingly, they also claim some familiarity with concepts that are entirely made up, such as the *plates of parallax, ultra-lipid,* and *cholarine*. In one study, roughly 90 percent claimed some knowledge of at least one of the nine fictitious concepts we asked them about.

Even worse, "the more well-versed respondents considered themselves in a general topic, the more familiarity they claimed with the meaningless terms associated with it in the survey." This makes it tough to argue with these "incompetent individuals," because when compared with the experts, "they were less able to spot competence when they saw it."

In other words, the least-competent people were the least likely to know they were wrong or to know that others were right, the most likely to try to fake it, and the least able to learn anything.

Dunning and Kruger have several explanations for this problem. In general, people don't like to hurt each other's feelings, and in some workplaces, people and even supervisors might be reluctant to correct incompetent friends or colleagues. Some activities, like writing or speaking, do not have any evident means of producing immediate feedback. You can only miss so many swings in baseball before you're forced to admit you might not be a good hitter, but you can mangle grammar and syntax every day without ever realizing how poorly you speak.

The problem of the "least competent" is an immediate challenge to discussions between experts and laypeople, but there's not much we can do about a fundamental characteristic of human nature. Not everyone, however, is incompetent, and almost no one is incompetent at everything. What kinds of errors do more intelligent or agile-minded people make in trying to comprehend complicated issues? Not surprisingly, ordinary citizens encounter pitfalls and biases that befall experts as well.

CONFIRMATION BIAS: BECAUSE YOU KNEW THIS ALREADY

"Confirmation bias" is the most common—and easily the most irritating—obstacle to productive conversation, and not just between experts and laypeople. The term refers to the tendency to look for information that only confirms what we believe, to accept facts that only strengthen our preferred explanations, and to dismiss data that challenge what we already accept as truth. We all do it, and you can be certain that you and I and everyone who's ever had an argument with anyone about anything has infuriated someone else with it.

For example, if we think left-handed people are evil (it's where the word *sinister* comes from, after all), every left-handed murderer proves our point. We'll see them everywhere in the news, since those are the stories we will choose to remember. No amount of data on how many more right-handed killers are on Death Row will sway us. Every lefty is proof; every righty is an exception. Likewise, if we've heard Boston drivers are rude, the next time we're visiting the Hub we'll remember the ones who honked at us or cut us off. We will promptly ignore or forget the ones who let us into traffic or waved a thank you. (For the record, *Forbes* in 2023 named Arizona and Rhode Island as the states with the "most confrontational" drivers. Massachusetts didn't even crack the top ten.)

In the 1988 film *Rain Man*, the autistic character Ray is a perfect, if extreme, example of confirmation bias. Ray is a savant whose mind is like a computer: it can do complex calculations at great speed, and it contains a giant repository of unrelated facts. But Ray, due to his condition, cannot arrange those facts into a coherent context. Whatever Ray's mind remembers is more important than all the other facts in the world.

Thus, when Ray and his brother must fly from Ohio to California, Ray panics. Every U.S. airline has, at some point, suffered a terrible disaster, and Ray can remember the dates and body counts *of every single one*. Focused on these terrifying exceptions, Ray refuses to get on any of the available flights. When the exasperated brother asks which company Ray will trust, he quietly names Australia's national airline. "Qantas," he says. "Qantas never crashed." Of course, Qantas does not fly domestically within the United States, and so Ray and his brother set off to drive cross-country, which is vastly more dangerous than flying. But because Ray has no databank of awe-inducing automobile crashes in his head, he gladly gets in the car.

We're all a little bit like Ray. We focus on the data that confirm our fears or fuel our hopes. We remember things that make an impression on us and ignore less dramatic realities. And when we argue with each other, or when we consult the advice of an expert, most of us have a hard time letting go of those memories, no matter how irrational it may be to focus on them.

To some extent, this is a problem not of general intelligence, but of education. People simply do not understand numbers, risk, or probability, and few things can make discussion between experts and laypeople more frustrating than this "innumeracy," as the mathematician John Allen Paulos memorably called it. For people who believe flying is dangerous, there will never be enough safe landings to outweigh the fear of the one crash. "Confronted with these large numbers and with the correspondingly small probabilities associated with them," Paulos wrote in 2001, "the innumerate will inevitably respond with the non sequitur, 'Yes, but what if you're that one,' and then nod knowingly, as if they've demolished your argument with their penetrating insight."[4]

Human beings can get quite creative with the "but what if I'm the one unlucky case" argument. Back in the early 1970s, I had an uncle who lived in rural Greece. He was a tough, athletic man, but he had a terrible fear of flying, which was preventing him from going to London to seek medical treatment for a serious ailment. My father tried to assure him with the fatalistic suggestion that while everyone will leave the earth one way or another, it's likely not his time to go. My uncle, like so many people who fear flying, resorted to a common objection: "Yes, but what if it's the *pilot's* time to go?"

None of us is perfectly rational, and most of us fear situations in which we are not in control. My uncle was an uneducated man born in a village in Greece in the early years of the twentieth century. I am an educated man of the twenty-first century with a good grasp of statistics and history—and yet I'm not much better about flying on those nights I've been buckled into the seat of a jetliner during some bumpy approaches into Providence. At moments like that, I try to think about the thousands of aircraft on approach all over the world, and the incredibly small chance that my plane will hit the Disaster Lottery. Usually, I fail miserably: all the flights that may be safely landing from Vancouver to Johannesburg are completely irrelevant to me as I grip the arms of my seat while my aircraft skims the house-tops of Rhode Island.

The late science fiction writer and medical doctor Michael Crichton used an example from the early days of the AIDS epidemic in the 1980s to show how people so often believe that they will always draw the shortest straw. The disease was poorly understood at the time, and a friend called Crichton for reassurance. Instead, she ended up nettled at the doctor's insistence on logic:

> I try to explain about risk. Because I have recently noticed how few people really understand the risks they face. I watch people keep guns in their houses, drive without seatbelts, eat artery-clogging French food, and smoke cigarettes, yet they never worry about these things. Instead they worry about AIDS. It's kind of crazy.
>
> "Ellen. Do you worry about dying in a car crash?"
> "No, never."

"Worry about getting murdered?"

"No."

"Well, you're much more likely to die in a car accident, or be murdered by a stranger, than to get AIDS."

"Thanks a lot," Ellen says. She sounds annoyed. "I'm so glad I called you. You're really reassuring, Michael."[5]

A decade later, AIDS was better understood and the hysteria faded. Nonetheless, many innumerate Americans still worry more about exotic diseases or terrorist attacks than about talking on their mobile phones while driving home after having a few drinks at the local pub.

Notice, too, how this bias almost never works in the other direction. Few of us are certain of being the exception in a *good* way. We'll buy a lottery ticket, fantasize about it for a moment, and then put it in our pocket and forget about it. No one heads to a car dealership or a realtor with tomorrow's Powerball number. We are gripped by irrational fear rather than irrational optimism because confirmation bias is, in a way, a kind of survival mechanism. Good things come and go, but dying is forever. Your brain doesn't much care about all those other people who survived a plane ride or a one-night stand: they're not you. Your intellect, operating on limited or erroneous information, is doing its job, trying to minimize any risk to your life, no matter how small. When we fight confirmation bias, we're trying to correct for a basic function—a feature, not a bug—of the human mind.

Whether the question is mortal peril or one of life's daily dilemmas, confirmation bias comes into play because people must rely on what they already know. They cannot approach every problem as though their minds are clean slates. This is not the way memory works, and more to the point, it would hardly be an effective strategy to begin every morning trying to figure everything out from scratch.

Scientists and researchers tussle with confirmation bias all the time as a professional hazard. They, too, must make prior assumptions in order to set up experiments or explain puzzles, which in turn means they're already bringing some baggage to their projects. They make guesses and use intuition, just like the rest of us, since it would waste a lot of time for every research program to begin from the assumption that no one knows anything and nothing ever happened before today.[6] "Doing before knowing" is a common problem in setting up any kind of careful investigation: after all, how do we know what we're looking for if we haven't found it yet?[7]

Researchers learn to recognize this dilemma early in their training, and they don't always succeed in defeating it. Confirmation bias can lead even the most experienced experts astray. Doctors, for example, will sometimes get attached to a diagnosis and then look for evidence of the symptoms they suspect already exist in a patient while ignoring markers of another disease or injury. We have a prejudice against uncertainty; even though every researcher is told that "a negative result is still a result," no one really wants to discover that their initial assumptions went up in smoke and that the right answer is still yet to be found.

This is how, for example, a 2014 study of public attitudes about gay marriage went terribly wrong. A graduate student claimed he'd found statistically reliable proof that if opponents of gay marriage talked about the issue with someone who was actually gay, they were likelier to change their minds. His findings were endorsed by a senior faculty member at Columbia University who had signed on as a coauthor of the study. It was a remarkable finding that basically amounted to proof that reasonable people can be talked out of homophobia.

The only problem was that the ambitious young researcher had falsified the data. The discussions he claimed he was analyzing never took place. When others outside the study reviewed it and raised alarms, the Columbia professor pulled the article. The student, who was about to start work on a bright future as a faculty member at Princeton, found himself out of a job.

Why didn't the faculty and reviewers who should have been keeping tabs on the student find the fraud right at the start? Because of confirmation bias. As the journalist Maria Konnikova later reported in the *New Yorker*, the student's supervisor admitted that he wanted to believe in its findings. He and other scholars *wanted* the results to be true, and so they were less likely to question the methods that produced their preferred answer. "In short, confirmation bias—which is especially powerful when we think about social issues—may have made the study's shakiness easier to overlook," Konnikova wrote in a review of the fiasco.[8] Indeed, it was "enthusiasm about the study that led to its exposure," because other scholars, hoping to build on the results, found the fraud only when they delved into the details of research they thought had already reached the conclusion they preferred.

This is why scientists, when possible, run experiments over and over and then submit their results to other people in a process called "peer review." This process—when it works—calls upon an expert's colleagues (his or her peers) to act as well-intentioned but rigorous devil's advocates. This usually takes place in a "double-blind" process, meaning that the researcher and the referees are not identified to each other, the better to prevent personal or institutional biases from influencing the review.

This is an invaluable process. Even the most honest and self-aware scholar or researcher needs a reality check from someone less personally invested in the outcome of a project. (The proposal for the book you're reading right now was peer-reviewed: that doesn't mean that the scholars who read it agreed with it, but that they were asked to consider the arguments and present whatever objections or advice they might have.) The ability to serve as a referee is often the role of a senior expert, since the ability to find and to recognize evidence that challenges or even disconfirms a hypothesis is something that takes quite a while to learn. Scholars and researchers spend a good part of their careers trying to master it as one of their core skills.

These reviews and revisions are invisible to laypeople because they all take place before the final product is released. The public only becomes aware of these processes when they go wrong—and when peer review goes wrong, it can go horribly wrong. The whole enterprise, instead of producing expert assurances of quality, can turn into fakery, backscratching, score settling, favoritism, and all the other petty behavior to which human beings are prone. In the case of the gay-marriage study, the fraud was discovered, and the system belatedly worked—but not in time to stop the article's initial publication.

In modern life outside of the academy, however, arguments and debates have no external review. Facts come and go as people find convenient at the moment. Thus, confirmation bias makes attempts at reasoned argument exhausting because it produces arguments and theories that are *nonfalsifiable*. It is the nature of confirmation bias itself to dismiss all contradictory evidence as irrelevant, and so *my* evidence is always the rule, *your* evidence is always a mistake or an exception. It's impossible to argue with this kind of explanation, because by definition it's never wrong.

An additional problem here is that most laypeople have never been taught, or they have forgotten, the basics of the "scientific method." This is the set of steps that lead from a general question to a hypothesis, testing, and analysis. Although people commonly use the word "evidence," they use it too loosely; the tendency in conversation is to use "evidence" to mean "things which I perceive to be true," rather than "things that have been subjected to a test of their factual nature by agreed-upon rules."

At this point, laypeople might object to all this as just so much intellectual hokum. Why does the average person need all this scholarly self-awareness? There's always common sense. Why isn't that good enough?

Most of the time, laypeople do not need any of this scholarly apparatus. In day-to-day matters, common sense serves us well and is usually better than needlessly complicated explanations. We don't need to know, for example, exactly how fast a car can go in a rainstorm before the tires begin to lose contact with the road. Somewhere there's a mathematical formula that would allow us to know the answer with great precision, but our common sense needs no such formula to tell us to slow down in bad weather, and that's good enough.

When it comes to untangling more complicated issues, however, common sense is not sufficient. Cause and effect, the nature of evidence, and statistical frequency are far more intricate than common sense can handle. Many of the thorniest research problems often have counterintuitive answers that by their nature defy our common sense. (Simple observation, after all, told early humans that the sun revolved around the earth, not the other way around.) The simple tools of common sense can betray us and make us susceptible to errors both great and small, which is why laypeople and experts so often talk past each other, even on relatively trivial issues such as superstitions and folk wisdom.

WIVES' TALES, SUPERSTITION, AND CONSPIRACY THEORIES

"Old wives' tales" and other superstitions are classic examples of confirmation bias and nonfalsifiable arguments. Many superstitions have some kind of grounding in experience. While it's a superstition that you shouldn't walk under ladders, for example, it's also true that it's *dangerous* to walk under a ladder. Whether you'll have bad luck all day by annoying a house painter is a different matter, but it's just foolish to walk under his ladder.

Superstitions are especially prone to confirmation bias, and they survive because common sense and confirmation bias sometimes reinforce each other. Are black cats unlucky? Cats, black or otherwise, by their nature tend to get underfoot, but we might only remember the black ones who trip us up. I have for many years lived with a lovely black cat named Carla, and I can confirm that she is, on occasion, a menace to my navigation of the stairs. A superstitious person might nod here knowingly; the fact that Carla is also the *only* cat in the house, of course, or whether other cat owners have tumbled over their tabbies, will mean nothing.

The most extreme cases of confirmation bias are found not in the wives' tales and superstitions of the ignorant, but in the conspiracy theories of more educated or intelligent people. Unlike superstitions, which are simple, conspiracy theories are horrendously complicated. Indeed, it takes a reasonably smart person to construct a really interesting conspiracy theory, because conspiracy theories are actually highly complex explanations. They are also challenging intellectual exercises, both for those who hold them and those who would disprove them. Superstitions are generally easy enough to disprove. Any statistician can verify that my cat is probably no more or less dangerous than any other on a staircase. Deep down, we know it anyway, which is why superstitions tend to be little more than harmless habits.

Conspiracy theories, by contrast, are frustrating precisely because they are so intricate. Each rejoinder or contradiction only produces a more complicated theory. Conspiracy theorists manipulate all tangible evidence to fit their explanation, but worse, they will also point to the *absence* of evidence as even stronger confirmation. After all, what better sign of a truly effective conspiracy is there than a complete lack of any trace that the conspiracy exists? Facts, the absence of facts, contradictory facts: everything is proof. Nothing can ever challenge the underlying belief.

These kinds of overcomplicated explanations violate the concept of "Occam's Razor" (sometimes spelled "Ockham"), named for the medieval monk who advocated the straightforward idea that we should always begin from the simplest explanation for anything we see. We should only work our way up toward more complicated explanations if we need them. This is also called the "law of parsimony," meaning that the most likely explanation is the one that requires the fewest number of logical leaps or shaky assumptions.

Imagine, for example, that we hear a noise, followed by someone swearing loudly in the next room. We run to the room and see a man, alone, holding his foot and jumping around with a grimace on his face. There's an empty crate and broken bottles of beer all over the floor. What happened?

Most of us will derive a simple explanation that the man dropped the crate on the floor, hurt his foot, and yelped an expletive. We heard the crash and we've seen people swear when injured. We have a good grasp of what other people look like when they're in pain, and the fellow is obviously hurting. It does not take many assumptions to create a reasonable explanation. It might not be a complete explanation, but it's a sensible first cut, given the available evidence.

But wait. Maybe the man is addicted to alcohol, and he's swearing because he's angry that he dropped the crate and the beer is now gone. Or maybe he's a temperance advocate, and he smashed the beer to the floor himself while cursing its vile existence. And perhaps he's holding his foot and jumping around because he is from a little-known culture in the far Canadian Arctic where people's faces are usually covered by parkas and they therefore express sorrow (or joy, or anger) by holding their feet and jumping. Or maybe he's a foreigner who thinks that certain pungent Anglo-Saxon words mean "Help, I dropped a crate of beer on my foot."

This is where the law of parsimony comes in. Any one of those oddball and highly unlikely possibilities could be true, but it would be ridiculous to jump right to such immensely complicated theorizing when we have a far more direct and serviceable explanation staring us right in the face. We have no idea if the man is a teetotaler or a drunk, whether he's from Canada or Cleveland, or whether his native language is English. While we can conduct some eventual investigation to find out whether any of those things are true, to *start* from any of those assumptions violates both logic and human experience.

If conspiracy theories are so complicated and ridiculous, why do they have such a hold on the popular imagination in so many societies? And make no mistake: they are in fact very popular and have been for centuries. Modern America is no exception. In the 1970s, for example, the novelist Robert Ludlum excelled at creating such conspiracies in a hugely popular series of novels, including one about a circle of political killers who were responsible for the assassination of President Franklin Roosevelt. (But wait, you say: FDR wasn't assassinated. *Exactly.*) Ludlum sold millions of books and created the fictional super-assassin Jason Bourne, who was the main character in a string of lucrative movies in the twenty-first century. Books, films, and television shows from *The Manchurian Candidate* in the early 1960s to *Stranger Things* five decades later have had millions of fans.

In modern American politics, conspiracy theories abound. President Barack Obama is a secret Muslim who was born in Africa. President George W. Bush was part of the plot to attack America on 9/11. The Queen of England was a drug dealer. The US government is spraying mind-controlling chemicals in the air through the exhaust ports of jet aircraft. COVID vaccines contain tracking microchips. The Jews control everything—except when the Saudis or Swiss bankers are controlling everything.

One reason we all love a good conspiracy thriller is that it appeals to our sense of heroism. A brave individual against a great conspiracy, fighting forces that would defeat the ordinary person, is a trope as old as the many legends of heroes themselves. American culture loves the idea of the talented amateur (as opposed, say, to the experts and elites) who can take on entire governments—or even bigger organizations—and win. James Bond, after all, didn't confront the gigantic terrorist enterprise SPECTRE until the British author Ian

Fleming realized he needed something bigger than Soviet communism for Bond to fight when his novels started to move to the Hollywood screen for American audiences.

More important and more relevant to the death of expertise, however, is that conspiracy theories are deeply attractive to people who have a hard time making sense of a complicated world and who have no patience for less dramatic explanations. Such theories also appeal to a strong streak of narcissism. Some people would choose to believe in complicated nonsense rather than accept that their own circumstances are the result of issues beyond their control, or beyond their intellectual capacity to understand, or even their own fault.

Conspiracy theories are also a way for people to give context and meaning to events that frighten them. Without a coherent explanation for why terrible things happen to innocent people, they would have to accept such occurrences as nothing more than the random cruelty of either an uncaring universe or an incomprehensible deity. These are awful choices, and even thinking about them can induce the kind of existential despair that leads a character in the nineteenth-century classic *The Brothers Karamazov* to make a famous declaration about tragedy: "If the sufferings of children go to make up the sum of the sufferings necessary to buy truth, then I protest that the truth is not worth such a price."

The only way out of this dilemma is to imagine a world in which our troubles are the fault of powerful people who had it within their power to avert such misery. In such a world, a loved one's incurable disease is not a natural event: it is the result of some larger malfeasance by industry or government. Revelations of the horrid behavior of a celebrity are not evidence that someone we admire is evil: it is a plot to smear a beloved figure. Even the loss of our favorite sports team might be a fix. ("I don't want to see the Buffalo Bills winning the Super Bowl," the chief villain in *The X-Files* said in a 1996 episode. "As long as I'm alive, that doesn't happen.") Whatever it is, *somebody* is at fault, because otherwise we're left blaming only God, pure chance, or ourselves.

Just as individuals facing grief and confusion look for reasons where none may exist, so, too, will entire societies gravitate toward outlandish theories when collectively subjected to a terrible national experience. Conspiracy theories and the flawed reasoning behind them, as the Canadian writer Jonathan Kay has noted, become especially seductive "in any society that has suffered an epic, collectively felt trauma. In the aftermath, millions of people find themselves casting about for an answer to the ancient question of why bad things happen to good people."[9] This is why conspiracy theories spiked in popularity after World War I, the Russian Revolution, the assassination of John F. Kennedy, the terror attacks of September 2001, and the COVID pandemic, among other historical events.

Today, some conspiracy theories are reactions to the economic and social dislocations of globalization, just as they were to the aftermath of war and the advent of rapid industrialization in the 1920s and 1930s. This is not a trivial obstacle when it comes to the problems of expert engagement with the public; nearly 30 percent of Americans in the mid-2010s, for example, thought "a secretive elite with a globalist agenda is conspiring to eventually rule the world," and 15 percent thought media or government add secret "mind-controlling" technology to TV broadcasts. Conspiracy theories about the possible murder of Princess Diana of the United Kingdom are still popular more than a quarter century after her death in a car accident. And in 2023, a University of Chicago study found that 12 percent of Americans accepted some version of the QAnon conspiracy theory that "Satanic pedophiles" control the US government.[10]

Such conspiracy theories are not harmless. At their worst, conspiracy theories can produce a moral panic in which innocent people get hurt, such as the "Satanic panic" of the 1980s, when some American parents became convinced that Satanic sex cults were operating inside children's day-care centers.[11] A similar panic, the rise of the QAnon movement—which believes, among other things, that prominent Americans are murdering children and harvesting their body fluids—has been vastly more destructive. The QAnon cult, which grew out of what seems now to be a malicious Internet prank that got out of control, gained adherents in the U.S. Congress and played a role in the violent attempt to overturn the American presidential election on January 6, 2021.[12]

If trying to get around confirmation bias is difficult, trying to deal with a conspiracy theory is impossible. Someone who believes that the oil companies are suppressing a new car that can run on seaweed is unlikely to be impressed by your new Prius or Tesla. (That's the energy-efficient car the industrial barons will *allow* you to have.) The people who think alien bodies were housed at Area 51 won't change their minds if they take a tour of the base. (The alien research lab is underground, you see.)

Arguing at length with a conspiracy theorist is not only fruitless but sometimes dangerous, and I do not recommend it. It's a treadmill of nonsense that can exhaust even the most tenacious teacher. Such theories are the ultimate bulwark against expertise, because of course every expert who contradicts the theory is *ipso facto* part of the conspiracy. As the writer Jef Rouner has put it in such an argument, "you have already lost your stand, and can do nothing more here."

> Ultimately, you are having a different interaction from the one you think you are. . . . You have to remember that the sort of person who readily subscribes to conspiracy theories already fears that there are vast, powerful forces maliciously allied against the areas of life that mean the most to them. Any denial of the threat increases the power of the threat by virtue of its being allowed to operate undetected.[13]

That's a place in a conversation where none of us wants to be.

Until QAnon, these large-scale cases of irrationality were few and far between. Now they are commonplace, even if their audiences are still small. But even people who do not believe in hallucinatory theories often harbor a daily unwillingness to accept expert advice, and this resistance is rooted in the same kind of populist suspicion of those perceived as smarter or more educated than the general public. The damage might be less dramatic, but it is no less tangible, and sometimes quite costly.

STEREOTYPES AND GENERALIZATIONS

"You can't generalize like that!" Few expressions are more likely to arise in even a mildly controversial discussion. People resist generalizations—boys tend to be like *this*, girls tend to be like *that*—because we all want to believe we're unique and that we cannot be pigeonholed that easily.

What most people usually mean when they object to "generalizing," however, is not that we shouldn't generalize, but that we shouldn't *stereotype*, which is a different issue. The problem in casual discourse is that people often don't understand the difference between stereotypes and generalizations, and this makes conversation, especially between experts and laypeople, arduous and exhausting. (I realize, of course, that I am generalizing here. But bear with me.)

The difference matters. Stereotyping is an ugly social habit, but generalization is at the root of every form of science. Generalizations are probabilistic statements, based on observable facts. They are not, however, explanations in themselves—another important difference from stereotypes. They're measurable and verifiable. Sometimes generalizations can lead us to posit cause and effect, and in some cases we might even observe enough to create a theory or a law that under constant circumstances is always true.

It is a generalization, for example, to say that "people in China are usually shorter than people in America." That may or may not be true. People who mistake this for a stereotype will immediately rush to find exceptions, and discussion will quickly run into a ditch: "I think Chinese people tend to be shorter than Americans." "You can't generalize like that! Chinese-born basketball player Yao Ming is seven and a half feet tall!"

The existence of an unusually tall Chinese basketball player proves nothing either way. We can settle this question only by going to the United States and China, measuring people, and seeing how often our assumption is true. If it's the case that Chinese people overall are shorter than Americans, then we've only noted something that is factually true enough times that we would not be wrong to assert it as a general but not infallible rule.

The hard work of explanation comes after generalization. *Why* are Americans taller than the Chinese? Is it genetic? Is it the result of a different diet? Are there environmental factors at work? There are answers to this question somewhere, but whatever they are, it's still not wrong to say that Americans tend to be taller than the Chinese, no matter how many slam-dunking exceptions we might find.

To say that *all* Chinese people are short, however, is to stereotype. The key to a stereotype is that it is impervious to factual testing. A stereotype brooks no annoying interference with reality, and it relies on the clever use of confirmation bias to dismiss all exceptions as irrelevant. (Racists have mastered this mode of argument: "All Brazilians are thieves except this one lady I work with, but she's different.") Stereotypes are not *predictions*, they're *conclusions*. That's why it's called "prejudice": it relies on pre-judging.

The tangle comes when we make generalizations that are negative or rooted in arguable criteria. No one can really dispute a generalization about height; it's something easily measurable in ways we all accept. Nor do we impute any sort of moral or political character to height. "Tall, aren't you?" a femme fatale says to the literary detective Phillip Marlowe in the 1939 novel *The Big Sleep*. "I didn't mean to be," Marlowe replies. It's witty precisely because we know being short or tall isn't something we control or for which we should apologize.

Negative generalizations, however, raise hackles, especially when they are based on arguable definitions. To say that "Russians are more corrupt than Norwegians," for example, is true but only if we adopt a shared definition of "corrupt." By Western definitions, Russia is plagued by corruption (and frankly, by Russian legal definitions as well), but it's also a perfectly reasonable objection to note that one culture's "bribe" is another culture's "gift." This is why generalizations need to be as carefully formulated as possible if they are to serve as basis for future research. There is a clear difference between "Russians in official positions are more willing to break their own laws in conducting government business than Norwegians in similar offices" as opposed to a broader statement that "Russians are more corrupt than Norwegians."

If we apply those narrower filters, we have a statement that is far less inflammatory and measurably true. Again, however, we have no idea why it's generally true. We know only that if we apply the same criteria consistently—that is, if we watch the same Russian and Norwegian officials process the same transactions enough times—we can establish something that is more often true than false. It may be that Russian laws are outdated and impossible to follow even for the most honest bureaucrat. (That's a bit of a stretch, but there's an element of truth in it, and it is, in my experience, an argument often made by many Russians themselves.) That's where more research comes in: to establish the *why* after confirming the *what*.

Of course, in daily conversation, none of this matters very much. These things may be true in some narrow, definable sense, but who wants to hear things that, if given without context, sound only like inflammatory assertions? Conversations among laypeople, and between laypeople and experts, can get difficult because human emotions are involved, especially if they are about things that are true in general but might not apply to any one case or circumstance.

That's why one of the most important characteristics of an expert is the ability to remain dispassionate, even on the most controversial issues. Experts must treat everything from cancer to nuclear war as problems to be solved with detachment and objectivity. Their distance from the subject enables open debate and consideration of alternatives, in ways meant to defeat emotional temptations, including fear, that lead to bias. This is a tall order, but otherwise conversation is not only arduous but sometimes explosive.

I'M OK, YOU'RE OK—SORT OF

There are other social and psychological realities that hobble our ability to exchange information. No matter how much we might suffer from confirmation bias or the heavy hand of the Dunning-Kruger Effect, for example, we don't like to tell people we know or care about that they're wrong. (At least not to their face.) Likewise, as much as we enjoy the natural feeling of being right about something, we're sometimes reluctant to defend our actual expertise. We all find it hard to separate the information, erroneous or otherwise, that serves as the foundations of our political and social beliefs from our self-image and our conceptions about who we are.

In 2014, for example, an international study reached a surprising and perhaps counterintuitive conclusion: people will go to great lengths to give each other a fair hearing and to weigh all opinions equally, even when everyone involved in the conversation knows there are substantial differences in competence between them. The authors of the study (which included people from China, Iran, and Denmark) suggest that this is an "equality bias" built into us, based on a human need to be accepted as part of a group. When two people were involved in repeated discussions and decision-making—and establishing a bond between the participants was a key part of the study—researchers found that the less capable people advocated for their views more than might have been expected, and that the more competent member of the conversation deferred to those points of view even when they were demonstrably wrong.[14]

At first, this sounds like nothing more than good manners and a desire for acceptance. Each party wanted to stay relevant to the other, rather than risk disrupting the relationship. The less competent person wanted to be respected and involved by not being seen as wrong or uninformed. The more competent person, meanwhile, did not want to alienate anyone by being consistently right.

This might make for a pleasant afternoon, but it's a lousy way to make decisions. As Chris Mooney, a *Washington Post* science writer, noted, this kind of social dynamic might grease the wheels of human relationships, but it can do real harm when facts are at stake. The study, he wrote, underscored "that we need to recognize experts more, respect them, and listen to them. But it also shows how our evolution in social groups binds us powerfully together and enforces collective norms but can go haywire when it comes to recognizing and accepting inconvenient truths."[15]

Why can't people simply accept these differences in knowledge or competence? This is an unreasonable question, since it amounts to saying, "Why don't people just accept that other people are smarter than they are?" (Or, conversely, "Why don't smart people just explain more clearly—and nicely—why other people are dumber than they are?") The reality is that social insecurity trips up both the intelligent and the ignorant. We all want to be liked.

In a similar vein, few of us want to admit to being lost in a conversation, especially when so much information is now so easily accessible. Social pressure has always tempted even intelligent, well-informed people to pretend to know more than they do, but this impulse is magnified in the Information Age. Karl Taro Greenfeld, a novelist and writer, described this kind of anxiety a decade ago in a meditation on why people attempt to "fake cultural literacy":

> What we all feel now is the constant pressure to know enough, at all times, lest we be revealed as culturally illiterate. So that we can survive an elevator pitch, a business meeting, a visit to the office kitchenette, a cocktail party, so that we can post, tweet, chat, comment, text as if we have seen, read, watched, listened. What matters to us, awash in petabytes of data, is not necessarily having actually consumed this content firsthand but simply knowing that it exists—and having a position on it, being able to engage in the chatter *about* it. We come perilously close to performing a pastiche of knowledgeability that is really a new model of know-nothingness.[16]

People skim headlines or articles and share them on social media, but they do not read them. Nonetheless, because people want to be perceived by others as intelligent and well informed, they fake it as best they can.

As if all of this weren't enough of a challenge, the addition of politics makes things even more complicated. Political beliefs among both laypeople and experts work in much the same way as confirmation bias. The difference is that beliefs about politics and other subjective matters are harder to shake, because our political views are deeply rooted in our self-image and our most cherished beliefs about who we are as people.

As Konnikova put it in her examination of the fraudulent gay-marriage study, confirmation bias is more likely to produce "persistently false beliefs" when it stems "from issues closely tied to our conception of self." These are the views that brook no opposition and that we will often defend beyond all reason, as Dunning noted:

> Some of our most stubborn misbeliefs arise not from primitive childlike intuitions or careless category errors, but from the very values and philosophies that define *who we are* as individuals. Each of us possesses certain foundational beliefs—narratives about the self, ideas about the social order—that essentially cannot be violated: To contradict them would call into question our very self-worth. As such, these views demand fealty from other opinions.

Put another way, what we believe says something important about how we see ourselves as people. We can take being wrong about the kind of bird we just saw in our backyard, or who the first person was to circumnavigate the globe, but we cannot tolerate being wrong about the concepts and facts that we rely upon to govern how we live our lives.

Take, for example, a common American kitchen-table debate: the causes of unemployment. Bring up the problem of joblessness with almost any group of laypeople and every possible intellectual problem will rear its head. Stereotypes, confirmation bias, half-truths, and statistical incompetence all bedevil this discussion.

Consider a person who holds firmly, as many Americans do, to the idea that unemployed people are just lazy and that unemployment benefits might even encourage that laziness. Like so many examples of confirmation bias, this could spring from personal experience. Perhaps it proceeds from a lifetime of continuous employment, or it may be the result of knowing someone who is genuinely averse to work. Every "help wanted" sign—which confirmation bias will note and file away—is further proof of the laziness of the unemployed. A page of job advertisements or a chronically irresponsible nephew constitutes irrefutable evidence that unemployment is a personal failing rather than a problem requiring government intervention.

Now imagine someone else at the table who believes that the nature of the American economy itself forces people into unemployment. This person might draw from experience as well: he or she may know someone who moved to follow a start-up company and ended up broke and far from home, or who was unjustly fired by a corrupt or incompetent supervisor. Every corporate downsizing, every racist or sexist boss, every failed enterprise is proof that the system is stacked against innocent people who would never choose unemployment over work. Unemployment benefits, rather than subsidizing indolence, are a lifeline and perhaps the only thing standing between an honest person and complete ruin.

There's a real argument to be had, of course, about the degree to which any of this is true, but these two people—admittedly, drawn as caricatures for our purposes here—are not going to be the ones to have it. It's unarguable that unemployment benefits suppress the urge to work in at least *some* people; it's also undeniable that *some* corporations have a history of ruthlessness at the expense of their workers, whose reliance on benefits is reluctant and temporary. This conversation can go on forever, because both the Hard Worker on one side and the Kind Heart on the other can adduce anecdotes, carefully vetted by their own confirmation bias, that are always true but are in no way dispositive.

There's no way to win this argument, because in the end, there are no answers that will satisfy everyone. Laypeople want a definitive answer from the experts, but none can be had because there is not one answer but many, depending on circumstances. When do benefits encourage sloth? How often are people thrown out of work against their will, and for how long? These are nuances in a broad problem, and especially where our self-image is involved, nuance isn't helpful. Unable to see their own biases, most people will simply drive each other crazy arguing, rather than accept answers that contradict what they already think about the subject. The social psychologist Jonathan Haidt summed it up neatly when he observed that when facts conflict with our values, "almost everyone finds a way to stick with their values and reject the evidence."[17]

This tendency is in fact so strong that a fair number of people, regardless of political affiliation, will shoot the messenger rather than hear something they don't like. A 2015 study, for example, tested the reactions of both liberals and conservatives to certain kinds of news stories, and it found that "just as conservatives discount the scientific theories that run counter to their worldview, liberals will do exactly the same."[18] (As we will see in Chapter 7, a similar dynamic emerged between the right and left at the outset of the COVID pandemic, but while liberals mostly corrected course, anti-science attitudes deepened and hardened on the right when political leaders employed attacks on expertise as signifiers of partisan loyalty.)[19] Even more disturbing, the study found that when exposed to scientific research that challenged their views, both liberals and conservatives reacted by doubting the *science*, rather than themselves. "Just reading about these polarizing topics," one of the authors noted, "is having a negative effect on how people feel about science."

This is why, as we'll see later in this book, the only way to resolve these debates in terms of policy choices is to move them from the realm of research to the arena of politics and democratic choice. If democracy is to mean anything at all, then experts and laypeople must solve complicated problems together. First, however, they face the challenge of overcoming the widening gulf between them. More education seems like an obvious solution, but in the next chapter we'll see that education, at least at the college level, is now part of the problem.

Chapter 3

Higher Education

The Customer Is Always Right

Those persons whom nature has endowed with genius and virtue should be rendered by liberal education worthy to receive and able to guard the sacred deposit of the rights and liberties of their fellow citizens.

Thomas Jefferson

Mr. Braddock: Would you mind telling me what those four years of college were for? What was the point of all that hard work?
Benjamin: You got me.

The Graduate

THOSE MAGICAL SEVEN YEARS

Higher education is supposed to cure us of the false belief that everyone is as smart as everyone else. Unfortunately, in the twenty-first century the effect of widespread college attendance is just the opposite: the great number of people who have been in or near a college think of themselves as the educated peers of even the most accomplished scholars and experts. College is no longer a time devoted to learning and personal maturation; instead, the stampede of young Americans into college and the consequent competition for their tuition dollars have produced a consumer-oriented experience in which students learn, above all else, that the customer is always right.

Before World War II, most people did not finish high school, and few went to college. In this earlier time, admissions to top schools were dominated by privileged families, although sometimes young men and a very few women could scrape up the money for tuition or earn a scholarship. It was an exclusive experience often governed as much by social class as by merit. (This remains true even today for families with very high incomes, whose children are still disproportionately likely to be admitted to top schools.)[1] Still, college attendance was an indication of potential, and graduation was a mark of achievement. A university degree was rare, serving as one of the signposts dividing experts and knowers from the rest of society.

Today, attendance at postsecondary institutions is a mass experience. As a result of this increased access to higher education, the word "college" itself is losing meaning, at least in terms of separating educated people from everyone else. "College graduate" today means a lot of things. Unfortunately, "a person of demonstrated educational achievement" is not always one of them.

Bashing colleges and universities is an American tradition, as is bashing the faculty who teach in them. (I was a member of several during my teaching career.) Stereotypes abound, including the stuffy (or radical, or irrelevant) professor in front of a collection of bored children who themselves came to campus for any number of activities except education. "College boy" was once a zinger aimed by older people at young men, with the clear implication that education was no substitute for maturity or wisdom.

But this book isn't about why colleges are screwed up. For one thing, they're not actually that much of a mess, despite the beliefs of increasing numbers of Americans (many of whom have never worked in higher education or even set foot on a college campus). And I don't have enough pages for the many *real* problems facing institutions of higher education. The problem we'll examine in this chapter is why fewer people respect learning and expertise, and how colleges and universities paradoxically became an important part of that trend.

I say this while remaining a defender of the American university system, including the much-maligned liberal arts. As the son of a working-class family, I am personally a beneficiary of wider access to higher education in the twentieth century and the social mobility it provided. The record of these institutions is unarguable. Universities in the United States are still the leading intellectual powerhouses in the world. I continue to have faith in the ability of America's post-secondary schools to produce both knowledge and knowledgeable citizens.

Still, the fact of the matter is that many of those American higher educational institutions are failing to provide to their students the basic knowledge and skills that form expertise. More important, they are failing to provide the ability to *recognize* expertise and to engage productively with experts and other professionals in daily life. The most important of these intellectual capabilities, and the one most under attack in American universities, is critical thinking: the ability to examine new information and competing ideas dispassionately, logically, and without emotional or personal preconceptions.

This is because attendance at a postsecondary institution no longer guarantees a "college education." Instead, colleges and universities now provide a full-service experience of "going to college." These are not remotely the same thing, and students now graduate believing they know a lot more than they actually do. Today, if an expert says, "Well, I went to college," it's hard to blame the public for answering, "Who hasn't?" Americans with college degrees now broadly think of themselves as "educated" when in reality the best that many of them can say is that they've continued on in some kind of classroom setting after high school, with wildly varying results.

The influx of students into America's postsecondary schools has driven an increasing commodification of education. Students at most schools today are treated as *clients*, rather than as students. Younger people, barely out of high school, are pandered to both materially and intellectually, reinforcing some of the worst tendencies in students who have not yet learned the self-discipline that once was essential to the pursuit of higher education. Colleges now are marketed as if they were multiyear vacation packages, rather than as a contract with an institution and its faculty for a course of educational study. This commodification of the college experience itself as a product is not only destroying the value of college degrees but is also undermining confidence among ordinary Americans that college means anything.

This is a deeper problem than the usual student stunts and intellectual fads on campuses that capture the public imagination from time to time. There will always be a certain amount of foolishness to a lot of campus life. As a Tufts University professor, Dan Drezner, has written, "One of the purposes of college is to articulate stupid arguments in stupid ways and then learn, through interactions with fellow students and professors, exactly how stupid they are."[2] College life, especially at the most elite schools, is insulated from society, and when young people and intellectuals are walled off from the real world, strange things can happen.

Some of this is just so much expensive inanity, harmless in itself. Nor is eye-rolling silliness at educational institutions all that new. Over a decade ago, for example, parents of students at Brown University were shelling out serious money so their children could take part in things like "Campus Nudity Week." (One female Brown participant said in 2013 that "the negative feedback" about the event "has helped prepare her for life after college." One can only hope.) In the end, however, I've never been all that worried about naked students amok in the streets of Providence. Instead, my concerns about colleges and how they've accelerated the death of expertise rest more with what happens—or isn't happening—in the classroom.

At its best, college should aim to produce graduates with a reasonable background in a subject, a willingness to continue learning for the rest of their lives, and an ability to assume roles as capable citizens. Instead, for many people college has become, in the words of a graduate of a well-known party school in California, "those magical seven years between high school and your first warehouse job." College is no longer a passage to educated maturity and instead is only a delaying tactic against the onset of adulthood—in some cases, for the faculty as well as for the students.

Part of the problem is that there are too many students, a fair number of whom simply don't belong in college. The new culture of education in the United States is that everyone should, and must, go to college. This cultural change is important to the death of expertise, because as programs proliferate to meet demand, schools become diploma mills whose actual degrees are indicative less of *education* than of *training*, two distinctly different concepts that are increasingly conflated in the public mind. In the worst cases, degrees affirm neither education nor training, but attendance. At the barest minimum, they certify only the timely payment of tuition.

This is one of those things professors are not supposed to say in polite company, but it's true. Young people who might have done better in a trade sign up for college without a lot of thought given to how to graduate, or what they'll do when it all ends. Four years turns into five, and increasingly six or more. A limited course of study eventually turns into repeated visits to an expensive educational buffet laden with plenty of intellectual junk food, and with very little adult supervision to ensure that the students choose nutrition over nonsense.

The most competitive and elite colleges and universities have fewer concerns in this regard, as they can pick and choose from applicants as they wish and fill their incoming classes with generally excellent students. These students will get a full education, or close to it, and then usually go on to profitable employment. Other institutions, however, end up in a race to the bottom. All these children, after all, are going to go to college somewhere, and so schools that are otherwise indistinguishable on the level of intellectual quality compete to offer better pizza in the food court, plushier dorms, and more activities besides the boring grind of going to class.

Not only are there too many students, there are too many professors. The very best national universities, the traditional sources of university faculty, are promiscuously pumping out PhDs at a rate far higher than any academic job market can possibly absorb. (I saw this glut of doctorates firsthand as a member of many hiring committees.) Lesser schools that have no business offering advanced degrees—and many of which barely qualify as glorified high schools even at the undergraduate level—offer doctorates of such low quality that they themselves would never hire their own graduates. Scads of unemployed PhDs, toting mediocre dissertations in any number of overly esoteric subjects, roam the academic landscape literally willing to teach for food.

Even the term "professor" has been denatured by overuse. Once a rare title, American postsecondary institutions now use it at will. Anyone who teaches in anything above the level of a high school is now a professor, from the head of a top department at a major research university to a part-time instructor in a local community college. And just as every teacher is a "professor," so, too, is every small college now a "university," a phenomenon that has reached ridiculous proportions. Tiny local schools that once served area residents have reemerged as "universities," as though they now have a particle collider behind the cafeteria.

The emergence of these faux universities is in part a response to an insatiable demand for degrees in a culture where everyone thinks they should go to college. Schools and colleges have created a destructive spiral of credential inflation the same way governments cause monetary inflation: by printing more paper. A high school diploma was once the requirement for entering the trades or beginning a profession. But everybody has one of those now, including people who can't even read. Consequently, many colleges now serve to verify the completion of high school, and so a master's degree now fills the requirement once served by a bachelor's degree. Students are going broke running around in this educational hamster wheel, without learning very much.[3]

How to solve all this is a crucial question for the future of American education. In 2016, a Democratic Party presidential candidate, Senator Bernie Sanders, said that a college degree today is the equivalent of what a high school degree was fifty years ago—and that therefore everyone should go to college just as everyone now attends high school. Six years later, President Joe Biden tried to push through a large-scale forgiveness of student debt—but without any effort to alleviate the conditions that encouraged all that debt in the first place. Both Sanders and Biden avoided the reality that treating colleges as remedial high schools is a significant part of how we got here in the first place. The larger point, however, is that the cumulative result of too many "students," too many "professors," too many "universities," and too many degrees is that college attendance is no longer a guarantee that people know what they're talking about.

The failures of the modern university are fueling attacks on the very knowledge those same institutions have worked for centuries to create and to teach to future generations. Intellectual discipline and maturation have fallen by the wayside. The transmission of important cultural learning—including everything from how to construct a logical argument to the foundational DNA of American civilization—is no longer the mission of the customer-service university.

WELCOME, CLIENTS!

College is supposed to be an uncomfortable experience. It is where a person leaves behind the rote learning of childhood and accepts the anxiety, discomfort, and challenge of complexity that leads to the acquisition of deeper knowledge—hopefully, for a lifetime. A college degree, whether in physics or philosophy, is supposed to be the mark of a truly "educated" person who not only has command of a particular subject, but also has a wider understanding of his or her own culture and history. It's not supposed to be easy.

This is no longer how college is viewed in modern America either by the providers or by the consumers of higher education. College as a client-centered experience caters to adolescents instead of escorting them away from adolescence. Rather than disabusing students of their intellectual solipsism, the modern university ends up reinforcing it. Students can leave campus without fully accepting that they've met anyone more intelligent than they are, either among their peers or their teachers. (This assumes that they even bother to make any distinction between peers and teachers at all.) They accept their degree as a receipt for spending several years around a lot of interesting people they and their families have paid for a service.

This is not to say that today's students are intellectually incompetent. Most of the young people at competitive schools have already mastered the rituals of test taking, recommendations, extracurricular activities, and other college-bound merit badges, and they arrive ready to take advantage of the great opportunities placed before them. Unfortunately, once they defeat the admissions maze and arrive at college, they too often spend the next four years being undereducated but overly praised, especially if they are determined to navigate their way through school on a diet of lightweight coursework. They might even suspect as much, and as a result they risk developing a toxic combination of insecurity and arrogance that serves them poorly once they're beyond the embrace of their parents and the comforting walls of their schools.

Meanwhile, at less competitive schools, students have far fewer worries during the application process, which might seem like a relief but is a problem in itself. As the economic writer Ben Casselman pointed out in 2016, most college applicants "never have to write a college entrance essay, pad a résumé or sweet-talk a potential letter-writer," because as a former college admissions officer noted, more than three-quarters of American undergraduates attend colleges that accept at least half their applicants. Only 4 percent attend schools that accept 25 percent or less, and fewer than 1 percent attend elite schools that accept fewer than 10 percent of their applicants, numbers that remained mostly unchanged in 2022.[4] Students at these less competitive institutions then struggle to finish, with only half completing a bachelor's degree within six years.

Many of these incoming students are not qualified to be in college and need significant remedial work. The colleges know it, but they accept students who are in over their heads, stick them in large (but cost-efficient) introductory courses, and hope for the best. Why would schools do this and obviously violate what few admissions standards they might still enforce? The answer, of course, is money. Even poorly prepared students take out loans and pay tuition; some will finish and some won't, but for a few years the institution gets paid either way, and somewhere a young person can say he or she has at least "some college."

Even without these financial pressures, the stampede toward college by unprepared students is also due to a long-standing culture of affirmation and self-actualization that forbids confronting children with failure. As Robert Hughes wrote back in 1995, America is a culture in which "children are coddled not to think they're dumb."[5] A junior high school teacher in Maryland captured the essence—and persistence—of this problem two decades later in a 2014 article she published in the *Washington Post* after she decided to quit her profession. She said that her school administration gave her two instructions that to her were "defining slogans for public education." One was that students were not allowed to fail. The other foreshadowed the client-centered approach to college: "If they have D's or F's, there is something that you are not doing for them."[6]

I encountered this in my teaching career numerous times, and not just among children or young college undergraduates. I had graduate students tell me that if they did not get an A in my class, their lesser grade would be evidence of poor instruction on my part. I also had students who nearly failed my class ask me for—and, in some cases, *demand*—a recommendation for a graduate program or a professional school. College students may not be dumber than they were thirty years ago, but their sense of entitlement and their self-confidence have grown considerably.

Parenting obviously plays a major role here. Overprotective parents have become so intrusive that a former dean of first-year students at Stanford wrote an entire book in which she said that this "helicopter parenting" was ruining a generation of children. These are the parents who defend and coddle their children even into high school and college, doing their homework for them—the Stanford dean politely calls this "overhelping"—and in general participating in every aspect of their child's life.[7] Some are worse than others: parents in some cases are moving to the same town as their children's colleges to be near them while they attend school. This is not "helicopter parenting" but more like "close air-support jet fighter parenting."

Another problem, paradoxically enough, is affluence. This sounds like a remarkable claim at a time when so many parents and young people are worrying about how to meet educational costs. But the fact of the matter is that more people than ever before are going to college, mostly by tapping a virtually inexhaustible supply of ruinous loans. Buoyed by this government-guaranteed money, and in response to aggressive marketing from tuition-driven institutions, teenagers from almost all of America's social classes now shop for colleges the way the rest of us shop for cars.

The campus visit is a good example of the shopping ritual that teaches children to choose colleges for any number of reasons besides an education. Each spring and summer, the highways fill with children and their parents on road trips to visit schools not to which the young clients have been accepted, but to which they are only *considering* applying. These are not just rich kids touring the Ivy League; friends with teenage children regularly tell me about hitting the road to visit small colleges and state schools I've never heard of. Every year, these parents ask me for my advice, and every year, I tell them it's a bad idea. Every year, they thank me for my input and do it anyway. By the end of the process, the entire family is cranky and exhausted, and the question of what the schools actually teach seems almost an afterthought.

Usually, the youngsters like most of the schools, because to a teenager stuck in high school, all colleges seem like pretty great places. Some choices, of course, quickly drop off the radar. An ugly town, a dingy campus, a decrepit dormitory, and that's that. Other times, prospective students fall in love with a school and then spend months agonizing like anxious suitors, hoping that a school they chose while they were barely past their sixteenth birthdays will give them the nod and change the course of their lives.

The idea that adolescents should first think about why they want to go to college at all, find schools that might best suit their abilities, apply only to those schools, and then visit the ones to which they're *accepted* is now alien to many parents and their children. Ask the parents why they drove their sons and daughters all over Creation to visit schools they may have no desire to attend—or to which they have almost no chance of admittance—and the answer rarely varies: "Well, they wanted to see it." The sentence few of them add is: "And we chose to spend the money to do it." College applications, at fifty bucks a pop or more, aren't cheap, but it's a lot more expensive to go road-tripping from Amherst to Atlanta.

This entire process means not only that children are in charge, but that they are already being taught to value schools for some reason other than the education it might provide. Schools know this, and they're ready for it. In the same way the local car dealership knows exactly how to place a new model in the showroom, or a casino knows exactly how to perfume the air that hits patrons just as they walk in the door, colleges have all kinds of perks and programs at the ready as selling points, mostly to edge out their competitors over things that matter primarily to kids.

Driven to compete for teenagers and their loan dollars, educational institutions promise an experience rather than an education. (I am leaving aside for-profit schools here, too many of which are mills that create debt and that in general I exclude from the definition of "higher education.") There's nothing wrong with creating an attractive student center or offering a slew of activities, but at some point it's like having a hospital entice heart patients to choose their cardiology department for a coronary bypass because it has great food.

Children and young adults are more empowered in this process at least in part because loan programs have shifted control over tuition from parents to students. There is also the more general trend, however, that parents for some decades have abdicated more and more decisions about many things to their children. Either way, it is hard to disagree with the *Bloomberg* columnist Megan McArdle's observation that decisions over the whole business have migrated from parents to children, with predictable results when "students are more worried about whether their experience is unpleasant than are parents."[8]

Undergraduate institutions play to these demands in every way. For example, some schools now try to accommodate the anxiety many high school students face about living with strangers. Once upon a time, learning to live with a roommate was part of the maturing process but one that was understandably dreaded by children still living with their parents. No longer, as a faculty member at Arizona State wrote about an emerging trend over the past decade:

> At many colleges, new students already have been introduced to their roommates on social media and live in luxurious apartment-like dorms. That ensures they basically never have to share a room or a bathroom, or even eat in the dining halls if they don't want to. Those were the places where previous generations learned to get along with different people and manage conflicts when they were chosen at random to live with strangers in close and communal quarters.[9]

If a student chooses to go to Arizona State because he or she likes the idea of never eating in a dining hall, something is already wrong with the entire process. Many young people, of course, have made worse choices for even sillier reasons.

Students are young and parents love their kids. Fair enough. But when the entire carnival of applications and admissions is over, the faculty must teach students who have walked into their classrooms with expectations completely unrelated to the actual requirements of gaining a college education. Today, professors do not instruct their students; instead, the students instruct their professors, with an authority that comes naturally to them. A group of Yale students in 2016, for example, demanded that the English department abolish its Major English Poets course because it was too larded with white European males: "We have spoken," they said in a petition. "We are speaking. Pay attention."[10] (Just imagine a professor punctuating a lecture by saying: "I have spoken.")

Sometimes, hypersensitivity to student objections can result in damage to careers, institutions, and the cause of education itself. In 2022, a student at Hamline University objected to an art history professor showing a famous painting of the Prophet Muhammad.

The professor, an adjunct without the protections of tenure, was fired after what the American Association of University Professors later called a "de facto campaign of vilification," that was "encouraged and promoted" by Hamline administrators, including accusations of Islamophobia.[11] The school's president made things worse when she made the baffling argument that academic freedom must not "infringe upon the rights of students."[12] To their credit, Hamline's faculty rejected this tepid defense of academic freedom and voted overwhelmingly to ask their president to step down. (She soon announced her retirement.) The university later backtracked and apologized in the face of a lawsuit from the instructor. But the damage was already done, and all because of the inflamed sensitivities of one student and some incompetent administrators.[13]

As a professor at an elite school once said to me, "Some days, I feel less like a teacher and more like a clerk in an expensive boutique."

And why shouldn't he? These are children who have been taught to address adults by their first names since they were toddlers. They have been given "grades" meant to raise their self-esteem rather than to spur achievement. And many of them have matriculated after being allowed to peruse colleges as though they were inspecting a condo near a golf course. This stream of small but meaningful adult concessions to children and their self-esteem corrodes their ability to learn, and it inculcates a false sense of achievement and overconfidence in their own knowledge that lasts well into adulthood.

When I first arrived as a faculty member at Dartmouth at the end of the 1980s, I was told a story about a well-known (and, at the time, still-living) member of the faculty that in a small way illustrates this problem and the challenge it presents to experts and educators. The renowned astrophysicist Robert Jastrow gave a lecture on President Ronald Reagan's plan to develop space-based missile defenses, which he strongly supported. An undergraduate challenged Jastrow during the question-and-answer period, and by all accounts Jastrow was patient but held to his belief that such a program was possible and necessary. The student, realizing that a scientist at a major university was not going to change his mind after a few minutes of arguing with a sophomore, finally shrugged and gave up.

"Well," the student said, "your guess is as good as mine."

Jastrow stopped the young man short. "No, no, no," he said emphatically. "*My* guesses are much, *much* better than yours."

Professor Jastrow has since passed away, and I never got the chance while I was in Hanover to ask him what happened that day. But I suspect that he was trying to teach some life lessons that are increasingly resisted by college students and citizens alike: that admission to college is the beginning, not the end, of education and that respecting a person's *opinion* does not mean granting equal respect to that person's *knowledge*. Whether national missile defenses are a wise policy is still debatable. What hasn't changed, however, is that the guesses of an experienced astrophysicist and a college sophomore are not equivalently good.

This is more than some Ivy League smart-alecks cracking wise with their professors. To take a less rarified example, a young woman in 2013 took to social media for help with a class assignment. (Where she lives or where she was studying is unclear, but she described herself as a future doctor.) She apparently was tasked with researching the deadly chemical substance Sarin, and, as she explained to thousands on Twitter, she needed help because she had to watch her child while doing her assignment. In minutes, her request was answered by Dan Kaszeta, the director of a security consulting firm in London and a top expert in the field of chemical weapons, who volunteered to help her.

What happened next transfixed many readers. (Jeffrey Lewis, an arms expert in California, captured and posted the exchange online.) "I can't find the chemical and physical properties of sarin gas [sic] someone please help me," the student tweeted. Kaszeta offered his help. He corrected her by noting that Sarin isn't a gas and that the word should be capitalized. As Lewis later wryly noted, "Dan's help [met] with a welcome sigh of relief from our beleaguered student."

Actually, it met with a string of expletives. The student lectured the expert in a gale-force storm of outraged ego: "yes the [expletive] it is a gas you ignorant [expletive]. sarin is a liquid & can evaporate . . . shut the [expletive] up." Kaszeta, clearly stunned, tried one more time: "Google me. I'm an expert on Sarin. Sorry for offering to help." Things did not improve before the exchange finally ended.

One smug Dartmouth kid and one angry Twitter user could be outliers, and they're certainly extreme examples of trying to deal with students. But faculty both in the classroom and on social media continue to report that incidents where students take correction as an insult are occurring more frequently. Unearned praise and hollow successes build a fragile arrogance in students that can lead them to lash out at the first teacher or employer who dispels that illusion, a habit that proves hard to break in adulthood.

CAN'T I JUST EMAIL YOU?

Client servicing and the treatment of expertise as a product are evident in colleges today, even in the smallest things. Consider, for example, the influence of email, which encourages all kinds of odd behavior that students would usually hesitate to display in person.

Even if we leave aside the occasional bad decision after a weekend of partying to write something and hit "send," email encourages a misplaced sense of intimacy that erodes the boundaries necessary to effective teaching. As we'll see in the next chapter, this is a characteristic of interactions over electronic media in general, but the informality of communication between teachers and students is one more example of how college life can contribute to the eroding respect for experts and their abilities.

Email became common on campuses in the early 1990s, and within a decade, professors noticed the changes wrought by instant communications. In 2006, the *New York Times* asked college educators about their experiences with student email, and their frustration was evident. "These days," the *Times* wrote, "students seem to view [faculty] as available around the clock, sending a steady stream of e-mail messages . . . that are too informal or downright inappropriate." As a Georgetown theology professor told the *Times*, "The tone that they would take in e-mail was pretty astounding. 'I need to know this and you need to tell me right now,' with a familiarity that can sometimes border on imperative."[14] I regularly saw such emails in my own career. In many, the salutation to me was "Hey," followed by a long string of disjointed prose, and then capped by a request: "Thoughts?"

Email, like social media, is a great equalizer, and it makes students comfortable with the idea of messages to teachers as being like any communication with a customer-service department. This has a direct impact on respect for expertise because it erases any distinction between the students who ask questions and the teachers who answer them. As the *Times* noted,

> While once professors may have expected deference, their expertise seems to have become just another service that students, as consumers, are buying. So students may have no fear of giving offense, imposing on the professor's time or even of asking a question that may reflect badly on their own judgment.
>
> Kathleen E. Jenkins, a sociology professor at the College of William and Mary in Virginia, said she had even received e-mail requests from students who missed class and wanted copies of her teaching notes.

When faced with these kinds of faculty complaints about email, one Amherst sophomore said, "If the only way I could communicate with my professors was by going to their office or calling them, there would be some sort of ranking or prioritization taking place. Is this question worth going over to the office?"

To which a faculty member might respond: *that's exactly the point.* Professors are not intellectual valets or on-call pen pals. They do not exist to resolve every student question instantly—including, as one UC Davis professor reported, advice about whether to use a binder or a subject notebook. One of the things students are supposed to learn in college is self-reliance, but why bother looking something up when the faculty member is only a few keystrokes away?

The COVID pandemic accelerated this trend when it shifted many high school and college classes to online versions taught using cameras and conferencing software. For many years before the pandemic, I taught hybrid courses—that is, in residence but with an option for some students to watch a live feed of the class in real time—and while it's always better to have a student in the room with the teacher, distance education is invaluable for people who are simply too far from the classroom or whose work and life schedules prevent class attendance.

But when classes switched to a purely online mode for two years, I—along with many of my colleagues at other institutions—was amazed that students came to "class" with their feet propped up on pillows, their phones nearby, and their televisions on. (For my part, I sat at a desk.) Students would keep up a steady stream of chat to each other during class—and then ask for parts of the lecture to be repeated because of their multiple distractions. These were not underachieving students; rather, the shift to learning from home undermined the habits both of decorum and discipline that help students focus in the classroom. The pandemic was a trying time, but where schooling is concerned, I can only hope that it finally buried the misbegotten concept that education can be virtualized.

Higher education is designed to help students overcome their intellectual indiscipline, not to encourage it. For many reasons, including the risk to their jobs, professors are sometimes hesitant to take charge, especially if they are untenured or adjunct faculty. Some of them, of course, treat children as their equals because they have absorbed the idea that the students really are their peers, a mistake that hurts both teaching and learning. Some educators even repeat the old saw that "I learn as much from my students as they learn from me!" With due respect to my colleagues in the teaching profession who use this expression, I am compelled to say: if that's true, *then you're not a very good teacher.*[15]

The solution to this reversal of roles in the classroom is for teachers to reassert their authority. To do so, however, would first require overturning the entire notion of education as client service. Tuition-conscious administrators would hardly welcome such a counterrevolution in the classroom, but in any case, it would likely be deeply unpopular with the clients.

For many years, Father James Schall at Georgetown University would unsettle his political philosophy students at the very first class meeting by handing out an essay he'd written called "What a Student Owes His Teacher." Here's a sample:

Students have obligations to teachers. I know this sounds like strange doctrine, but let it stand.

The first obligation, particularly operative during the first weeks of a new semester, is a moderately good will toward the teacher, a trust, a confidence that is willing to admit to oneself that the teacher has probably been through the matter, and, unlike the student, knows where it all leads. I do not want here to neglect the dangers of the ideological professor, of course, the one who imposes his mind on what is. But to be a student requires a certain modicum of humility.

Thus, the student owes the teacher trust, docility, effort, thinking.[16]

Schall (a friend and mentor who has since passed away) made that essay required reading for many years before retiring. One can only imagine the howls of outrage it would provoke now on most campuses to tell students they need to work harder, have more perspective about their own talents, and trust their teachers. Many faculty members today might agree with Schall, but they cannot risk aggravating the students, because, as everyone in any service industry knows, the customer is always right.

Students, well intentioned or otherwise, are poorly served by the idea that students and teachers are intellectual and social equals and that a student's opinion is as good as a professor's knowledge. Rather than disabusing young people of these myths, college too often encourages them, with the result that people end up convinced they're smarter than they are. As the social psychologist David Dunning has noted, "The way we traditionally conceive of ignorance—as an absence of knowledge—leads us to think of education as its natural antidote. But education, even when done skillfully, can produce illusory confidence."[17]

Just imagine how difficult things get when education isn't done skillfully.

THE GENERIC UNIVERSITY

An administrator at a small college—excuse me, a "university"—could well read this chapter and protest that I am unfairly excoriating businesses for acting like businesses. Higher education, after all, is an industry, and it is no sin if the corporations in it compete with each other. The business analogy, however, fails when the schools themselves do not deliver what they've promised: an education. The game begins long before a prospective student fills out an application. Even as colleges have moved toward intellectually low-impact programs surrounded by lifestyle improvements and nonacademic activities, they have attempted simultaneously to inflate their importance and burnish their brands. My earlier comment about the proliferation of "universities" was not a stray observation: it's happening, and it has been going on since at least the 1990s. Like so much else associated with the current maladies of higher education, it is a change driven by money and status.

One reason these small schools become universities is to appeal to students who want to believe they're paying for something in a higher tier—that is, for a regional or national "university," rather than a local college.[18] State colleges and community colleges are lower-status institutions, when compared with four-year universities, in the eyes of college-bound high school students (and especially foreign students, who bring sizable tuition checks with them). Hence, many of them have tried to distinguish themselves with an attempted rebranding as "universities."

A more prosaic motivation behind this name game is to find new funding streams by grafting graduate programs onto small colleges. The competition to pull in more money and the consequent proliferation of graduate programs have thus forced these new "universities" into a degree-granting arms race. Not only are schools adding graduate programs in professional degrees like business administration, but many of them are bloating their undergraduate programs with additional coursework for a master's degree.

Faced with this competitive pressure from other schools doing likewise, some of these fledgling universities then step up their game and add doctoral programs. And because these small schools cannot support a doctoral program in an established field, they construct esoteric interdisciplinary fields that exist only to create new credentials. It's not hard to see how this ends up creating degrees that do not signal a corresponding level of knowledge.

All of this borders on academic malpractice. The creation of graduate programs in colleges that can barely provide a reasonable undergraduate education cheats both graduates and undergrads. Small colleges do not have the resources—including the libraries, research facilities, and multiple programs—of large universities, and repainting the signs at the front gates cannot magically create that kind of academic infrastructure. Turning Smallville College into Generic University might look good on the new stationery, but it is the kind of move that can push what might have been a serviceable local college into a new status as a half-baked university.

This rebranding dilutes the worth of all postsecondary degrees. When everyone has attended a university, it gets that much more difficult to sort out actual achievement and expertise among all those "university graduates." People eager to misinform their fellow citizens will often say that they have a university education, or even a graduate degree, and that they are therefore to be taken seriously. The only thing more disheartening than finding out these folks are lying about possessing multiple degrees is to find out that they're telling the truth.

Students will likely object that the demands of their major are a lot more work than I'm giving credit for here. Perhaps, but that depends on the major itself. The requirements of a degree in a STEM field (science, technology, engineering, mathematics), a demanding foreign language, or a rigorous degree in the humanities can be a different matter than a major in communications or visual arts or—as much as it pains me to say it—political science. Every campus has "default majors," chosen when a student has no real idea what to do, some of which are off-ramps from more demanding programs after students learn the limits of their abilities.

At the risk of being misunderstood, I should clarify a few points. First, it's not news to me or anyone else in higher education that even the best schools have "gut" courses, the class a student can pass by exchanging oxygen for carbon dioxide for a set number of weeks. Perhaps it might be shocking for a career professor to admit this, but there's nothing wrong with easy or fun courses. I would even defend at least some of them as necessary. There *should* be classes where students can experiment with a subject, take something enjoyable, and get credit for learning something.

The problem comes when too many courses start to look like gut courses. They exist in the humanities, the social sciences, and yes, even in the sciences, and their numbers, at least by my subjective judgment, are growing. No field is immune, and a look through the offerings of many programs around the country—as well as a compilation of the grades given in them—suggests that what were once isolated professorial vices are now common departmental habits.

I should also note that I am not making an argument here for slimming colleges down to a bunch of STEM departments with a smattering of English or history majors. I deplore those kinds of arguments, and I have long objected to what I see as an assault on the liberal arts. Too often, those who denigrate the liberal arts are really advocating for nothing less than turning colleges into trade schools. Art history majors always take the cheap shots here, even though many people don't realize that a lot of art history majors go on to some very lucrative careers. In any case, I don't want to live in a civilization where there are no art history majors or, for that matter, film studies, philosophy, or sociology majors.

The question is how many students in these majors are learning anything, or whether there need to be so many students taking these subjects at third-string institutions—especially if supported by taxpayer dollars. There is no way around the reality that students are too often wasting their money and obtaining the illusion of an education by gravitating toward courses or majors that either shouldn't exist or whose enrollments should be restricted to the small number of students who intend to pursue them seriously and with rigor. This, too, is one of the many things faculty are not supposed to say out loud, because to resentful parents and hopeful students, it sounds like baseless elitism.

It might be elitism, but it's not baseless. Many small schools were once called "teachers' colleges" and served that purpose well. Their history or English departments fulfilled the perfectly useful function of producing history and English teachers. Today, however, these tiny "universities" offer anthropology or the philosophy of science as though their students are slated for graduate study at Stanford or Chicago. These majors are sometimes built around the interests of the few faculty members who teach them, or offered as a way to fatten the catalog of a school that otherwise might not seem intellectually sturdy enough to prospective students.

There's nothing wrong with personal fulfillment or following your bliss—if you can afford it. If a small college has a history course that interests you, by all means, take it. It might be terrific. But students who choose majors with little thought about where their school stands, what academic resources it can offer in that program, or where it places graduates from those programs will risk leaving campus (whenever they finally finish) with less knowledge than they've been led to believe, a problem at the core of a lot of needless arguments with people who are deeply mistaken about the quality of their own education.

When rebranded universities offer courses and degree programs as though they are roughly equivalent to their better-known counterparts, they are not only misleading prospective students but also undermining later learning. The quality gap between programs risks producing a sense of resentment: if you and I both have university degrees in history, why is your view about the Russian Revolution any better than mine? Why should it matter that your degree is from a top-ranked department, but mine is from a program so small it has a single teacher? If I studied film at a local state college, and you went to the film program at the University of Southern California, who are you to think you know more than I? We have the same degree, don't we?

These kinds of comparisons and arguments about the differences between colleges and their various degrees and programs get under the skin pretty quickly. The student who gained admission to a top school and finished a degree there resents the leveling that comes with an indifferent comparison to his or her fellow major from an unknown public "university." Meanwhile, the student who worked day and night to get the same degree bridles at the implication that his or her achievement means less without a pedigree.

There's plenty of bad faith in these arguments, which are often little more than social one-upmanship. A lousy student who attended a good school is still a lousy student; a diligent student from a small institution is no less intelligent for the lack of a famous pedigree. The fact remains, however, that taking a course at a regional college with an overworked adjunct is usually a lot different than studying at a top university with an accomplished scholar. It might be true, but saying so immediately generates huffy cries of snobbery, and everyone walks away angry.

We may not like any of these comparisons, but they matter in sorting out expertise and relative knowledge. It's true that great universities can graduate complete dunderheads. Would-be universities, however, try punch above their intellectual weight for all the wrong reasons, including marketing, money, and faculty ego. In the end, they are doing a disservice to both their students and society. Studying the same thing might give people a common language for further discussion of a subject, but it does not automatically make them peers.

Colleges and universities also mislead their students about their own competence through grade inflation. Collapsing standards so that schoolwork doesn't interfere with the fun of going to college is one way to ensure a happy student body and relieve the faculty of the pressure of failing anyone. As *Bloomberg*'s McArdle wrote, this attempt to lessen the unpleasant aspects of college on the customers should be no surprise when classroom seats are a commodity rather than a competitively earned privilege.

> You see the results most visibly in the lazy rivers and rock-climbing walls and increasingly luxurious dorms that colleges use to compete for students, but such a shift does not limit itself to extraneous amenities. Professors marvel at the way students now shamelessly demand to be given good grades, regardless of their work ethic, but that's exactly what you would expect if the student views themselves as a consumer, and the product as a credential, rather than an education.[19]

Or as the *Washington Post* writer Catherine Rampell describes it, college is now a deal in which "students pay more in tuition, and expect more in return—better service, better facilities and better grades."[20] Less is demanded of students now than even a few decades ago. There is less homework, shorter trimester and quarter systems, and technological innovations that make going to college more fun but less rigorous. When college is a business, you can't flunk the customers.

College isn't always rock climbing and kayaking, but there can be no doubt that the trend is toward deemphasizing grades by inflating them. As a group of professors wrote in the *Chronicle of Higher*

Education in 2023, there is no constituency for keeping grade inflation under control:

> Why is grade inflation happening? We answer this with a question: Who wants tougher grading standards? Administrators want high graduation rates. Departments want to attract students to enroll in their courses and major in their subject areas. Faculty who are easier graders are rewarded with higher scores in teaching evaluations. Furthermore, as colleges increase the number of adjuncts they employ, these less-stable faculty members may worry more about the impact of student satisfaction and enrollment on their continued employment, and increase grades accordingly.[21]

When grades matter less, students find other things to do. A University of Chicago study found in 2011 that "it does not take a great deal of effort to demonstrate satisfactory academic performance in today's colleges and universities" and so college students today decide to invest time in other activities in college.[22] Some of those "other activities" are noble and enriching. Many others are the sorts of things parents would probably just as soon not know about.

When it comes to the death of expertise, the effect of lighter workloads and easier grades should be obvious: students graduate with a high GPA that doesn't reflect a corresponding level of education or intellectual achievement. (Again, I am leaving aside certain kinds of degrees here, and talking about the bulk of majors taken in the United States today.) "I was a straight-A student at a university" does not mean today what it did in 1960 or even 1980. A study of two hundred colleges and universities up through 2009 found that A was the most commonly given grade, an increase of nearly 30 percent since 1960 and over 10 percent just since 1988. By 2016, grades in the A and B range accounted for more than 80 percent of all grades in all subjects, a trend that continues unabated.[23]

Every institution, when confronted with these facts, blames every other institution around it. The problem, of course, is that no one university or program can take a stand against grade inflation without harming its own students: the first faculty to deflate their grades instantly make their students seem less capable than those from other institutions. This, as Rampell correctly noted, means that the default grade is no longer the "gentleman's C" of the 1950s, but a "gentleman's A," now bestowed more as an entitlement for course completion than as a reward for excellence.

Princeton, Wellesley, and Harvard, among others, established committees in the early twenty-first century to investigate the problem of grade inflation. Princeton adopted a policy that tried to limit the faculty's ability to give A grades in 2004, an experiment that was rolled back by the faculty itself less than a decade later. At Wellesley, humanities departments tried to cap the average grade at a B+ in their courses; those courses lost a fifth of their enrollments and the participating departments lost nearly a third of their majors.

Experienced educators have grappled with this problem for years. I was one of them, and like my colleagues, I did not find a universal solution. The two most important facts about grade inflation, however, are that it exists and that it suffuses students with unwarranted confidence in their abilities. Almost every institution of higher education is complicit in what is essentially collusion on grades, driven on one side by market pressures to make college fun, to make students attractive to employers, and to help vulnerable professors escape the wrath of dissatisfied students, and on the other by irresponsible notions about the role of self-esteem in education.

RATE ME GENTLY

Another way colleges and universities enhance the notion that students are clients, and thus devalue respect for expertise, is to encourage the students to evaluate the educators standing in front of them as though they are peers. Student evaluations came out of the movement for more "relevance" and student involvement after the 1960s. They are still with us, and in an era where businesses, including education, are obsessed with "metrics," they are used and abused more than ever.

When I was a professor, I supported the use of student evaluations as one of several measures of teaching ability. I will immodestly say that mine, throughout my entire career, were always good—I was commended for my teaching at Dartmouth, and I won awards for it at both the Naval War College and the Harvard Extension School—and so I have no personal axe to grind here. I'm also a former academic administrator who had to review the evaluations of other faculty as part of my duties overseeing a department. I've read thousands of these evaluations over the years, from students at all levels, and they're a worthwhile exercise if they're handled properly. Nonetheless, the whole idea is now out of control, with students rating professional men and women as though they're reviewing a movie or commenting on a pair of shoes.

Evaluations usually fall into a gray area, where most teachers are competent and most students generally like the courses. Student ratings are most useful in spotting trends; a multiyear look at evaluations can identify both the best and the worst teachers, especially if the readers are adept at decoding how students write such reports. ("She's boring," for example, often means "she actually expected me to read the book she assigned instead of just entertaining me.") In my own classes, I used them to spot things in my courses that were working as well as what might be missing the mark, such as books or lectures that I should drop or keep, or to let me know if my own sense of whether I had an especially good or weak term was shared by the students.

Still, there's something wrong with a system that asks a student how much they liked their education. College isn't a restaurant. (I sometimes hear a Yelp review as I'm reading these evaluations: "The basic statistics course was served a bit cold, but it was substantial, while my partner chose a light introduction to world religions that had just a hint of spice.") Evaluating teachers creates a habit of mind in which the layperson becomes accustomed to judging the expert, despite being in an obvious position of having inferior knowledge of the subject material.

Student evaluations are also a hypersensitive indicator, influenced by the tiniest and most irrelevant things, from the comfort of the seats to the time of day the course is offered. A certain number of them should be ignored. And some of them are just strange, to the point where professors will exchange stories of the worst or weirdest evaluations they've gotten. One of my colleagues once gave a detailed lecture on British naval history, for example, and a military student's only comment was that the teacher needed to press his shirt. A top historian I knew was regularly ridiculed on evaluations for being short. I was once told by an undergraduate that I was a great professor but that I needed to lose some weight. (That one was accurate.) Another student disliked me so much that he or she said on my evaluation that they would pray for me.

As entertaining as these evaluations are, the process encourages students to think of themselves as the arbiters of the talent of the teachers. And when education is about making sure clients are happy, a college's reliance on evaluations forces weaker or less secure teachers to become dancing bears, striving to be loved or at least liked, so that more students will read the reviews and keep the class (and the professor's contract) alive for the next term. This creates and sustains a vicious circle of pandering and grade inflation. Students should be involved in their education as more than observers or receptacles for information, but they should not be the final referees of quality in a classroom (One solution I campaigned for among my colleagues was to allow a peer or senior colleague to observe their teaching as an added input alongside student evaluations. I submitted myself for such annual observations even as a senior and tenured faculty member.) Engagement and debate are the lifeblood of a university, and professors are not above criticism of either their ideas or their teaching ability. But the industrial model of education has reduced college to a commercial transaction, where students are taught to be picky consumers rather than critical thinkers.

COLLEGE IS NOT A SAFE SPACE

Young men and women are not as irresponsible as we sometimes portray them in the media or the pop culture, or in our mind's eye, for that matter. We laugh at college movie comedies and fondly remember our own irresponsible moments as students, and then we sternly lecture our children never to be like us. We applaud student activism if we like the cause, and we deplore it if we disagree. Adults, in general, tend to be sour critics of the generations that follow them.

None of this, however, excuses colleges for allowing their campuses to turn into circuses. It was probably inevitable that the anti-intellectualism of American life would invade college campuses, but that is no reason to surrender to it. And make no mistake: campuses in the United States are increasingly surrendering their intellectual authority not only to children, but also to activists who are directly attacking the traditions of free inquiry that scholarly communities are supposed to defend.

I have plenty of strong opinions on what I see as assaults on the free exchange of ideas, but we need not rehearse here the many arguments over draconian speech codes, attacks on guest speakers, and academic freedom. The more relevant point when it comes to the death of expertise is that campus fads, such as "safe spaces" and speech codes, do in fact corrode the ability of colleges to produce people capable of critical thought. (And remember, "critical thinking" isn't the same thing as "relentless criticism.") In the same way that shopping for schools teaches young men and women to value a school for reasons other than an education, these accommodations to young activists encourage them to believe, once again, that the job of a college student is to enlighten the professors instead of the other way around.

There are so many examples of this it is almost unfair to point to any one policy or controversy at any one university. The problem is endemic to American universities and has recurred, in waves of varying strength, since the early 1960s. What is different today, and especially worrisome when it comes to the creation of educated citizens, is how the protective, swaddling environment of the modern university infantilizes students and thus dissolves their ability to conduct a logical and informed argument. When feelings matter more than rationality or facts, education is a doomed enterprise. Emotion is an unassailable defense against expertise, a moat of anger and resentment in which reason and knowledge quickly drown. And when students learn that emotion trumps everything else, it is a lesson they will take with them for the rest of their lives.

Colleges are supposed to be the calm environment in which educated men and women determine what's true and what's false, and where they learn to follow a model of scholarly inquiry no matter where it takes them. Instead, many colleges have become hostages to students who demand that their feelings override every other consideration. They no doubt believe in their right to make this demand because their lives, up until then, have been lived in a therapeutic culture that leaves no thought unexpressed and no feeling invalidated.

Still, student activism is a normal part of college life. Adolescents are *supposed* to be passionate; it's part of being a teen or a twenty-something. I'm still old-fashioned enough that I expect educated men and women to be leaders among the voters by virtue of a better education, and so I applaud tomorrow's voters exercising their political reasoning in debate and discussion.

Unfortunately, the new student activism is regressing back to the old student activism of a half century ago: intolerance, dogmatism, and even threats and violence. Ironically (or perhaps tragically), students are mobilizing extreme language and demands over increasingly small things. While Baby Boomers might well claim that they were busting up the campus for peace in 1967, there's some truth to the notion that young men about to be drafted and sent to an Asian jungle were understandably emotional about the subject. Members of minority groups who were not fully citizens in the eyes of the law until the early 1960s justifiably felt they were out of less spectacular options than protest, even if nothing excuses the violence that ensued.

Today, by contrast, students explode over imagined slights that are not even remotely in the same category as fighting for civil rights or being sent to war. Students now build majestic Everests from the smallest molehills, and they descend into hysteria over pranks and hoaxes. In the midst of it all, the students are learning that emotion and volume can always defeat reason and substance, thus building about themselves fortresses that no future teacher, expert, or intellectual will ever be able to breach.

An infamous example of how emotion can overcome reason and proportion occurred at Yale in 2015, when a house master's wife had the temerity to tell minority students to ignore Halloween costumes they thought offensive. This provoked a campuswide temper tantrum that included professors being shouted down by screaming students. "In your position as master," one student howled in a professor's face, "it is your job to create a place of comfort and home for the students. . . . Do you understand that?!"

Quietly, the professor said, "No, I don't agree with that," and the student unloaded on him:

"Then why the [expletive] did you accept the position?! Who the [expletive] hired you?! You should step down! If that is what you think about being a master you should step down! *It is not about creating an intellectual space! It is not! Do you understand that? It's about creating a home here.* You are not doing that!"[24] [emphasis added]

Yale, instead of disciplining students in violation of their own norms of academic discourse, apologized to the tantrum throwers. The house master eventually resigned from his residential post, while staying on as a faculty member. His wife, however, resigned her faculty position and left college teaching entirely.

To faculty everywhere, the lesson was obvious: the campus of a top university is not a place for intellectual exploration. It is a luxury home, rented for nine months at a time, by children of the elite who may shout at faculty as if they're berating clumsy maids in a colonial mansion.

A month after the Yale fracas, protests at the University of Missouri flared up after a juvenile incident in which a swastika was drawn on a bathroom wall with feces. Exactly what Missouri's flagship public university was supposed to do, other than to wash the wall, was unclear, but the campus erupted anyway. "Do you know what systemic oppression is?!" a student yelled at the flustered Mizzou president. "Google it!" she hollered. Student journalists were harassed and threatened, in one case by a faculty member (ironically enough, by one with a courtesy appointment in the journalism school). After a few more days of these theatrics, the university's president resigned. The chancellor and a professor who had refused to cancel classes after the protests both followed suit. Some months later, the adjunct journalism professor who had confronted a student was fired.

Missouri, however, isn't Yale. It does not have a nearly inelastic demand for its services. Applications and donations soon took a hit in the wake of the protests and resignations.[25] Within two years, enrollment in the freshman class dropped by 35 percent. "The university administration," the *New York Times* reported in 2017, "acknowledges that the main reason is a backlash from the events of 2015, as the campus has been shunned by students and families put off by, depending on their viewpoint, a culture of racism or one where protesters run amok."[26] When the smoke cleared, Missouri's flagship university was left with fewer faculty, administrators, applicants, and donations, all because of a racist prank and the reaction of a group of students, enabled by an even smaller group of faculty, that reversed the roles of teachers and learners at a major public university.

Interestingly, this is a subject that often unites liberal and conservative intellectuals. The British scholar Richard Dawkins, something of a scourge to conservatives because of his views on religion, was perplexed by the whole idea of "safe spaces," the places American students demand as a respite from any form of political expression they might find "triggering." Dawkins minced no words: "A university is not a 'safe space,'" he said on Twitter. "If you need a safe space, leave, go home, hug your teddy and suck your thumb until ready for university."

Likewise, after the Yale and Missouri events, the *Atlantic* writer Conor Friedersdorf noted that "what happens at Yale does not stay there" and that tomorrow's elites were internalizing values not of free expression but of sheer intolerance. "One feels for these students," Friedersdorf later wrote. (I do not, but Friedersdorf is more understanding than I am.) "But if an email about Halloween costumes has them skipping class and suffering breakdowns, either they need help from mental-health professionals or they've been grievously ill-served by debilitating ideological notions they've acquired about what ought to cause them pain."[27]

Some opportunistic figures on the American right have gone on the offensive against colleges and universities, claiming that the solution (at least for publicly funded schools) is to gut the institutions and establish direct political control over higher education. They seek to abolish tenure, dissolve majors they don't like, and mandate ideologically conservative curricula overseen by legislators instead of educators—a recipe for successive cycles of politicization by whoever controls the state legislature. Such "solutions" are no solution at all; these irresponsible and cloddish measures are about politics rather than education.[28]

It's true that Americans of both parties have doubts about the economic worth of an increasingly expensive college degree, but the populist right's attack is based on ideology, not money. The number of Republicans who see college as a negative influence on American life grew by more than twenty points in two years, from 2015 to 2017— in other words, from the year before to the year after Donald Trump's 2016 election victory. Another poll found that in 2015, 56 percent of Republicans expressed confidence in higher education, a number that plunged to 19 percent by 2023.[29] Colleges have plenty of problems, but the rapid and decisive turn against higher education on the right is more the result of propaganda rather than considered debate.

I admit, however, that I have little idea how to fix the dysfunction on many college campuses, especially since so many of these problems begin *before* students get to college. Like most professors—I hope—I did what I could in my own classroom. I held my students to clear standards. I expected them to learn how to formulate their views and to argue them calmly and logically. I graded them on their responses to the questions I asked on their exams and on the quality of their written work, not on their political views. I demanded that they treat other students with respect and that they engage the ideas and beliefs of others in the classroom without excessive emotionalism or personal attacks.

But I was always haunted by the realization that once the students left my classroom, I could not moderate their arguments forever. I could not prevent them from dismissing others, from rejecting facts, from denouncing well-intentioned advice, or from demanding that their feelings be accepted in place of the truth. If they've spent four years showing such disrespect for their professors and their institutions, they cannot be expected to respect their fellow citizens. And if college graduates can no longer be counted on to lead reasoned debate and discussion in American life, and to know the difference between knowledge and feeling, then we're indeed in the kind of deep trouble no experts—or politicians—can fix.

Chapter 4

Let Me Google That for You

How Unlimited Information Is Making Us Dumber

> My mind now expects to take in information the way the Net distributes it: in a swiftly moving stream of particles. Once I was a scuba diver in the sea of words. Now I zip along the surface like a guy on a Jet Ski.
>
> Nicholas Carr

> Although the Internet could be making all of us smarter, it makes many of us stupider, because it's not just a magnet for the curious. It's a sinkhole for the gullible. It renders everyone an instant expert. You have a degree? Well, I did a Google search!
>
> Frank Bruni

> Do not believe everything you read on the Internet, especially quotes from famous people.
>
> Abraham Lincoln (probably)

THE RETURN OF STURGEON'S LAW

Ask any professional or expert about the death of expertise, and most of them will immediately blame the same culprit: the Internet. People who once had to ask the advice of specialists in any given field now plug search terms into a browser and get answers in seconds. Why rely on people with more education and experience than you—or, worse, go to the trouble of making appointments with them—when you can just get the information yourself?

Chest pain? Ask your computer. "Why does my chest hurt?" will generate more than 1.2 billion results (at least on the search engine I just used) in exactly 0.45 seconds. A stream of information will fill your screen, with helpful advice from sources ranging from the National Institutes of Health to other outfits whose bona fides are a tad less reputable. Some of these sites will even walk the would-be patient through a diagnosis. Your doctor might have a different opinion, but who is he to argue with a glowing screen that will answer your question in less than half a second?

In fact, who is anyone to argue with anyone? In the Information Age, there's no such thing as an irresolvable argument. Each of us is now walking around with more accumulated information on a smartphone or tablet than ever existed in the entire Library of Alexandria. At the beginning of this book, I mentioned the character Cliff Clavin from the classic television show *Cheers*, the local know-it-all who routinely lectured the other regulars in a Boston pub on every subject under the sun. But Cliff couldn't exist today: at the first claim of "it's a known fact," everyone in the bar could pull out a phone and verify (or more likely disprove) any of Cliff's claims.

Put another way, technology has created a world in which we're *all* Cliff Clavin now. And that's a problem.

Despite what irritated professionals may think, however, the Internet is not the primary cause of challenges to their expertise. Rather, the Internet has accelerated the collapse of communication between experts and laypeople by offering an apparent shortcut to erudition. It allows people to mimic intellectual accomplishment by indulging in an illusion of expertise provided by a limitless supply of facts.

Facts, as experts know, are not the same as knowledge or ability. And on the Internet, "facts" are sometimes not even facts. In the various skirmishes in the campaigns against established knowledge, the Internet is like artillery support: a constant bombardment of random, disconnected information that rains down on experts and ordinary citizens alike, deafening all of us while blowing up attempts at reasonable discussion.

Internet users have created many humorous laws and corollaries to describe discussion in the electronic world. The tendency to bring up Nazi Germany in any argument inspired Godwin's Law (which asserts that any online argument, if it goes on long enough, will include comparisons to the Nazis) and the related *reductio ad Hiterlum*. The deeply entrenched and usually immutable views of Internet users are the foundation of Pommer's Law, in which the Internet can only change a person's mind from having *no* opinion to having a *wrong* opinion. There are many others, including my personal favorite, Skitt's Law: "Any Internet message correcting an error in another post will contain at least one error itself."

When it comes to the death of expertise, however, the law to bear in mind is an observation coined long before the advent of the personal computer: Sturgeon's Law, named for the legendary science-fiction writer Theodore Sturgeon. In the early 1950s, highbrow critics derided the quality of popular literature, particularly American science fiction. They considered sci-fi and fantasy writing a literary ghetto, and almost all of it, they sniffed, was worthless. Sturgeon angrily responded by noting that the critics were setting too high a bar. Most products in most fields, he argued, are of low quality, including what was then considered serious writing. "Ninety percent of *everything*," Sturgeon decreed, "is crap."

Where the Internet is concerned, Sturgeon's Law of 90 percent might be lowballing. The sheer size and volume of the Internet, and the inability to separate meaningful knowledge from random noise, mean that good information will always be swamped by lousy data and weird detours. Worse, there's no way to keep up with it all, even if any group or institution wanted to try. In 1994, there were fewer than three thousand websites online, and they loaded onto personal computers at the slow pace of a modem connected to a telephone line. By 2023, there were more than *one billion* sites. Most of them are accessible at virtually instantaneous speed and easily found through searches. Most of them are searchable and will arrive before your eyes in mere seconds, regardless of their quality.

The good news is that even if Sturgeon's Law holds, that's still one hundred million pretty good websites. These include all the major news publications of the world (many of which are now read more in pixels than on paper), as well as the home pages of think tanks, universities, research organizations, and any number of important scientific, cultural, and political figures. The bad news, of course, is that finding all of this information means plowing through a blizzard of useless or misleading information posted by everyone from well-intentioned grandmothers to terrorists. Some of the smartest people on earth have a significant presence on the Internet. Some of the stupidest people on the same planet, however, reside just one click away on the next page or hyperlink.

The countless dumpsters of nonsense parked on the Internet are a Sturgeon's Law nightmare. People who already are faced with confusing choices about getting information from a few dozen news channels on their televisions now face millions upon millions of web pages produced by anyone willing to pay for an online presence. The Internet is without doubt a great achievement that continues to change our lives for the better by allowing more people more access to information—and to each other—than ever before in history. But it also has a dark side that is exerting important and deeply negative effects on the ways people gain knowledge and respond to expertise.

The most obvious problem is that the freedom to post anything online floods the public square with bad information and half-baked thinking. The Internet lets a billion flowers bloom, and most of them stink, including everything from the idle thoughts of random bloggers and the conspiracy theories of cranks all the way to the sophisticated campaigns of disinformation conducted by groups and governments. Some of the information on the Internet is wrong because of sloppiness, some of it is wrong because well-meaning people just don't know any better, and some of it is wrong because it was put there out of greed or even sheer malice. The medium itself, without comment or editorial intervention, displays it all with equal speed. The Internet is a vessel, not a referee.

This, of course, is no more and no less than an updated version of the basic paradox of the printing press. As the writer Nicholas Carr pointed out, the arrival of Gutenberg's invention in the fifteenth century set off a "round of teeth gnashing" among early humanists, who worried that "printed books and broadsheets would undermine religious authority, demean the work of scholars and scribes, and spread sedition and debauchery."[1]

Those medieval naysayers weren't entirely wrong. The printing press was used to mass-produce Bibles, to teach people to read, and eventually to empower the literacy that drives so much of human freedom. Of course, it also enabled the dissemination of insanity like the *Protocols of the Elders of Zion*, taught people to confuse words with facts, and supported the creation of totalitarian propaganda that undermined that same human freedom. The Internet is the printing press at the speed of fiber optics.

In addition to enabling torrents of misinformation, the Internet is weakening the ability of laypeople and scholars alike to do basic research, a skill that would help everyone to navigate this wilderness of bad data. This might seem an odd claim coming from a former member of the scholarly community, because I gladly admit that Internet access has always made my work as a writer a lot easier. In the 1980s, I had to put together a dissertation by lugging around armloads of books and articles. Today, I keep browser bookmarks and folders full of electronically readable articles at my fingertips. How can that not be better than the hours I spent going blind in front of copiers and microfiche machines in the bowels of a library?

In some ways, the convenience of the Internet is a tremendous boon, but mostly for people already trained in research and who have some idea what they're looking for. It's much easier to subscribe to the electronic version of, say, *Foreign Affairs* or *International Security* than it is to decamp to the library or impatiently check an office mailbox. This is no help, unfortunately, for a student or an untrained layperson who has never been taught how to judge the provenance of information or the reputability of a writer.

Libraries, or at least their reference and academic sections, once served as a kind of first cut through the noise of the marketplace. Visiting a library was an education in itself, especially for a reader who took the time to ask for help from a librarian. The Internet, however, is nothing like a library. Rather, it's a giant repository where anyone can dump anything, from a first folio to a faked photograph, from a scientific treatise to pornography, from short bulletins of information to meaningless electronic graffiti. It's an environment almost entirely without regulation, which opens the door to content being driven by marketing, politics, and the uninformed decisions of other laypeople rather than the judgment of experts.

Can fifty million Elvis fans really be wrong? Of course they can.

In practice, this means that a search for information will cough up whatever algorithm is at work in a search engine, often provided by for-profit companies using criteria that are largely opaque to the user. But even when searches produce links to encyclopedias, plugging words into a browser window isn't research: it's asking questions of programmable machines that themselves cannot truly understand human beings. (While artificial intelligence and programs such as ChatGPT can mimic human interaction, software cannot reproduce the idiosyncratic curiosity or the illogical but insightful leaps of intuition that characterize both the wonderful and maddening nature of human intellect.) Research requires the ability to find authentic information, summarize it, analyze it, write it up, and present it to other people. It is not just the province of scientists and scholars, but a basic set of skills a high school education should teach every graduate because of its importance in any number of jobs and careers. But why bother with all that tedious hoop-jumping when the screen in front of us already has the answers, generated by the millions in just seconds, and beautifully laid out in colorful, authoritative-looking websites?

The deeper issue here is that the Internet is changing the way we read, the way we reason, even the way we *think*, and all for the worse. We expect information instantly. We want it broken down, presented in a way that is pleasing to our eye—no more of those small-type, fragile textbooks, thank you—and we want it to say what we want it to say. People do not do "research" so much as they "search for pretty pages online to provide answers they like with the least amount of effort and in the shortest time." The resulting flood of information, always of varying quality and sometimes of uncertain sanity, creates a veneer of knowledge that leaves people worse off than if they knew nothing at all. It's an old saying, but it's true: it ain't what you don't know that'll hurt you, it's what you do know that ain't so.

Finally, and perhaps most disturbingly, social media is making us meaner, shorter-fused, and incapable of conducting discussions where anyone learns anything. The major problem with instantaneous communication is that it's *instantaneous*. While the Internet enables more people to talk to each other than ever before—a distinctly new historical condition—everyone talking immediately to everyone else might not always be such a good idea. Sometimes, human beings need to pause and to reflect, to give themselves time to absorb information and to digest it. Instead, the Internet is an arena in which people can react without thinking, and thus in turn they become invested in defending their gut reactions rather than accepting new information or admitting a mistake—especially if it's a mistake pointed out by people with greater learning or experience.

WHAT'S FAKE ON THE INTERNET: EVERYTHING

There aren't enough pages in this or any other book to catalog the amount of bad information on the Internet. Miracle cures, conspiracy theories, faked documents, misattributed quotes—all of these and more are the crabgrass and weeds that have rapidly overgrown a global garden of knowledge. The healthier but less sturdy grasses and flowers don't stand a chance.

Durable old urban legends and conspiracy theories, for example, have been reconditioned and given new life online. We've all heard stories of alligators in the sewers, improbable celebrity deaths, and libraries that fell down because no one counted on the weight of the books in them, told and retold mostly by word of mouth. On the Internet, these stories are presented with beautiful layouts and graphics. They now spread so fast through email and social media that there are groups, like the admirable project at Snopes.com and other fact-checking organizations, who do nothing but stomp out these intellectual wastebasket fires all day long.

Unfortunately, they're shoveling against the tide. People do not come to the Internet so that their bad information can be corrected, or their cherished theories disproven. Rather, they ask the electronic oracle to confirm them in their ignorance. In 2015 a *Washington Post* writer, Caitlin Dewey, worried that fact-checking could never defeat myths and hoaxes because "no one has the time or cognitive capacity to reason all the apparent nuances and discrepancies out."[2] In the end, she sighed, "debunking them doesn't do a darn thing."

Two months after she wrote those words, Dewey and the *Post* threw in the towel and ceased her weekly "what was fake on the Internet" column. There was no way to keep up with the madness, especially once hoaxers figured out how to make money out of spreading myths for precious clicks on websites. "Frankly," Dewey told her readers, "this column wasn't designed to address the current environment. This format doesn't make sense." More alarming were the conversations Dewey had with professional researchers who told her that "institutional distrust is so high right now, and cognitive bias so strong *always*, that the people who fall for hoax news stories are frequently only interested in consuming information that conforms with their views—even when it's demonstrably fake" (emphasis in the original).[3] Dewey and the *Post* fought the Internet, and the Internet won.

A lot of nonsense, particularly in politics, thrives on the reach and staying power of the Internet. A stubborn group of cranks might still believe the earth is flat or that Americans never walked on the moon, but eventually all the pictures from space are good enough for the rest of us. When it comes to urban legends like Barack Obama's African birth, George W. Bush's orchestration of the 9/11 terror attacks, or the US Treasury's secret plan to replace the dollar with a global currency, astronauts with cameras cannot help. Social media, websites, and chat rooms turn myths, stories heard from a "friend of a friend," and rumors into "facts."

As the British writer Damian Thompson has explained, instant communication is empowering people and groups dedicated to crackpot ideas, some of them quite dangerous. Thompson calls this "counterknowledge," in that it all flies in the face of science and is completely impervious to contrary evidence.

> Now, thanks to the internet . . . a rumor about the Antichrist can
> leap from Goths in Sweden to an extreme traditionalist Catholic

sect in Australia in a matter of seconds. Minority groups are becoming ever more tolerant of each other's eccentric doctrines. Contacts between black and white racists, which began tentatively decades ago, are now flourishing as the two groups swap conspiracy stories.[4]

In a slower, less-connected world, these kinds of groups could not reinforce their beliefs with instantaneous affirmation from other extremists online. The free movement of ideas is a powerful driver of democracy, but it always carries the risk that ignorant or evil people will bend the tools of mass communication to their own ends and propagate lies and myths that no expert can dispel.

Worse, bad information can stay online for years. Unlike yesterday's newspaper, online information is persistent and will pop up in subsequent searches after appearing just once. Even when falsehoods or mistakes are deleted at the source, they'll show up in an archive somewhere else. If the stories in them go "viral" and travel the electronic world in days, hours, or even minutes, they're effectively impossible to correct.

For example, in 2015 the conservative gadfly Allen West broke a make-believe scoop that President Obama was forcing members of the US military to pray like Muslims for Ramadan.[5] West's website juxtaposed a blaring headline—"Look what our troops are being FORCED to do"—against a picture of US soldiers kneeling with their heads to prayer mats. It was a startling visual and the story spread rapidly through social media.

No such thing had occurred. West had recycled a picture, taken several years earlier, of actual *Muslims* in the US military at prayer. Even after objections were raised to the misleading picture (by me, among others), West did not pull the story. Removing the post wouldn't have mattered, since it was already archived on blogs and other sites. People surfing the Internet who have neither the training nor the time to ascertain the provenance of the information will from now on come across not only the original story but also thousands of repetitions of it and never know that the whole thing is bunk.

In 2020, West was elected the chair of the Texas Republican Party. He stepped down after 11 months and ran in the Texas gubernatorial primary election in an attempt to unseat the Republican incumbent, Governor Greg Abbott, whom he opposed over issues that included COVID policies about mask mandates and lockdowns. He also refused vaccination. In 2021, in the midst of the campaign, both Abbott and his wife were hospitalized with COVID; both received monoclonal antibody treatments.[6] In the election, West lost decisively to Abbott, garnering 12 percent of the vote. As of 2023, West is the executive director of a right-wing legal organization and has nearly half a million readers following his Substack account.

Today, no one need be frustrated by fussy fact-checkers or resolute editors. Just as a nicely bound book could once mislead people into thinking its contents were authoritative, so, too, do slick websites provide the visual cues of reliability and authenticity that help uninformed readers spread bad information faster than any headline that William Randolph Hearst could have imagined. Experts and other professionals who insist on the dreary rigor of logic and factual accuracy cannot compete with a machine that will always give readers their preferred answer in sixteen million colors.

OF COURSE IT'S SAFE, I GOOGLED IT

Leaving aside slick, self-produced websites and the inevitable Facebook posts and memes that crowd the Internet, the search for quick answers has also facilitated the growth of entire industries based on selling bad ideas to the public and charging them for the privilege of being misinformed. I refer here not to online journalism—that's in the next chapter—but rather to the many outlets, often fronted by celebrities, that offer advice meant to supplant and replace established knowledge from experts.

Are you a woman concerned about your reproductive health? I have no experience in these matters, but I'm told by the women in my life that regular visits to the gynecologist are not something they particularly enjoy. Now that the Internet has arrived, however, women have an alternative source of information other than medical professionals: the actress Gwyneth Paltrow has her own "lifestyle magazine," GOOP.com, and she can discuss with you, in the privacy of your home or via your smartphone, the many things women can do to maintain their gynecological health, including steaming their vaginas.

If you're unfamiliar with this practice, Ms. Paltrow highly recommends it. "You sit on what is essentially a mini-throne," she said in 2014, "and a combination of infrared and mugwort steam cleanses your uterus, et al. It is an energetic release—not just a steam douche—that balances female hormone levels. If you're in [Los Angeles], you have to do it."

Actual gynecologists, however, do not recommend that women in Los Angeles or anywhere else steam any of their middle anatomy. A gynecologist named Jen Gunter took to her own (distinctly less glamorous) website with a clear alternative recommendation:

> Steam isn't going to get into your uterus from your vagina unless you are using an attachment with some kind of pressure and MOST DEFINITELY NEVER EVER DO THAT. Mugwort or wormwood or whatever when steamed, either vaginally or on the vulva, can't possibly balance any reproductive hormones, regulate your menstrual cycle, treat depression, or cure infertility. Even steamed estrogen couldn't do that.
>
> If you want to feel relaxed get a good massage.

If you want to relax your vagina, have an orgasm.[7]

Paltrow's site, however, is the epitome of hip, at least for a particular demographic. A satirist named Laura Hooper Beck captured the credulousness of Paltrow's fans perfectly: "Basically, if a doctor tells me to do it, I'm gonna take a hard pass. But if a skinny blonde in an ugly wig tells me that blowing hot air up my vagina is going to cure everything I've ever suffered from, including a bad relationship with my mother, well, then, I'm gonna listen to Gwyneth Paltrow, because girlfriend knows science."[8]

The trend of celebrity oddball health advice has only gotten worse. As a *Guardian* columnist noted in 2023:

> Tennis star Novak Djokovic, for example, has suggested that he thinks you can purify water with positive thinking. Rightwing provocateur Jordan Peterson has extolled the health benefits of only eating beef. Tech bros, meanwhile, are obsessed with "biohacking," or treating their bodies like machines. Bloomberg recently published a feature about a 45-year-old multimillionaire software entrepreneur called Bryan Johnson who has a team of 30 doctors devoted to monitoring his body and trying to reverse his ageing process.[9]

Paltrow herself was back in the news in 2023 when she went on a podcast and described her dietary habits, which *People* magazine described as an "anti-inflammatory diet of bone broth and vegetables" but critics called unhealthy and bordering on an eating disorder. Paltrow also admits that she gets nutrients via an intravenous tube, which is also not a practice most doctors would recommend. ("I love IVs, I'm an early IV adopter," she said on TikTok.)

It's easy—too easy, I know—to make fun of vacuous celebrities, and since this is now more about steam and vaginas than I've ever written in my entire career, let's leave Paltrow and her health advice aside. There is nevertheless an important point here about the influence of the Internet on the death of expertise, because in an earlier time, a sensible American woman would have had to exert a great deal of initiative to find out how a Hollywood actress parboils her plumbing. Now, a woman searching for answers on everything from fashion to uterine cancer could accidentally spend more time reading GOOP than talking to her doctor.

Celebrities abusing their status as celebrities is nothing new, but the Internet amplifies their effect. In 2015, the *New York Times* columnist Frank Bruni got a call from Robert F. Kennedy, Jr., son of the senator and presidential candidate assassinated in 1968. It was important, Kennedy told Bruni, that they meet. Kennedy was insistent about correcting Bruni on the issue of vaccination. Like too many other Americans, Kennedy was lugging around ill-informed paranoia about vaccines causing, in Kennedy's words, "a holocaust" among American children. Bruni later recalled of the meeting: "I had sided with the American Medical Association, the American Academy of Pediatrics, the National Institutes of Health and the Centers for Disease Control and Prevention. [But] Kennedy knew better."[10]

Kennedy did what many Americans do in such situations: he decided beforehand what he believed—that some sort of conspiracy was afoot—and then went looking for sources to buttress that belief. As Bruni pointed out, "The anti-vaccine agitators can always find a renegade researcher or random 'study' to back them up. This is erudition in the age of cyberspace: You surf until you reach the conclusion you're after. You click your way to validation, confusing the presence of a website with the plausibility of an argument."

Eight years later, Kennedy ran for president. He filed a request for a restraining order against Google for taking his anti-vaccine videos off YouTube (which Google owns). Kennedy claimed that his campaign was being undermined by the removal of the videos, which he argued was being done because of "coercion" from the United States government. In August 2023, a federal judge denied Kennedy's request. The judge added that Kennedy might not even have a free speech case: "The coronavirus still poses a health risk to certain individuals, and it would not serve the public interest to let medical misinformation proliferate on YouTube."[11] The day the decision was announced, Kennedy was holding down more than 12 percent of a national presidential poll against incumbent Joe Biden.

Internet grazing—mistakenly called "research" by laypeople—makes interactions between experts and professionals arduous. Once again, confirmation bias is a major culprit: although many stories on the Internet are false or inaccurate, the one-in-a-billion story where Google gets it right and the experts get it wrong goes viral. In a tragic case in 2015, for example, a British teenager was misdiagnosed by doctors who told her to "stop Googling her symptoms."[12] The patient insisted she had a rare cancer, a possibility the doctors dismissed. She was right, they were wrong, and she died.

The British teen's story made big news, and a rare mistake likely convinced a great many people to be their own doctors. Of course, people who have died because they used a computer to misdiagnose their heart disease as indigestion never make the front page. But none of that matters. These David-and-Goliath stories (a teenager against her team of doctors) feed the public's insatiable confirmation bias and fuel their cynicism about established knowledge while bolstering their false hopes that the solutions to their problems are just a few mouse clicks away.

Once upon a time, books were at least a marginal barrier to the rapid dissemination of misinformation, because books took time to produce and required some investment and judgment on the part of a publisher. "I read it in a book" meant "this probably isn't crazy, because a company spent the money to put it between two covers and publish it." This was never entirely true about books, of course; some of them are carefully fact-checked, peer reviewed, and edited, while others are just slammed between covers and rushed to bookstores.

Nonetheless, books from reputable presses go through at least a basic process of negotiation between authors, editors, reviewers, and publishers, including the book you're reading right now. Books from self-published "vanity presses," by contrast, are looked down upon by reviewers and readers alike, and with good reason. Today, however, the Internet is the equivalent of hundreds of millions of vanity presses all cranking out whatever anyone with a keyboard wants to say, no matter how stupid—or how vile. (As *National Journal*'s Ron Fournier has said, in the age of the Internet, "every bigot is a publisher.") There's a fair amount of wisdom and information hiding out there, but there's no escaping Sturgeon's Law.

Accessing the Internet can make people dumber than if they had never engaged a subject at all. The very act of searching for information makes people think they've learned something, when in fact they're more likely to be immersed in yet more data they do not understand. This happens because after enough time surfing, people no longer can distinguish between things that may have flashed before their eyes and things they actually *know*.

Seeing words on a screen is not the same as reading or understanding them. When a group of experimental psychologists at Yale investigated how people use the Internet, they found that "people who search for information on the Web emerge from the process with an inflated sense of how much they know—even regarding topics that are unrelated to the ones they Googled."[13] This is a kind of electronic version of the Dunning-Kruger Effect, in which the least competent people surfing the web are the least likely to realize that they're not learning anything.

People looking for information, say, about "fossil fuels" might end up scrolling past many pages on a related term, like "dinosaur fossils." After enough websites fly by, they eventually lose the ability to recognize that whatever they just read about either subject isn't something they knew before they looked at a screen. Instead, they just assume that they knew things about both dinosaurs and diesel fuel because they're just that smart. Unfortunately, people thinking they're smart because they searched the Internet is like thinking they're good swimmers because they got wet walking through a rainstorm.

The Yale team somewhat gently described this problem as "mistaking outsourced knowledge for internal knowledge." A blunter way of putting it would be to say that people can't remember most of what they see while blowing through dozens of mouse clicks. As the writer Tom Jacobs observed, searching "appears to trigger an utterly unjustified belief in one's own knowledge—which, given the increasingly popular habit of instinctively looking online to answer virtually any question, is a bit terrifying."[14]

It may well be terrifying, but it's definitely annoying. These mistaken assertions of gained knowledge can make the job of an expert nearly impossible. There is no way to enlighten people who believe they've gained a decade's worth of knowledge because they've spent a morning with a search engine. Few words in a discussion with a layperson can make an expert's heart sink like hearing "I've done my own research."

How can exposure to so much information fail to produce at least some kind of increased baseline of knowledge, if only by electronic osmosis? How can people read so much yet retain so little? The answer is simple: few people are bothering to read what they find.

As a University College of London (UCL) study found, people don't read the articles they encounter during a search on the Internet. Instead, they glance at the top line or the first few sentences and then move on. Internet users, the researchers noted, "are not reading online in the traditional sense; indeed, there are signs that new forms of 'reading' are emerging as users 'power browse' horizontally through titles, contents pages and abstracts going for quick wins. It almost seems that they go online to avoid reading in the traditional sense."[15] This is the *opposite* of reading, aimed not so much at learning but at winning arguments or confirming a preexisting belief.

Children and younger people are especially vulnerable to this tendency. The UCL study suggested that this is because they "have unsophisticated mental maps of what the internet is, often failing to appreciate that it is a collection of networked resources from different providers," and so they spend little time "evaluating information, either for relevance, accuracy or authority." These youngsters "do not find library-sponsored resources intuitive and therefore prefer to use Google or Yahoo! instead," because these services "offer a familiar, if simplistic solution, for their study needs." Teachers and other experts are not immune from the same temptations. "Power browsing and viewing," according to the study, "appear to be the norm for all. The popularity of abstracts among older researchers rather gives the game away." (And the news gets worse: YouTube channels are now targeting children with artificial intelligence programs that are supposedly about science and technology but instead pummel kids with conspiracy theories about the existence of electricity-producing pyramids, the denial of human-caused climate change, and the existence of aliens.)[16]

"Society," the UCL study's authors conclude, "is dumbing down."

This already serious problem might even be a bit scarier than it looks. Internet users tend to gravitate toward, and to believe, whichever results of a search come up first in the rankings, mostly without regard to the origins of those results. After all, if the search engine trusted it enough to rank it highly, it must be worthwhile. This is why anyone pushing content on the Internet looks at ways to improve where their product shows up in a search: if you sell soup, you'll do what you can to rattle a search engine so that people looking for soup recipes are instead steered toward coupons for your brand of soup.

But what if you're selling something more important than soup, like a political candidate? There is at least some evidence that search-engine rankings can alter people's perceptions of political reality. In 2014, two psychologists completed a study of what they called the "search engine manipulation effect" and claimed that their tests showed an ability "to boost the proportion of people who favored any candidate by between 37 and 63 percent after just one search session," and that this potentially constitutes a "serious threat to the democratic system of government."[17] It's too early to say that search engines are undermining democracy—at least yet—but it's hard to argue with the reality that most laypeople can no longer tell the difference between real information and whatever a search engine burps up.

THE WISDOM OF MEGA-CROWDS

Obviously, nonexperts are not always wrong about everything, nor are experts always right. Once in a blue moon, a teenager can get it right and a team of doctors can get it wrong. Experts are important, but ordinary people do manage to live their lives every day without the advice of professors, intellectuals, and other know-it-alls. The Internet, used properly, can help laypeople reach out to each other for basic information that might be too costly or difficult to access from professionals. In fact, the Internet, like the stock market and other mechanisms that aggregate the public's guesses and hunches about complicated matters, can produce moments where laypeople outperform experts.

The way in which a lot of wrong guesses can be milled into one big right guess is a well-established phenomenon. Unfortunately, the way people think the Internet can serve as a way of crowd-sourcing knowledge conflates the perfectly reasonable idea of what the writer

James Surowiecki has called "the wisdom of crowds" with the completely unreasonable idea that the crowds are wise because each member of the mob is also wise.

Sometimes, people without any specialized knowledge can make a better guess at something in a large group than any one member of the group. This tends to be true especially for decisions where the amalgamation of a lot of guesses might produce a better aggregate guess than any one expert's opinion. Surowiecki recounted the story, for example, of an English county fair in 1906, when the public was asked to guess the weight of an ox. The average of the guesses was better than any one person's guess and ended up almost exactly on the mark.[18] Likewise, the world's stock exchanges collectively are generally better than any one stock analyst at betting on stocks.

There are a lot of reasons crowds are better at estimation than individuals, including the way in which a large number of guesses among a lot of people can help to wash out a certain amount of confirmation bias, misperception, or any other number of errors. It also allows people with only partial information to bring those small amounts of knowledge to a problem and help solve it, much in the way a thousand people can complete a huge jigsaw puzzle even though each of them may only have a few pieces.

To take one example, in 2004 the unbiased eye of the crowd cost one of the most prominent journalists in America at the time his job. At the height of the ongoing US presidential campaign, longtime CBS news anchor Dan Rather and his producers went on the air with a story about incumbent President George W. Bush's military record. CBS claimed to have documents from the early 1970s proving that Bush ditched his Air National Guard unit and never finished his required service. Bush, a commander-in-chief who at that point had led America into two major wars, was running against Senator John Kerry, a decorated war hero, and the charge was naturally electrifying in a race that focused heavily on military issues.

Bush supporters objected to what they claimed was dodgy sourcing and sloppy reporting, but in the end ordinary people on the Internet, not angry partisans, brought the story down. Laypeople with no experience in journalism but who spent plenty of time around computers noticed that the font in the documents closely matched those generated by Microsoft's Word software. Obviously, in 1971 the Air Force used typewriters. Microsoft and its programs didn't exist then. The documents had to be fakes.

Faced with this crowd-sourced challenge to the story, CBS ordered an investigation. The network ended up repudiating the documents and the story. The segment's producer was fired. Dan Rather, convinced to this day that he was right and everyone else was wrong, retired and sued his old employer. He lost.

So who needs experts? If we ask the same question enough times, or set enough people to work on the same subject, why not rely on their collective wisdom instead of seeking the flawed or biased opinion of only a handful of self-anointed Wise Ones? If one person is smart and a hundred smarter, then a billion communicating instantly must be even smarter still.

Enthusiasts of the online reference site Wikipedia, among others, have argued that the future rests with this kind of collective knowledge rather than with the expert vetting of references and information. In theory, with a public and open encyclopedia to which anyone can contribute, the sheer number of people watching over each entry should root out error and bias. The articles would be geared toward the inquisitive minds of ordinary human beings rather than the narrow interests of a panel of scholars or editors. Not only would the entries be in a constant and evolving state of accuracy, but the articles themselves by definition would constitute a collection about things that deeply engage the readers instead of a systematic but useless compendium of esoteric knowledge.

Unfortunately, things have not always worked out that way, and Wikipedia is a good lesson in the limits of the Internet-driven displacement of expertise. As it turns out, writing articles about any number of complicated subjects is a lot more difficult than guessing the weight of a bull. Although many well-intentioned people have contributed their time as Wikipedia editors, for example, some of them were also employed by companies and celebrity public relations firms that had an obvious interest in how things appeared in an encyclopedia for the masses. (Nine out of ten Wikipedia contributors are also male, which would likely raise flags among readers—if readers knew it.)

Even with the best of intentions, crowd-sourced projects like Wikipedia suffer from an important but often unremarked distinction between laypeople and professionals: volunteers do what interests them at any given time, while professionals employ their expertise every day. A hobby is not the same thing as a career. As a saying attributed to the British writer Alastair Cooke goes, "Professionals are people who can do their best work when they don't feel like it." The enthusiasm of interested amateurs is not a consistent substitute for the judgment of experts.

Wikipedia's initial efforts fell prey to inconsistency and a lack of oversight, which is exactly what might have been expected from a group homework project. A researcher who studied these trends suggested that Wikipedia after 2007 should have changed its motto from "the encyclopedia that anyone can edit" to "the encyclopedia that anyone who understands the norms, socializes him or herself, dodges the impersonal wall of semi-automated rejection and still wants to voluntarily contribute his or her time and energy can edit."[19]

Eventually, Wikipedia imposed stricter editing controls, but those restrictions in turn discouraged new contributors. As a 2013 article in the *MIT Technology Review* noted, the size of the volunteer force that built Wikipedia and "must defend it against vandalism, hoaxes, and manipulation" has "shrunk by more than a third since 2007 and is still shrinking." Wikipedia still struggles to maintain the quality of its own articles, even measured by its own criteria:

> Among the significant problems that aren't getting resolved is the site's skewed coverage: its entries on Pokemon and female porn stars are comprehensive, but its pages on female novelists or places in sub-Saharan Africa are sketchy. Authoritative entries remain elusive. Of the 1,000 articles that the project's own volunteers have tagged as forming the core of a good encyclopedia, most don't earn even Wikipedia's own middle-ranking quality scores.[20]

Wikipedia does have "featured articles," which must be "well-written," "comprehensive," and "well-researched," including "a thorough and representative survey of the relevant literature," with claims verified against "high-quality reliable sources."

In other words, what Wikipedia really wants is for its best pieces to be just like peer-reviewed scholarship—only without using actual peers. Peer review is a difficult beast to manage even in optimal conditions, with editors trying to assign oversight to the best in each field while avoiding professional rivalries and other conflicts of interest. Translating this process into a project for millions of people with minimal supervision was an unreasonable goal. For something like Wikipedia to work, practically every subject-matter expert in the world would have to be willing to babysit every entry.

Of course, if measured by readership, Wikipedia works just fine. And on some subjects, Wikipedia is a perfectly serviceable source of information. As the MIT article noted, articles are skewed "toward technical, Western, and male-dominated subject matter," so when it comes to tangible—and, more important, uncontroversial—information, Wikipedia has succeeded in bringing together a lot of data in a reliable and stable format. (Personally, I love that Wikipedia is a great source for the plot of almost any movie, no matter how small or obscure.) If you want to know who discovered strontium, who attended the Washington Naval Conference in 1922, or a quick explanation of last year's Nobel Prizes, Wikipedia is much better than a random search engine.

Once any kind of political agenda gets involved, things get a lot dicier. The Wikipedia entry on the chemical weapon Sarin, for example, became an arena for infighting among people who had conflicting agendas over whether the Syrian government used the substance on its own people. Even the basic science fell under attack. A London-based analyst, Dan Kaszeta—the Sarin expert I mentioned in the last chapter who learned a hard lesson about trying to help a college student—told me in late 2015 that

> if someone were to rely on the current Wikipedia page for accurate information about the chemical warfare agent Sarin, they would be misled by half-truths and numerous vague statements not supported by the supplied references. Some of the information on the Wiki page, while technically correct in some aspects, is worded in ways that are misleading. Some of the statements are false.

Kaszeta added that he "spent many hours after the 2013 use of Sarin in Syria correcting misconceptions about Sarin, many of which were doubtless attributable to errors and half-truths on relevant Wikipedia pages."

What people misunderstand about Wikipedia and other online resources, and about the wisdom of crowds in general, is that knowledge is about a lot more than assembling a box of factoids or making coin-toss predictions. Facts do not speak for themselves. Sources like Wikipedia are valuable for basic data as a kind of perpetually updating almanac, but they're not much help on more complex matters.

Crowds can be wise. Not everything, however, is amenable to the vote of a crowd. The Internet creates a false sense that the opinions of many people are tantamount to a "fact." How a virus is transmitted from one human being to another is not the same thing as guessing how many jelly beans are in a glass barrel. As the comedian John Oliver has complained, you don't need to gather opinions on a fact: "You might as well have a poll asking: 'Which number is bigger, 15 or 5?' or 'Do owls exist?' or 'Are there hats?'"

Likewise, public policy is not a parlor game of prediction; it is about long-term choices rooted in thoughtful consideration of costs and alternatives. Asking crowds to guess about specific events in short-term, mental dart-throwing matches just isn't much help when trying to navigate in difficult policy waters. "Will Bashar Assad of Syria use chemical weapons at some point in the next year" is an even bet, like putting a chip on one color in roulette. It's a yes-or-no question, and at some point, you've either won or lost the bet. It's not the same question as "*Why* would Bashar Assad use chemical weapons?" and it is light-years away from the dilemma of "What should America *do* if Bashar Assad uses chemical weapons?" The Internet, however, conflates all three of these questions, and it turns every complicated issue into a poll with a one-click radio button offering a quick solution.

The ease with which people can weigh in on these issues, and even sometimes get a prediction about them right when experts might have been wrong, bolts another layer of anti-intellectual armor to the resistance among laypeople to views more informed than their own.

I UNFRIEND YOU

Learning new things requires patience and the ability to listen to other people. The Internet and social media, however, are making us less social and more confrontational. Online, as in life, people are clustering into small echo chambers, preferring only to talk to those with whom they already agree. The writer Bill Bishop called this "the big sort" in a 2008 book, noting that Americans now choose to live, work, and socialize more with people like themselves in every way. The same thing happens on the Internet.

We're not just associating with people more like ourselves, we're actively breaking ties with everyone else, especially on social media. A 2014 Pew research study—and this was before the hyperpolarization of the Trump era in American politics—found that liberals are more likely than conservatives to block or unfriend people with whom they disagreed, but mostly because conservatives already tended to have fewer people with whom they disagreed in their online social circles in the first place. (Or as a *Washington Post* review of the study put it, conservatives have "lower levels of ideological diversity in their online ecosystem.")[21] A 2021 study led by researchers at Princeton found that the self-sorting process is now practically a reflex, with people now sorting themselves into silos or "epistemic bubbles" online without even realizing it.[22] Worse, multiple studies find that access to broadband connections actually *increases* political polarization, because—unsurprisingly—people go online to find others who share their preexisting views, and thus to confirm and strengthen their biases rather than to interact with those who disagree.[23]

This unwillingness to hear out others not only makes us all more unpleasant with each other in general, but also makes us less able to think, to argue persuasively, and to accept correction when we're wrong. When we are incapable of sustaining a chain of reasoning past a few mouse clicks, we cannot tolerate even the smallest challenge to our beliefs or ideas. This is dangerous because it both undermines the role of knowledge and expertise in a modern society and corrodes the basic ability of people to get along with each other in a democracy.

Underlying much of this ill temper is a false sense of equality and the illusion of egalitarianism created by the immediacy of social media. I have a Twitter account and a Facebook page, and so do you, so we're peers, aren't we? After all, if a top reporter at a major newspaper, a diplomat at the Kennedy School, a scientist at a research hospital, and your Aunt Rose from Reno all have an online presence, then all of their views are just so many messages speeding past your eyes. Every opinion is only as good as the last posting on a home page.

In the age of social media, people using the Internet assume that everyone is equally intelligent or informed merely by virtue of being online. As the *New York Times* movie critic A. O. Scott once put it,

On the Internet, everyone is a critic—a Yelp-fueled takedown artist, an Amazon scholar, a cheerleader empowered by social media to Like and to Share. The inflated, always suspect authority of ink-stained wretches like me has been leveled by digital anarchy. Who needs a cranky nag when you have a friendly algorithm telling you, based on your previous purchases, that there is something You May Also Like, and legions of Facebook friends affirming the wisdom of your choice?[24]

The anonymity of social media tempts users into arguing as though every participant is the same, a group of peers starting from the same level of background and education. This is a rule very few people would use in real life, but on the Internet, the intellectual narcissism of the random commenter displaces the norms that usually govern face-to-face interactions.

This strange combination of distance and intimacy poisons conversation. Reasonable arguments require participants to be honest and well intentioned. Actual proximity builds trust and understanding. We are not just brains in a tank processing disparate pieces of data; we hear out another person in part by relying on multiple visual and auditory cues, not just by watching their words stream past our eyes. Teachers, especially, know that the same material delivered at a distance or on a screen has a different impact than personal interaction with a student who can ask questions, furrow a brow, or show an expression of sudden understanding.

Distance and anonymity remove patience and presumptions of goodwill. Rapid access to information and the ability to speak without having to listen, combined with the "keyboard courage" that allows people to say things to each other electronically they would never say in person, kill conversation. As the writer Andrew Sullivan has noted, this is in part because nothing on the Internet is dispositive, and so every participant in a debate demands to be taken as seriously as every other.

> And what mainly fuels this is precisely what the Founders feared about democratic culture: feeling, emotion, and narcissism, rather than reason, empiricism, and public-spiritedness. Online debates become personal, emotional, and irresolvable almost as soon as they begin. Yes, occasional rational points still fly back and forth, but there are dramatically fewer elite arbiters to establish which of those points is actually true or valid or relevant.[25]

Twitter, Facebook, Reddit, and other online sites can be outlets for intelligent discussion, but too often these and other venues become nothing more than a fusillade of assertions, certainties, poor information, and insults rather than actual exchanges. Visual media such as TikTok and YouTube make it even more difficult to pause and apply reason to images and videos.

To be sure, the Internet is also facilitating conversations among people who might never otherwise have encountered each other. Introverts might argue that an arena like Reddit or the comments section of an online journal opens the door for more interaction from people who in an earlier time might have been reluctant to engage in a public discussion. Unfortunately, allowing anyone to express a view means that almost anyone *will* express a view, which is why so many publications, from the *Toronto Sun* to the *Daily Beast*, have been shutting down their online comments sections.

The Internet, as David Dunning points out, sharpens the problem of misinformation in multiple ways, especially when refuting a dumb idea requires repeating it at least once in the course of the discussion. This creates a minefield for teachers and other experts who risk confirming a mistake merely by acknowledging its existence:

> Then, of course, there is the problem of rampant misinformation in places that, unlike classrooms, are hard to control—like the Internet and news media. In these Wild West settings, it's best *not* to repeat common misbeliefs at all. Telling people that Barack Obama is not a Muslim fails to change many people's minds, because they frequently remember everything that was said—except for the crucial qualifier "not."[26]

Experts trying to confront this kind of stubborn ignorance may think they're helping, when in fact they're basically trying to throw water on a grease fire. It doesn't work and only spreads the damage around.

The Internet is the largest anonymous medium in human history. The ability to argue from a distance, and the cheapened sense of equality it provides, is corroding trust and respect among all of us, experts and laypeople alike. Alone in front of the keyboard but awash in websites, newsletters, and online groups dedicated to confirming any and every idea, the Internet has politically and intellectually mired millions of Americans in their own biases. Social media outlets such as Facebook amplify this echo chamber; as Megan McArdle wrote in 2016, "Even if we are not deliberately blocking people who disagree with us, Facebook curates our feeds so that we get more of the stuff we 'like.' What do we 'like'? People and posts that agree with us."[27]

This is especially dangerous now that social media such as Facebook, TikTok, Instagram, and Twitter have become the primary sources of news and information for many Americans, and experts trying to break through this shell of political insularity and self-assured ignorance do so at their peril. It's difficult enough to argue with one person who has gotten something wrong; it's quite another to try to reason with someone as they gather pretty websites as "evidence" and marshal legions of anonymous, like-minded social media friends with equally uninformed views for support. Meanwhile, scholars and professionals who insist on logic, foundational knowledge, and basic rules about sources risk condemnation by twenty-first-century online users as nothing more than elitists who do not understand the miracles of the Information Age.

The pitfalls of social media, the Dunning-Kruger Effect, and the death of expertise all collided head-on in 2022 when the technology mogul Elon Musk bought Twitter. At the time the wealthiest man in the world, Musk claimed to be fed up with what he saw as censorship and opacity at Twitter, and he said he would solve all these issues by buying the platform. (He then tried to back out of the deal, but Twitter took him to court.) Better known for his car and space exploration companies, Tesla and SpaceX, Musk somehow convinced himself that he had the talent to run a giant social media enterprise. He promptly set about firing many of Twitter's staff and issuing various dictates, some of which he later ignored or rescinded. One idea he held to quite firmly, however, was that Twitter needed more Elon Musk, and he ramped up his pace of stunningly uninformed tweets about everything from vaccines to the Russian-Ukrainian war, all while apparently thinking he was doing a terrific job of restoring Twitter as an important public space.

Within a year, Twitter's revenue was down by nearly 60 percent and its overall value as a company dropped 66 percent. Tesla, meanwhile, shed 65 percent of its value, in part because of investor concerns over the distraction of Twitter. (Tesla has since rebounded somewhat, but it has not recovered its pre-Twitter value.)[28] Through it all, Musk was a case study in the Dunning-Kruger dynamic: In 2023, he impulsively rebranded Twitter as "X"—he is fascinated by the letter—in the belief that he is on the verge of creating a visionary new platform. In reality, as the writer David Frum once pointed out (on Twitter, ironically), Musk's greatest achievement so far is that he is now single-handedly responsible for the greatest destruction of value in the shortest period of time in the entire history of capitalism.

Musk's impulsive incompetence, bizarre and comical at the time, has since had a much darker implication for expertise and online information. Musk openly resented the system of verification at Twitter, in which the platform would vouch, with a small blue mark, that organizations and individuals—particularly those in the media or public figures likely to be impersonated—were who they claimed to be. (I had one for years.) Musk eliminated this system and offered the blue check for sale to any user; at the time same, he also invited back many accounts previously banned for offensive conduct, misinformation, and other offenses against the previous company's terms of service.

The result, as predictable as a sunrise, was that Twitter quickly was awash in fake accounts, racist trolls, and "promoted" tweets that mimicked news stories. The whole business was such a disaster that Musk quickly started re-verifying well-known users without even asking them—which was just as well, as many of them wanted nothing to do with him—but the damage was done, and Twitter (or X, or whatever it might be called when you read this) is now far less reliable as a source of information, especially about breaking events.

Websites and Internet polls and social media might be unreliable, but reporters can dig out the truth instead of getting pulled down in the whirlpool. Journalists can still serve as the arbiters of all this chaos, using the careful tools of investigation, sourcing, and fact-checking.

Or, as we'll see in the next chapter, perhaps not.

Chapter 5

The "New" New Journalism, and Lots of It

Charlie: Mom, I find it interesting that you refer to the *Weekly World News* as "The Paper." The paper contains *facts.*
May: This paper contains facts. And this paper has the eighth highest circulation in the whole wide world. Right? Plenty of facts. "Pregnant man gives birth." That's a fact.

So I Married an Axe Murderer

I READ IT IN THE PAPER

Did you know that chocolate can help you lose weight? Sure you do. You read it in the paper. In fact, you might have read it in several papers, and woe to any expert, including a doctor, who might have told you otherwise. After all, hiding the miraculous weight-decreasing qualities of the tastiest thing in the world is just the kind of thing experts would do. Thankfully, a German scientist, Johannes Bohannon of the Institute of Diet and Health, wrote a paper that was published in a journal and then joyfully covered in press throughout the world, and he verified what we have all suspected all along: chocolate is really good for you.

Except Johannes Bohannon doesn't exist. Neither does the Institute of Diet and Health. The journal that published the paper is real, but apparently it is less than scrupulous about things like peer review and editing. "Johannes" Bohannon was in fact a journalist named John Bohannon, who was (in Bohannon's words) "part of a team of gonzo journalists and one doctor" who wanted to "demonstrate just how easy it is to turn bad science into the big headlines behind diet fads."[1]

So chocolate won't make you thinner. But did you know that the West Bank and Gaza, the occupied Palestinian areas on two sides of Israel, are connected by a bridge, one on which the Israelis sometimes maliciously limit Palestinian traffic? You might well have read that one in the "news," too. In 2014, the online journal *Vox*—which bills itself as a source that explains complicated issues to everyone else—listed "11 crucial facts to understand the Israel-Gaza crisis." Fact number one included the Gaza–West Bank bridge.

It doesn't exist.

Vox corrected its error—the writer claimed he'd seen an article about a proposed bridge but didn't realize it was never built—but not before critics had a good laugh at *Vox*'s expense.

Vox for some years was a regular target for such criticism, and sometimes for good reason. The website branded itself as an effort at explanatory journalism, meant to provide facts about complicated stories; it soon developed a reputation, however, for getting tripped up by those same facts. In early 2016, for example, *Vox* ran a headline that said, "The most radical thing the Black Panthers did was give kids free breakfast." The Panthers, a radical group formed in the late 1960s that fused black nationalism and Marxism-Leninism, were involved in multiple cases of violence and murder, including shoot-outs with the police. They were not exactly the friendly staff of a day-care center. The *Vox* piece prompted the *Daily Beast* columnist Michael Moynihan to tweet, "Remember when 'explainer' writers had to know something about what they were explaining? Nor do I."

So, chocolate isn't a weight-loss miracle, and there's no bridge between Gaza and the West Bank. Maybe the Panthers were a bit rougher than we remember. But perhaps you weren't aware of the real meaning of Easter to Christians, which celebrates the resurrection of Jesus Christ directly up to Heaven. The *New York Times* said so in 2013. Now, the Gospels make some sort of reference to Jesus walking around for a bit first, which is probably the version that local parish priests and ministers relate every spring. Those members of the clergy might be smart, and there might even be some theology degrees scattered in among them, but who are they to argue with the *New York Times*?

There are well over a billion Christians in the world, and amazingly enough, a few of them caught the error. The *Times* quietly ran what might be one of the most understated corrections in newspaper history: "An earlier version of this article mischaracterized the Christian holiday of Easter. It is the celebration of Jesus's resurrection from the dead, not his resurrection into heaven."[2] That is a more accurate statement of the official version, but to get it wrong in the first place means that someone at the *Times* had no idea about Pentecost, the story of the "Doubting Thomas" or of other common cultural references derived from moments in the New Testament where Jesus appeared in person, rather than taking the direct elevator to the top floor on Easter Sunday.

If keeping up with all this misinformation tires you out, you can always retreat back to some fine literature and perhaps read one of the great novels by Evelyn Waugh. After all, Waugh was listed in 2016 by *TIME* magazine as one of the "100 greatest female writers of all time," so her work might well be worth a look.

Except, of course, that Evelyn Waugh (who lived until 1966) was a man. At least Waugh was properly associated with his work. In 2019, the *New York Times* attributed a wonderful quote about the power of poetry to Walt Whitman—"we read and write poetry because we are members of the human race"—which certainly sounds like something Whitman might have said, but in fact the line was from the 1989 film *Dead Poets Society*. Close enough.

These kinds of howlers aren't just a product of the Internet era. A front-page story in the *Washington Post* from more than thirty years ago, for example, referred to Ireland as a member of NATO, which would have been a shock not only to the famously neutral people of Ireland, but to both the Soviet Union and the United States. Everyone makes mistakes, including experts, journalists, editors, and fact-checkers. These things happen.

Unfortunately, however, these kinds of mistakes happen a lot more frequently in the new world of twenty-first-century journalism. Worse, because of the Internet, misinformation spreads a lot faster and sticks around a lot longer. In a world of constant information, delivered at high speed and available twenty-four hours a day, journalism is now sometimes as much a contributor to the death of expertise as it is a defense against it.

I realize it seems churlish to complain about the feast of news and information brought to us by the Information Age. (It's also somewhat of a professional hazard for me personally. After leaving the teaching profession, I began a new career as a writer for a national magazine, so I am now officially part of the problem.) But I'm going to complain anyway. Changes in journalism, like the increased access to the Internet and to college education, have had unexpectedly corrosive effects on the relationship between laypeople and experts. Instead of making people better informed, much of what passes for news in the twenty-first century often leaves laypeople—and sometimes experts—even more confused and ornery.

Experts face a vexing challenge: there's more news available, and yet people seem less informed, a trend that goes back at least a quarter century. Paradoxically, it is a problem that is worsening rather than dissipating. People know less about the world around them, and they are less interested in it, despite the availability of more information than ever before.

As long ago as 1990, for example, a study conducted by the Pew Trust warned that disengagement from important public questions was worse among people under thirty, the group that should have been most receptive to then-emerging sources of information like cable television and electronic media. This was a distinct change in American civic culture, as the Pew study noted:

> Over most of the past five decades younger members of the public have been at least as well informed as older people. In 1990, that is no longer the case. . . . Those under 30 know less than younger people once did. And, they are less interested in what's happening in the larger world around them. Social scientists and pollsters have long recognized that younger people have usually been somewhat less attuned to politics and serious issues. But the difference has been greatly sharpened.[3]

The children of those respondents fared no better. A 2011 University of Chicago study found that America's college graduates "failed to make significant gains in critical thinking and complex reasoning during their four years of college," but more worrisome, they "also failed to develop dispositions associated with civic engagement."[4] Like their parents, these young people were not only less informed than we might have expected, but they were also less interested in applying what little they might have learned to their responsibilities as citizens.

And *their* children are even worse off. A 2022 study found that teenagers were most likely to get news by "scrolling through their social feeds," relying mostly on what their friends already liked on Instagram and TikTok.[5] Thus, when a layperson's riposte to an expert consists of "I read it in the paper" or "I saw it on the news," it may not mean very much. Indeed, the information may not have come from "the news" or "the paper" at all, but from something that only looks like a news source—or it might have been a momentary distraction wedged between funny videos of cats. More likely, such an answer means "I saw something from a source I happen to like and it told me something I wanted to hear." At that point, the discussion has nowhere to go; the original issue is submerged or lost in the effort to untangle which piece of misinformation is driving the conversation in the first place.

How did this happen? How can people be more resistant to facts and knowledge in a world where they are constantly barraged with facts and knowledge? The short answer where journalism is concerned—in an explanation that could be applied to many modern innovations—is that technology collided with capitalism and gave people what they wanted, even when it wasn't good for them.

I realize that criticizing journalism and the modern news media puts me at risk of violating the Prime Directive for experts: never tell other experts how to do their jobs (especially as I am a relatively new member of that profession). While most of my career was outside of journalism, however, I was nonetheless a consumer of its products, and I relied on the media during my earlier careers as a teacher and a policy analyst. I had to navigate the hurdles every expert faces in communicating complex events and ideas to students and other laypeople every day, a problem I now face again when writing, for example, about foreign policy for a large audience.

TOO MUCH OF A GOOD THING IS TOO MUCH

The challenges to expertise and established knowledge created by modern journalism all flow from the same problem that afflicts so much of modern American life: there is too much of everything.

There are more sources of news in the twenty-first century than ever before. Thanks to radio, television, and the Internet, people can access those sources easily and share them electronically; thanks to universal education, they can read them and discuss them more widely than in the past. It's a banquet of information, served up with various kinds of garnish on any number of platters. So why do people remain resolutely ignorant and uninformed, and reject news, along with expert opinion and advice, even when it's all delivered to them almost without effort? Because there's too much of it, and it is too closely fused with entertainment.

Today, anyone with electricity is up to their neck in news from every direction whenever they want it. Most newspapers and local television stations in America are instantaneously available in electronic format and are updated regularly. Consumers with access to satellite or cable television—which is to say, almost anyone in most of the developed world—can take their pick of dozens of newscasts from around the planet. There is a news source for every taste and political view, with the line between journalism and entertainment sometimes intentionally obscured to drive ratings, views, and clicks.

To put this in perspective, the average American home in 1960 had three television stations available to it along with eight radio stations, one newspaper, and three or four magazines.[6] By 2014, the Nielsen rating organization estimated that the average US home had 189 television channels (60 more than it had in 2008) with consumers tuning in consistently to about 17 of those channels. Only a few years later, streaming services added even more options. Add to this the amount of media delivered to consumers through their mobile devices and home computers, estimated by a researcher at the San Diego Supercomputer Center in 2015 to be so much that the average person at that time would have needed more than fifteen hours a day to see or hear it all.[7]

But *more* of everything does not mean *more quality* in everything. (Sturgeon's Law is inescapable everywhere.) To say that the citizens of the United States now have many more sources of news than ever before is like saying that they also have more dining choices than ever before: it's true, but it doesn't mean that anyone's getting healthier by eating in America's nearly three hundred thousand cheap chain restaurants and fast-food outlets.

Affluence and technology lowered the barriers to journalism and to the creation of journalistic enterprises in the late twentieth and early twenty-first centuries, with predictable consequences. Not only could more young people afford to take internships and low-paid contributing gigs to break into media work, but this influx of cheap writing labor also served a need: growing bandwidth needed to be filled with more content. Once, limited page inches on paper required hard editorial decisions about quality and relevance. Now, more media and more outlets mean more competition; more competition means building loyalty among identifiable political and demographic niches in the audience. All of this competition is at the behest of the American consumer, who wants everything simpler, faster, prettier, and more entertaining.

Forty years ago, the media were more conscientious about separating "news" from everything else. This also meant, however, that the "news" was in fact not a fully realized picture of the world. Instead, it was a carefully curated and edited stream of information. The small number of networks and news outlets, and the relatively tiny amount of time devoted to news on television, meant that the public saw the world as it was viewed by the corporations who ran the networks. News organizations had to try to cover the broadest and most demographically marketable audience, and so newscasts in the United States through the 1960s and 1970s were remarkably alike, with calming, authoritative figures such as Walter Cronkite and

Harry Reasoner reporting even the most awful events with aplomb and detachment.

However, this also meant that not everything counted as news. There was more corporate and elite control over the news before the 1990s—and that wasn't entirely a bad thing. When each network had only thirty minutes in which to capture the day's events, an arms control treaty with the Soviet Union was likely to get more play than which celebrities were getting divorces. Networks rarely broke into their programming with news except for the dread-inducing "special reports," which were usually about a major disaster of some kind. If something important happened in the world, everyone in America had to wait for the paperboy—a solemn childhood office I occupied in the early 1970s—or for their evening newscast.

Not only is there more news, but there is more interactivity with the news. Americans no longer read whatever fits into a set number of newspaper columns, nor do they sit passively in front of a television and receive a digest of events. Instead, they're asked, constantly, what they think of the information they're being given, often in real time. TikTok and Twitter and Instagram and Facebook are the new news tickers, crowd-sourced streams of information that break news and spread rumors with equal force. Talk shows and news broadcasts— increasingly difficult to distinguish from each other—often ask viewers to weigh in via social media or on a website instant poll, with the clear assumption that the audience is watching the news with a smartphone, tablet, or laptop nearby.

Interactivity is also driving the selection of stories, which can make one yearn for the days of corporate editorial control. When the *Dallas Morning News* hired a new editor in 2015, it reached out to Mike Wilson, a journalist from the Internet news site FiveThirtyEight, which specializes in "data-driven" stories rather than breaking news. "I think what we need to throw out are some old notions of what our readers need," Wilson said in an interview after he was hired.

We just have to be more responsive to what the audience wants. I think the tradition in newspapers has been that we have set the agenda and we've told readers what we think they want to know. I think we need to come down off of that mountain a little bit and ask people, involve people in the conversation a little bit more.[8]

Larger papers agree. "How can you say you don't care what your customers think?" Alan Murray, who oversees online news at the *Wall Street Journal*, said in 2015. "We care a lot about what our readers think. But our readers also care a lot about our editorial judgment. So we're always trying to balance the two."[9]

Journalists and their editors swear up and down that they are not allowing the public to drive their selection and coverage of stories, but that is hard to believe. More than twenty years ago, a *New York Times* report tried to put the best face on it after describing how closely the *Washington Post* and other papers monitor their web traffic: "Rather than corrupt news judgment by causing editors to pander to the basest reader interests, the availability of this technology so far seems to be leading to more surgical decisions about how to cover a topic so it becomes more appealing to an online audience."[10] The *Post*'s readers, the story proudly notes, were less interested in the 2010 British elections than in Crocs (an ugly shoe fad), but that didn't make the *Post* alter its coverage. That might have been a relief to hear, but it was unsettling even back then that this assurance had to be given at all. Nothing has improved since then, especially with local and national publications downsizing and shedding the reporters and editors who once wrote important but not always audience-grabbing stories.[11]

To judge from the public's awareness of major issues, what readers need is not more input into the stories, but basic information, including the occasional map with a "You Are Here" pointer on it. In a less competitive, less crowded market, media outlets would not be so driven by what readers or viewers want in the same way, but in

THE DEATH OF EXPERTISE

a market glutted by information, it was only a matter of time before the tables were turned and journalists were asking readers what they would like to read instead of informing them about things they must know.

This fusing of entertainment, news, punditry, and citizen participation is a chaotic mess that does not inform people so much as it creates the illusion of being informed. Just as clicking through endless Internet pages makes people think they're learning new things, watching countless hours of television and scrolling through hundreds of headlines is encouraging laypeople to believe—erroneously—that they understand the news. Worse, their daily interaction with so much media makes them resistant to learning anything that takes too long or isn't entertaining enough.

This information overload isn't just overwhelming laypeople either. The fact is that everyone is drowning in data, including professionals who pay a lot of attention to news and who try to be discriminating consumers. In 2015 the *National Journal* surveyed people it called "Washington Insiders," mostly composed of congressional staff, federal government executives, and private-sector public affairs professionals, and asked them how they get their news. According to the study, it was now easier than ever for these "insiders" to obtain information, "but harder than ever for them to make sense of it all." Professionals in Washington, like everyone else, were "somewhat paralyzed" by a "glut" of news that left them "lacking confidence in individual sources and information."[12]

If professional policymakers and staff in Washington can't make sense of the news, how can anyone else? Who has enough time to sort through it all? The *National Journal* study even nodded to this time pressure by including a note that the study itself should take forty-five minutes to read in full, but only twenty to skim. The irony is both obvious and disturbing.

This endless stream of news and tailored interactive broadcasting predates the Internet and cable. It even predates television. Radio is where it all began; more accurately, radio is where people first immersed themselves in endless news and talk, in a medium that was supposedly killed off by television in the 1960s but found new life at the end of the twentieth century.

RADIO KILLED THE VIDEO STAR

While many professionals and experts tend to blame the Internet for the profusion of would-be know-it-alls lecturing them in their offices, others invoke the twenty-four-hour news cycle as another culprit, drowning people in stories and facts faster than they can absorb them. As with the accusations against the Internet, there's good reason for those complaints. Americans now watch the news as if they're in the situation room of the White House, hanging on every new scrap of information as if they were personally going to make the call on launching a war. (CNN for many years has appealed to this viewer vanity by calling its afternoon broadcast "The Situation Room.")

This doesn't explain, however, why Americans erroneously end up thinking they're better informed than the experts on the myriad issues flooding across their screens. For this, we must look a little more closely at how the public's relationship with the media developed after the 1970s. The decade of Watergate, "stagflation," and defeat in Vietnam is the benchmark not only because it was on the cusp of the addition of new technologies like cable, but also because those developments coincided with an accelerating collapse of trust in government and other institutions in American life. The growth of new kinds of media and the decline of trust are both intimately related to the death of expertise.

Television in the 1950s was supposed to displace radio for most kinds of programming. AM radio nonetheless dominated music and sports, with a wide audience reach but a tinny, monaural sound. This inferior sound quality couldn't compete with the obvious problem that human beings, equipped with two ears, prefer listening to everything in stereo. FM offered better sound—as the band Steely Dan promised in a hit song called "FM," there was "no static at all"—but it took until 1978 for FM radio broadcasts to reach more listeners than AM. Television, meanwhile, with its ability to add visual elements to its reports, grabbed the news and other staples of American life once primarily found on radio.

Radio wasn't dead, however. Especially on the AM band, radio offered something television could not: an interactive format. Relatively unhindered by the limits of airtime and cheap to produce, the idea behind talk radio was simple: give the host a microphone, hit the switch, and take calls from people who wanted to talk about the news and express their own views. With other forms of entertainment gravitating to television or to the richer sound of FM, it was an obvious choice for stations looking for affordable programming.

Talk radio had immense political consequences, and it provided the foundations for attacks on established knowledge that flowered later on social media. No one did more to drive the ascendance of talk radio than the broadcaster Rush Limbaugh. From the late 1980s until his death in 2021, Limbaugh created an alternative to the often stodgy world of Sunday-morning television punditry. Limbaugh wasn't the first; despite the belief held by many of his critics that the 1987 repeal of the US government's "Fairness Doctrine"—a rarely invoked requirement that holders of public broadcast licenses make room for opposing views on important subjects—powered Limbaugh's rise, politically oriented radio talk shows were scattered throughout the United States since at least the 1950s, often relegated to evenings and late nights. (To take one example, I grew up in

Western Massachusetts in the 1970s listening to an AM radio talker named Tracy Cole, an obnoxious and insulting host who was much like Limbaugh, and who regularly inveighed against liberal women, welfare cheats, and other targets.)[13]

Limbaugh, however, did something unique, by setting himself up as a source of truth in opposition to the rest of the American media. Syndication increased Limbaugh's reach, and within a few years of his first broadcasts, he was heard on more than six hundred stations nationwide. He told his listeners that the press and the national television networks were conspiring in a liberal echo chamber, and especially that they were in the tank for the new administration of President Bill Clinton. Not all of these charges were entirely fair, but not all of them were wrong either, and Limbaugh was able to mine the established media daily for examples of bias—of which there were plenty—and run with them. With three solid hours of uninterrupted airtime, Limbaugh had an advantage television wouldn't have until the expansion of cable.

Limbaugh and other talkers also built a loyal national base of followers by allowing them to call in and express their support. The calls were screened and vetted; according to a manager at one of Limbaugh's early affiliates, this was because Limbaugh felt that he was not a very good debater. Debate, however, was not the point: the object was to create a sense of community among people who already were inclined to agree with each other. Later, the Internet would overtake this kind of network building among people who rejected the mainstream media, but the phenomenon began on radio.

The television networks and print media were taken by surprise to find not only that millions of people were listening but that these listeners were turning against traditional sources of news. In 1970, Vice President Spiro Agnew charged the press with liberal bias, hauling off the immortal zinger (penned by the speechwriter William Safire) that the media was full of "nattering nabobs of negativism."

Twenty years later, talk radio made the same case—and this time the radio talkers made it stick.

The irony, of course, is that Limbaugh himself, along with other conservative radio hosts, soon *became* the mainstream. By the early twenty-first century, broadcast radio was again slumping as a market, but Limbaugh held on to twenty million listeners, and in 2008 he scored a $400 million contract whose size was second only to shock-jock Howard Stern's half-billion-dollar deal with Sirius satellite radio. The line between news and entertainment became even more blurred when comedian Joe Rogan signed a 2020 deal reportedly worth at least $100 million with streaming service Spotify. Rogan's programming is a free-form clubhouse environment, in which serious issues are discussed unseriously, and Rogan has come under fire not only for his use of offensive slurs but because of his embrace of anti-vaccine ideas. Nonetheless, he is one of the most influential public figures in America, especially among young men.[14] In the early age of television, video nearly put radio out of business; soon enough, however, television, talk radio, and streaming services would become complementary rather than competing media as radio's top stars moved to cable, and vice versa.

Liberal talk radio could not compete in this realm and had far less of an impact. Liberals might say this is because they refused to stoop to the level of their competitors. (The progressive radio host Randi Rhodes, on the now-defunct progressive network Air America, *did* call Hillary Clinton "a big fucking whore" on the air in 2008, which suggests that at least some liberals were willing to go the distance.) Conservatives, for their part, have argued that liberal talk radio, in a country dominated by liberal media outlets, was a solution to a nonexistent problem, because liberals already had plenty of places to be heard. For whatever reason, left-leaning talkers never gained traction. Alan Colmes, for example, was a popular progressive talker until his death in 2017, but he never gained more than a fraction of the audience commanded by Limbaugh or by Colmes's own former talk-show partner Sean Hannity (who divides his time between radio and a show on Fox News).

The rise of talk radio challenged the role of experts by reinforcing the popular belief that the established media—and virtually all other institutions—were dishonest and unreliable. Radio talkers didn't just attack established political beliefs: they attacked everything, plunging their listeners into an alternate universe where facts of any kind were unreliable unless verified by the host. In 2011, Limbaugh referred to "government, academia, science, and the media" as the "four corners of deceit," which pretty much covered everyone except Limbaugh.

There are many other examples. Glenn Beck once told his listeners that the Obama White House science adviser John Holdren was an advocate of compulsory abortion. (He wasn't, but the story still makes the rounds.) Hannity and others latched on to a rumor that the Egyptian government was going to legalize necrophilia. (Limbaugh asked who might provide the condoms for such an encounter.) The story, as the former *Christian Science Monitor* foreign correspondent Dan Murphy noted, was "utter hooey," but that didn't matter.

There is a reasonable argument that talk radio in the 1980s and 1990s was a necessary antidote to television and print outlets that had become politically complacent, ideologically monotonous, and too self-regarding. Limbaugh and his talk-radio imitators did not create middle America's resentment and distrust of the media, as Agnew's famous attack on the press showed. Radio talkers, however, fueled that distrust with renewed energy. Eventually, talk radio became as dogmatic and one-sided as the culture it claimed to be supplanting. Many of the new generation of podcasters and streamers, such as Rogan, have adopted a kind of unmoored nihilism, in which everything might be true, or everything might be a lie, that makes their predecessors on radio seem almost tame by comparison. Conservative talkers may have been able to bring forward debates that major television networks would prefer to have ignored, but they also intensified the voices of people who think that opinions are as good as facts, and that experts are no smarter, and far more mendacious, than anyone else.

AMERICA HELD HOSTAGE: DAY 16,000

The radio insurgency against the print and electronic media might not have spread farther than the AM band were it not for cable television and the Internet, two arenas that reinforced each other both as alternative sources of news and as platforms for attacks on established knowledge throughout the 1990s. Even Limbaugh, after conquering the best-seller lists with a foray into book writing, took a stab at syndicated television for a few years. A previously narrow media gate was now large enough to accommodate a stampede. Stories originating in one medium quickly bounced to another and then returned more loudly, like the ear-splitting feedback of a microphone held in front of a speaker.

The irony, however, is that neither cable nor the Internet pioneered the twenty-four-hour news cycle. For that, we can thank the late Ayatollah Khomeini of Iran.

In November 1979, Iranian revolutionaries overran the US embassy in Tehran, taking dozens of American personnel as hostages. The spectacle shocked Americans who saw it all happen nearly in real time. The Iranian hostage drama was something new, a story in between a war and a crisis: Vietnam was a slow-motion debacle that dragged on for a decade, while the Cuban missile crisis took place in two weeks, faster than television and newspapers could fully report it. The hostage taking was fast, and then slow, with a few days of violence followed by a long grind of waiting and worrying.

The news media were in a jam. On the one hand, Americans were in grave danger in a foreign country; on the other, nothing was actually *happening*. Like the comedian Chevy Chase announcing each week on *Saturday Night Live* that Spain's Francisco Franco was *still* dead, so, too, were network anchors left with little more to say than that the hostages were still hostages.

The ABC television network at the time decided to try something different by moving the daily Iran briefing to the late evening. This was also a marketing decision: ABC had no late-night programming against Johnny Carson's venerable talk show on its rival NBC, and news programming was, by comparison, cheap. ABC filled the evening slot with a new program called *Nightline* devoted solely to coverage of the crisis. Each night, ABC would splash the screen with "America Held Hostage," followed by the number of days of captivity. The anchor (usually the veteran ABC newsman Ted Koppel) would then fill the time by interviewing experts, journalists, and other figures associated with the crisis.

After 444 days of captivity, the hostages came home, but Koppel and *Nightline* stayed on and ran for many more years. Cable provided the technology for later imitators, but *Nightline* provided the model. The "breaking" alerts and the chyrons—those little ribbons of news factoids that now scroll across the bottom of the screen on news networks—all originated with a program that was, in effect, created on the fly in response to a crisis.

Another legacy of the *Nightline* era and the advent of the twenty-four-hour news cycle is the devaluation of expert advice in the media. As the Army War College professor Steven Metz has rightly noted, in an earlier time, "the public tended to defer to national security authorities who had earned their influence through experience and expertise as elected officials, military leaders, political appointees, academics, members of the media or think tank analysts." And then things changed:

Hard-earned expertise was unnecessary when there were hours of radio and television air time or online discussion boards to fill.... For decades now, deference to authority has eroded across the political landscape. The profusion of information and communication technology gave voice, and self-confidence, to people who previously would defer to authority.[15]

"Armed with a bit of information," Metz concludes, such people "opined on an ever-expanding array of issues." Producers and reporters enabled those would-be experts by asking them to speak on anything and everything, a temptation few people can resist. (I am among those who are not without sin on this.)

Nightline was a success, but broadcast networks still saw no reason to run news day and night. After all, what viewer wanted to watch nothing but news? In 1980, the entrepreneur Ted Turner took a chance that people would, in fact, watch endless amounts of news when his invention, the Cable News Network, went on the air. CNN was denigrated by broadcast news executives as "the Chicken Noodle Network," an add-water-and-stir porridge of headlines and features. Turner got the last laugh, as CNN not only became a cable juggernaut but also later spawned its own competitors, including one—Fox News—that would eventually overtake it in the ratings.

Instead of older white males reading the news in stentorian voices, Turner gave CNN a far glossier look. On June 1, 1980, thirty-nine-year-old David Walker and his thirty-one-year-old wife, Lois Hart, anchored the first moments of the new CNN, delivering a story about President Jimmy Carter visiting the civil rights leader Vernon Jordan in the hospital. The news was no longer a half hour of listening to America's soothing middle-aged uncles, men such as John Chancellor and Frank Reynolds, but an ongoing engagement with a roster of younger, more attractive anchors scattered throughout the day and night.

The twenty-four-hour news cycle had arrived, but it took a succession of crises and disasters throughout the 1980s and into the 1990s to capture an audience. The attempted assassination of President Ronald Reagan, the crash of a jet into the Potomac River in Washington, and the terrorist hijacking of a TWA flight, among others, all proved that Americans would leave their television sets tuned to a news channel for hours on end. Instead of a ritual where Americans gathered at a preset time or rushed to their sets at the heart-stopping words "we interrupt this broadcast," news became a kind of open buffet where viewers could visit and graze all day long.

The testimony of the law professor Anita Hill and her allegations of sexual harassment against Supreme Court nominee Clarence Thomas in 1991 proved that Americans would not only watch crises and disasters, but also stay riveted to their sets for political and courtroom dramas as well—especially if they involved sex or murder or, in the best case, both. In 1991, after judicial rulings allowed more cameras into courtrooms, Court TV arrived on cable. Americans became armchair legal experts by watching endless cases about rape, murder, and other assorted skullduggery.

CNN was already putting out more news than the average viewer could reasonably handle in a day, but the proliferation of cable outlets like Court TV was an expert's nightmare. In a 1991 review of the new network, *Entertainment Weekly* called Court TV "part C-SPAN, part *Monday Night Football*," although that might have been uncharitable to both. And by the time the spectacular 1995 murder trial of O. J. Simpson concluded, millions of laypeople had developed deep views on things they could not understand, from the statistics of DNA testing to the veracity of shoeprints. It was a ratings treasure trove, and it proved that what people really wanted from their news networks was not hours of boring news, but high-tension drama.

CNN launched a headlines-only channel in 1982. Devoted solely to news, it was supposed to be a rotating cycle of top stories every thirty minutes. Of course, that was too dry for the average viewer, and sure enough, the celebrity judge Nancy Grace soon camped out at what came to be renamed HLN. (Like Kentucky Fried Chicken renaming itself KFC to sidestep what it was doing to chickens—that is, frying them—HLN apparently needed to get "news" out of the title.)

HLN specialized in lurid stories interspersed with Grace's hyperbolic raging about justice. In a ghastly 2008 story, a mother in Florida named Casey Anthony was accused of murdering her toddler daughter. It was a disturbing story, a kind of rerun of the Simpson trial in which millions of people took sides quickly. HLN, however, didn't just cover Anthony's trial; Grace and others made it a staple of HLN's "news," running some *five hundred* stories about it.[16] By the time Anthony was acquitted in 2011, HLN's viewers were likely more versed in Florida murder statutes than in their own rights under the US Constitution. In 2022, HLN abandoned any pretense of updating viewers. It stopped producing live news coverage, and in the words of former CNN media reporter Brian Stelter, transformed "almost completely into a true-crime channel."[17]

There is no way to discuss the nexus between journalism and the death of expertise without considering the revolutionary change represented by the arrival of Fox News in 1996. The creation of the conservative media consultant Roger Ailes, Fox made the news faster, slicker, and, with the addition of news readers who were actual beauty queens, prettier. It's an American success story, in every good and bad way that such triumphs of marketing often are. (Ailes, in what seems almost like a made-for-television coda to his career, was forced out of Fox in 2016 after multiple allegations of sexual harassment were covered in great detail on the medium he helped create.)

Fox's history intersects with the death of expertise, however, in an important way: the arrival of Fox was, in its way, the ultimate expression of the partisan division in how people seek out sources of news in a new electronic marketplace. What Limbaugh tried to do with radio and a syndicated television show, Ailes made a reality with a network. Had Ailes not created Fox, someone would have, because the market, as talk radio proved, was already there. As the conservative author and Fox commentator, the late Charles Krauthammer, liked to quip, Ailes "discovered a niche audience: half the American people."

Fox, however, soon mutated into an openly partisan operation, thus putting the last nail in the coffin of the news broadcast as a nominally apolitical review of the day's events. Fox, like the radio talkers, positioned itself to be the alternative to the mainstream, a watchdog over a club to which it claimed it did not belong and to whom it owned nothing, and an advocate for a conservative movement that believed it had no real power in American culture despite its control by 2016 of a majority of elected offices across the United States.

Of course, the idea that Fox was unique, or that the major networks were somehow apolitical, was always a fiction. Media bias, of various kinds and in every venue, is real. Fox, for a time, tried to draw a line between its hard-news operations and its opinion programming, and for a time it succeeded. (Fox's national security reporting and its polling operations were particularly good.) Fox's influence is larger because of the sheer size of its audience, but Fox hosts were not wrong to argue that their competitors also featured partisan "infotainment" in their schedules.

The 2020 election, however, presented Fox with a dilemma. The Fox election desk had (rightly) declared Donald Trump the loser on election night, a move that infuriated both Trump and his supporters. The ensuing fiasco at Fox, in which the network allowed its anchors to report outlandish stories about election fraud that they themselves knew to be false, is another book in itself. Fox paid out more than three-quarters of a billion dollars to a voting machine company in order to settle a massive defamation lawsuit, and they soon fired one of their most unhinged hosts, Tucker Carlson. (Carlson, until that moment, was Fox's top rated and most highly paid star.) The network admitted that the stories were not true, but not in time: A June 2023 poll found that nearly a third of Americans—and 68 percent of Republicans, Fox's most loyal viewers—still believed that Joe Biden somehow stole the 2020 election from Trump.[18]

Little changed after Fox's gigantic payout, and the network remains a supremely corrosive part of the media landscape. The destructive synergy created by the combination of news, entertainment, and the Internet remains a problem of Gibraltarian proportions for experts trying to communicate with laypeople who already believe that everyone lies about everything, but who also somehow believe that staring at their phone while sitting on the subway will nonetheless keep them abreast of the world's events.

TRUST NO ONE

For thirty-five years, I opened almost every class I taught at the college and graduate level by telling my students that no matter what else they do, they should consume a balanced daily diet of news. I would tell them to follow the major newspapers; to watch at least two networks; to subscribe (online or otherwise) to at least one journal with which they consistently disagree.

I don't know if I had much success on that score. If my students were anything like other Americans, they tended to follow sources with which they already agree. In 2014, for example, a Pew survey asked Americans which television news sources they "trust the most to provide accurate information about politics and current events." The results are exactly what we would expect in a fractured media market: people gravitate toward sources whose views they already share. The modern media, with so many options tailored to particular views, is a huge exercise in confirmation bias. This means that Americans are not just *poorly* informed, they're *misinformed.*

There is a huge difference between these two maladies. Two decades ago, the problem was already obvious, as a study on public knowledge conducted at the time by the University of Illinois showed. The political scientist Anne Pluta later summed up the findings by noting that "uninformed citizens don't have any information at all, while those who are misinformed have information that conflicts with the best evidence and expert opinion." Not only do these people "fill the gaps in their knowledge base by using their existing belief systems," but over time those beliefs become "indistinguishable from hard data." And, of course, the most misinformed citizens "tend to be the most confident in their views and are also the strongest partisans."[19] Multiple studies since have confirmed these patterns, to the point where such findings are now truisms.

This is one reason why few Americans trust what little news, or newslike programming, they watch. Too many people approach the news with an underlying assumption that they are already well versed in the issues. They do not seek information so much as confirmation, and when they receive information they do not like, they will gravitate to sources they prefer because they believe others are mistaken or even lying. In an earlier time, those other sources were harder to find; when people had to make do with fewer outlets, they had to contend with news that was not specifically tailored to their prejudices. Today, hundreds of media outlets cater to even the narrowest agendas and biases.

This mindset, and the market that services it, creates in laypeople a combination of groundless confidence and deep cynicism, habits of thought that defeat the best attempts of experts to educate their fellow citizens. Experts can't respond to questions if most people already think they know the answers, nor does it help them to bring forward messages when so many people are already prone to shoot—or, at best, to ignore—the messengers. It's bad enough that people aren't keeping up with the news; it's worse when they don't trust what little news they do read and shop around until they find what they are looking for.

In part, American distrust of the media is just one symptom of the larger malady: Americans increasingly don't trust anyone anymore. They view all institutions, including the media, with disdain. Everybody hates the media—or, at least, everybody *claims* to hate the media. According to pollsters, news organizations are among the least trusted institutions in the United States; a Gallup poll in 2014 found that only four in ten Americans trust the media to report news "fully, accurately, and fairly," an all-time low.[20] But that was before Donald Trump turned his first national campaign into an ongoing assault on media, one that continues as of this writing while the former president fights dozens of felony indictments in multiple jurisdictions. Gallup asked again about trust in the media in 2016, and the numbers hit an even deeper record low; by 2022, trust had rebounded by a statistically insignificant two points.[21]

Of course, most people don't really hate the media. They just hate the media that deliver news they don't like or transmit views with which they don't agree. A Pew study in 2012 noted that two-thirds of Americans think news organizations in general are "often inaccurate," but that same number drops to less than a third when people are asked the same question about the news organization "you use most."[22] Almost a decade later, Pew found that Republicans distrust media they think are "mainstream," while Democrats trust those same outlets more.[23] This, as many observers have pointed out over the years, is much the same way everyone claims to hate Congress, when what they really mean is that they hate all the members of Congress *but their own*.[24] Likewise, people who hate "the media" still watch the "the news" or read "the paper," as long as it's one they already trust.

In a democracy, this level of cynicism about the media is poisonous. All citizens, including experts, need news. Journalists relay events and developments in the world around us, providing a reservoir of facts we use as the raw material for many of our own opinions, views, and beliefs. We have to rely on their judgment and their objectivity, because their reports are usually the first encounter the rest of us have with previously unknown events or facts. Around the world, journalists do their job amazingly well, often at risk to their own lives. And yet most Americans distrust the information they provide.

ARE THE VIEWERS SMARTER THAN THE EXPERTS?

Are the viewers and readers right to be so mistrustful? Why not assume that journalists (and their editors) know what they're doing? After all, some journalists, without doubt, are experts in the field on which they report. Some foreign correspondents, for example, are fluent in the language of their area and have a deep knowledge of other cultures. Some science reporters are themselves scientists or have a fair amount of scientific training. And I know from experience—I worked in the Massachusetts State House and the US Senate early in my career—that some political reporters understand and can explain the legislative process better than some members of Congress.

And yet there are journalists who think there's a bridge in Gaza or that Evelyn Waugh was a woman. This shallowness is not because journalism attracts unintelligent people, but because in an age when everything is journalism, and everyone is a journalist, standards inevitably fall. A profession that once had at least some barriers to entry is now wide open, with the same results we might expect if medicine, law enforcement, aviation, or archaeology were suddenly do-it-yourself projects.

This is partly the fault, as so much is these days, of "academizing" what used to be a trade. Rather than apprenticeships as part of a career track that includes writing obituaries and covering boring town meetings, journalism and communications are now undergraduate majors. These departments and programs crank out young people with little knowledge about the subjects of their correspondence. They are schooled in the structure of a story but not in the habits or norms of the profession. Many of them, accustomed to posting their deep thoughts online since high school, do not understand the difference between "journalism" and "blogging."

Veteran journalists, meanwhile, are being pushed out of newsrooms to make room for a younger generation who understand how to deliver clicks, as *The Nation* writer Dale Maharidge described in 2016.

> Old-school journalism was a trade, and legacy journalists find today's brand of personality journalism, with its emphasis on churning out blog posts, aggregating the labor of others, and curating a constant social-media presence, to be simply foreign. And the higher-ups share the new bias. One editor of a major national publication, who himself is well over 40, confided to me that he's reluctant to hire older journalists, that "they're stuck in the mentality of doing one story a week" and not willing to use social media.[25]

The market's focus on form rather than content, the need for speed, and the fashionable biases of the modern university combine to create a trifecta of misinformation.

Inexperienced writers can have a significant impact especially on the information available to the sizable number of people who primarily get their news through social media. Facebook, for example, uses news curators to decide what shows up in a reader's Facebook news feed. According to a 2016 exposé by Gizmodo.com, Facebook treated these reporters as low-level contractors while giving them immense power over the news:

> The trending news section [at Facebook] is run by people in their 20s and early 30s, most of whom graduated from Ivy League and private East Coast schools like Columbia University and NYU. They've previously worked at outlets like the *New York Daily News*, Bloomberg, MSNBC, and the *Guardian*. Some former curators have left Facebook for jobs at organizations including the *New Yorker*, Mashable, and Sky Sports.
>
> According to former team members interviewed by Gizmodo, this small group has the power to choose what stories make it onto the trending bar and, more importantly, what news sites each topic links out to. "We choose what's trending," said one. "There was no real standard for measuring what qualified as news and what didn't. It was up to the news curator to decide."[26]

Despite some changes at Facebook in later years, the obvious answer here is not to rely on Facebook for news. But many millions of people do, just as many also rely on Twitter—which itself has experimented for years with algorithms meant to alter what appears, and with what priority, in a user's Twitter stream, a process now in the hands of new owner Elon Musk, who at times reportedly decided personally what to boost—or what to suppress.[27]

In fairness to these younger reporters, they're often put in an impossible situation by the nature of the market. As the former Slate.com writer Will Saletan told me, complicated stories require a lot more time than just blurting out whatever produces a click. Saletan spent a year researching the food safety of genetically modified organisms (GMOs), a story that might exceed even the vaccine debate for the triumph of ignorance over science.[28] "You can't ask a young person to sort out this issue on the kind of time frame that's generally tolerated these days," Saletan said after his story—which blew apart the fake science behind the objections to GMOs—appeared. These kinds of stories require not only time but a willingness to do research and stay focused on dull details. As Saletan put it, "You really have to be a willful bastard to persist in researching a topic like [GMOs], which feels incredibly technical and boring when you're deep inside it, even if it excites passions when it becomes political." (Saletan later moved to the political site Bulwark.com, where he was given the time to produce an in-depth study of the political evolution of South Carolina Senator Lindsey Graham of more than one hundred pages.)

Sometimes the errors are trivial and amusing. In the great "chocolate helps you lose weight" hoax, for example, the hoaxers never thought they'd get as far as they did; they assumed that "reporters who don't have science chops" would discover the whole faked study was "laughably flimsy" once they reached out to a real scientist. They were wrong: nobody tried to vet the story with actual scientists. "The key," as the hoaxers later said, "is to exploit journalists' incredible laziness. If you lay out the information just right, you can shape the story that emerges in the media almost like you were writing those stories yourself. In fact, that's literally what you're doing, since many reporters just copied and pasted our text."[29]

A dumb story about chocolate as a weight-loss gimmick isn't going to hurt too many people. (Chocolate junkies don't need scientific reasons to indulge.) But when the coverage turns to more serious issues, journalists who are lost in the subject matter and weighted down by their ideological biases can cause more confusion than illumination. The writer Joshua Foust some years ago zeroed in on the practice of "embedding" journalists overseas with military forces, creating the illusion of experience among reporters who in fact had little idea where they were:

Far too many correspondents know nothing about the places they go to cover: whether Georgia or Afghanistan, basic knowledge is critically lacking from media accounts (one freelance reporter in Georgia told me that staff reporters were asking officials, "Where is Abkhazia?"). Personal experience suggests that the situation is largely the same in Afghanistan: "It's only a one-week embed," the thinking seems to go, "so I don't have to do too much work—I can learn as I go."[30]

Without any foundational knowledge, young writers have nothing to fall back on but a college education in journalism, which, in the words of former journalist Joel Engel, is too often a "homogenizing process" that "ensures conformity" and produces young journalists who come out of college "seeing what they believe."

This kind of outright ignorance or even professional malpractice can do grievous damage to real people and their communities. In 2014, for example, *Rolling Stone* suffered a massive journalistic failure in its reporting of a now-infamous story about a gang rape at the University of Virginia. A reporter, determined to find a story of sexual assault on an elite American campus, found one. Her editors published it, in grotesque detail. The whole story quickly unraveled, however, and turned out to be a hoax. The result was a smoking wreck of lawsuits and destroyed reputations.

Rolling Stone ended up retracting the story and asking the Columbia School of Journalism to conduct an investigation. The Columbia investigators concluded that the reporter Sabrina Erdeley and her editors had violated even basic rules of journalism, all in the name of a story that was, apparently, just too good to check.[31] The case continued to drag on for years, with one of the university's administrative deans named in the story—a woman who supposedly failed to act on the initial rape claim—eventually winning a suit against *Rolling Stone* for defamation. But not everyone learned a lesson. In a 2023 interview, the magazine's publisher at the time, Jann Wenner, looked back and said: "Other than this one key fact that the rape described actually was a fabrication of this woman [the supposed victim], the rest of the story was bulletproof."[32]

The rape, however, was central to the story's narrative, which itself was in part based on studies claiming that one in four (sometimes reported as one in five) women in America's colleges and universities will be sexually assaulted. These statistics helped to enable the *Rolling Stone* hoax, when the numbers themselves and the studies on which they were based should have raised concerns. As Slate's Emily Yoffe wrote in 2014, "the one-in-four assertion would mean that young American college women are raped at a rate similar to women in Congo, where rape has been used as a weapon of war."[33] Another study central to this dire narrative later turned out to have included "college aged men" who were as old as *seventy-one*, whose average age was over twenty-six, and none of whom actually lived on a college campus. But no matter: the statistic is still out there now more as a slogan than as a fact, and anyone arguing about it will say, understandably, that "they saw it in the news."

Similar to the "one in four" statistic is the now-common claim, repeated regularly in the American media, that US military veterans are killing themselves at an alarming rate because of the stress of fighting two major wars. "Twenty-two a day"—meaning twenty-two veteran suicides every twenty-four hours—has become the mantra both of veterans' service organizations as well as antiwar groups. Multiple stories have appeared in electronic and print media about the "epidemic" of veteran suicide in 2013 and after, with dramatic headlines and pictures of young men and women in uniform who'd ended their lives. The implications of the stories were clear: extended combat service is driving America's warriors to suicide, and a heartless government does not care.

When I first saw this statistic, I had a personal interest in pursuing the underlying studies. As a professor at the Naval War College, I worked every day with military officers, many of whom had seen combat. I was also briefly certified as a suicide-prevention counselor because of volunteer work I did many years ago in my younger days. As someone with at least some experience in suicide prevention, I was concerned about people killing themselves; as someone who worked with military personnel, I was worried about my students and friends; as a social scientist, I was bothered by a statistical argument that didn't seem plausible.

Unfortunately, the media were no help. Indeed, they were a fundamental part of the problem. It is true, in fact, that veterans are killing themselves at higher rates in the twenty-first century than in earlier years. But in part, that's because *everybody* has been killing themselves at higher rates—for reasons epidemiologists are still debating—and veterans are part of "everybody." Adding to the confusion, the studies that looked at "veteran" suicides also included everyone of any age who'd ever served in the military in any capacity, from reserve duty to sustained combat. In other words, a young person just home from a combat zone and a middle-aged man who'd done a few years in his local National Guard unit thirty years earlier were both counted as part of this new "epidemic" if they killed themselves at any point.

A beleaguered Veterans Administration—not exactly the most popular bureaucracy in America—tried in vain to note that according to a sizable 2012 study, suicides among veterans really hadn't changed all that much since 1999. The *New York Times* duly reported on this study with a headline that read "As Suicides Rise in U.S., Veterans Are Less of Total." The *Washington Post* headline implied an opposite conclusion: "VA Study Finds More Veterans Committing Suicide." Both headlines, amazingly, were about the same study, and both, in a strictly factual sense, were true.

The media, or at least some outlets, interviewed the scientist who wrote the study, but his answers made no difference to the narrative. "There is a perception that we have a veterans' suicide epidemic on our hands. I don't think that is true," said Robert Bossarte, the epidemiologist who conducted the study. "The rate is going up in the country, and veterans are a part of it."[34] Most of the stories didn't bother with this quote, nor did they include important benchmarks like the overall suicide rate in America or the suicide rate among men in the same age cohort as the young combat veterans. Nor were other occupations compared to the military, perhaps because relatively high rates among other groups—such as medical doctors, among others—would have taken some of the urgency out of the story.

The bad reporting continued with a slew of companion stories about how suicides among military personnel in 2012 outnumbered combat deaths. The message, of course, was that American soldiers were now more of a danger to themselves than the enemy. That's a grim picture, except for a small problem: it is statistically meaningless. The assertion that there were "more suicides than combat deaths" will always *by definition* be true in any year where US forces aren't involved in a lot of actual fighting. You can do this statistical trick with any year in which there isn't much combat: compare military suicides in, say, the late 1950s to combat deaths. To its credit, *TIME* ran a piece that got it right, even titling it "Military Suicides Top Combat Deaths—But Only Because the Wars Are Ending."[35] But, again, this should have been obvious to anyone who took even a moment to think about it, and it is remarkable that *TIME* or anyone else had to run such a story in the first place.

The point in all of this is that people genuinely concerned about veterans and suicide don't really know any more about what's going on with veterans today than they did before they read these stories. But they *think* they do, and heaven help the expert in any field who casts doubt on this public outrage or who even tries to explain the subject with a bit more nuance. Veterans are going crazy and killing themselves, and that's that. After all, *I read it in the paper.*

WHAT IS TO BE DONE

Some journalists are experts on the subjects of their reporting, but if they are not, how can experts do a better job helping them? I cannot, and will not, make recommendations here beyond hoping that newer journalists somehow acquire a background in the subject on which they write. That's generic advice and as far as I am willing to go when it comes to telling other professionals how to do their jobs. I say this while realizing fully that nothing can stop people from cherry-picking their sources, no matter how high quality the information available to them.

But I have a few admonitions for experts, and several for the consumers of journalism.

To experts, I will say: know when to say no. Some of the worst mistakes I ever made were when I was at the beginning of my career and I could not resist giving an opinion. Most of the time, I was right to think I knew more than the reporter or the readers, but that's not the point: I also found myself out on a few limbs I should have avoided. In fairness to journalists, I have found that they will respect and report your views accurately—only on a few occasions did I ever feel ambushed or misquoted—but they will also respect your principled refusal to go too far out of your lane. It is your obligation, not theirs, to identify that moment.

The consumers of news have some important obligations here as well. I have four recommendations for you, the readers, when approaching the news: be humbler, be ecumenical, be less cynical, and be a lot more discriminating.

Be humble. That is, at least begin by assuming that the people writing the story, whatever their shortcomings, know more about the subject than you do. At the least, try to remember that in most cases, the person writing the story has spent more time with the issue than you have. If you approach any story in the media, or any source of information already assuming you know as much as anyone else on the subject, the entire exercise of following the news is going to be a waste of your time.

Be ecumenical. Vary your diet. You wouldn't eat the same thing all day, so don't consume the same sources of media all day. When I worked in national politics, I subscribed to a half-dozen journals at any given time, across the political spectrum. Don't be provincial: try media from other countries, as they often report stories or have a view of which Americans are completely unaware. And don't say you "don't have the time." You do.

Be less cynical—or don't be *so* cynical. It's extremely rare that anyone is intentionally lying to you. Yes, the people writing the stories often have an agenda, and there will always be another Sabrina Erdeley out there. And yes, the journalists you're reading or watching will get some things wrong, often with an astonishing lack of self-awareness. None of them have a monopoly on the truth, but they're not all liars. They're doing the best they can, by their lights, and most of them would be glad to know you're keeping tabs by reading other sources of news and information.

Be more discriminating. If you see something in a major media outlet that doesn't seem right to you, finding some half-baked website isn't the answer. Websites that are outlets for political movements, or other, even worse enterprises—Fox News is an object lesson here—that cater specifically to zealots or fools, will do more harm than good in the search for accurate information. Instead, ask yourself questions when consuming media. Who are these writers? Do they have editors? Is this a journal or newspaper that stands by its reporting, or is it part of a political operation? Are their claims checkable, or have other media tried to verify or disprove their stories? Even something as simple as noting whether a publication candidly issues corrections can help steer you away from a poor source.

Conspiracy theorists and adherents of quack ideas about medicine, or government, or for that matter, the shape of the earth, will never believe anything that challenges their views, but most of us can do better. And remember: reading and following the news is a skill like any other at which we get better by repetition. The best way to become a good consumer of news is to be a *regular* consumer of news.

I've been unsparing in my criticism of the low level of foundational knowledge among Americans, about the narcissism and bias that prevent them from learning, about a college industry that affirms ignorance rather than cures it, about media who think their job is to entertain, and about journalists who are too lazy or too inexperienced to get their stories right. I've shaken my fist at most of the groups I think bear a great responsibility for the death of expertise and for undermining established knowledge just when we need it most.

I've let only one group off the hook so far: experts.

What happens when experts are wrong, and who should be responsible for deciding when to listen to them and when to ignore them? We'll confront this question in the next chapter.

Chapter 6

When the Experts Are Wrong

I have a confession to make: I have been wrong quite a lot lately. Maybe I am just especially bad at understanding how the world works, an interpretation my daughters might favor. I doubt, however, that this is the whole story.

Professor Francis Gavin

Even when the experts all agree, they may well be mistaken.

Bertrand Russell

NO EXPERTS NEED APPLY

In 2002, a distinguished historian wrote that the widely told tales of "No Irish Need Apply" signs in late nineteenth-century America were myths. The University of Illinois professor Richard Jensen said that such signs were inventions, "myths of victimization," passed down from Irish immigrants to their children until they reached the unassailable status of urban legends. For more than a decade, most historians accepted Jensen's scholarship on the matter. Opponents of Jensen's thesis were dismissed—sometimes by Jensen himself—as Irish-American loyalists. In a 2015 story that seemed to encapsulate the death of expertise, an eighth grader named Rebecca Fried claimed that Jensen was wrong, not least because of research she did on Google. She was respectful but determined. "He has been doing scholarly work for decades before I was born, and the last thing I want to do was show disrespect for him and his work," she said later. It all seemed to be just another case of a precocious child telling an experienced teacher—an emeritus professor of history, no less—that he had not done his homework.

As it turns out, she was right, and he was wrong. Such signs existed, and they weren't that hard to find. I am partly descended from Irish immigrants; I had heard the stories of the signs from older relatives who claimed to have seen them, but I had no basis for the claims other than these anecdotes. Among historians, however, scholars had wrestled with Jensen's claims for years, but they fought with his work inside the thicket of professional historiography. Young Rebecca, however, did what a sensible person would: she started looking through databases of old newspapers. She found the signs, as the *Daily Beast* later reported, "collecting a handful of examples, then dozens, then more. She went to as many newspaper databases as she could. Then she thought, *somebody had to have done this before, right?*" As it turned out, neither Jensen nor anyone else had apparently bothered to do this basic fact-checking.

Jensen later fired back, trying to rebut the work of a grade-schooler by claiming that he was right but that he could have been more accurate in his claims. Debate over his thesis, as the *Smithsonian* magazine later put it, "may still be raging in the comments section" of various Internet lists, but Fried's work proves "that anyone with a curious mind and a nose for research can challenge the historical status quo."[1] Miss Fried, for her part, later entered high school with a published article in the *Journal of Social History* already on her resume.

In the 1970s, America's top nutritional scientists told the United States government that eggs, among many other foods, might be lethal. There could be no simpler application of Occam's Razor, with a trail leading from the barnyard to the morgue. Eggs contain a lot of cholesterol, cholesterol clogs arteries, clogged arteries cause heart attacks, and heart attacks kill people. The conclusion was obvious: Americans need to get all that cholesterol out of their diet.

And so they did. Then something unexpected happened: Americans gained a lot of weight and started dying of other things. Eggs, it turned out, weren't so bad, or at least they weren't as bad as the foods that replaced them. In 2015 the government decided that eggs were acceptable, perhaps even healthy. As the columnist (and resident of egg-laden Vermont) Geoffrey Norman wrote at the time,

> A lot of [obese] people who got that way thought that they were following a government-approved diet. Egg consumption declined by over 30 percent when the government put them on its dietary blacklist. People have to eat, so they substituted other things for eggs. Things that helped to make them fat. The eggs they did not eat would not, it turns out, have clogged their arteries and killed them. The stuff they substituted for those eggs, however, might well have caused them to suffer from type 2 diabetes and worse.[2]

The egg scare was based on a cascade of flawed studies, some going back almost a half century. People who want to avoid eggs may still do so, of course. In fact, there are studies now that suggest that skipping breakfast entirely—which scientists also have long warned not to do—also isn't as bad as anyone thought.[3]

In 1982, one of the top experts on the Soviet Union, Seweryn Bialer, delivered a stern warning to readers of the prestigious journal *Foreign Affairs* that the USSR was a lot stronger than it looked at the time.

> The Soviet Union is not now nor will it be in the next decade in the throes of a true systemic crisis, for it boasts enormous unused reserves of political and social stability that suffice to endure the deepest difficulties. The Soviet economy, like any gigantic economy administered by intelligent and trained professionals, will

not go bankrupt. It may become less effective, it may stagnate, it may even experience an absolute decline for a year or two; but, like the political system, it will not collapse.[4]

A year later, Bialer won a Macarthur Foundation "genius grant." Two years after that, the Soviet Communist Party—obviously facing the throes of a true systemic crisis—chose Mikhail Gorbachev as its new leader. Less than eight years after Bialer's finger-wagging lecture, the Union of Soviet Socialist Republics ceased to exist.

In the months before the final Soviet collapse, an MIT professor, Stephen Meyer, testified before the US Senate Foreign Relations Committee. American political leaders watching events in the USSR were concerned about the security of thousands of Soviet nuclear weapons pointed at the United States, and Meyer, one of his generation's leading experts on Soviet military affairs, told everyone to calm down: Gorbachev was in control. "Hints of military coups" in the Soviet Union, he assured the assembled senators, were "pure flights of fancy."[5]

Meyer gave his testimony on June 6, 1991. Nine weeks later, Gorbachev was deposed in a coup led by a group that included the Soviet defense minister and the head of the feared security apparatus, the KGB. Chaos descended as tanks entered the streets of Moscow. But no matter: a year after the Soviet collapse, Meyer left the study of Russia and nuclear arms completely and worked instead on biodiversity issues, serving on various committees for the Massachusetts Department of Fisheries and Wildlife until his untimely death in 2006.

Bialer and Meyer were hardly a minority. As the historian Nick Gvosdev observed some years later, many Soviet experts substituted what they believed, or wanted to believe, about the USSR in place of "critical analysis of the facts on the ground." Two scholars of international relations noted that everyone else got it wrong, too. "Measured by its own standards, the [academic] profession's performance was embarrassing," Professors Richard Ned Lebow and Thomas Risse Kappen wrote in 1995. "None of the existing theories of international relations recognized the possibility that the kind of change that did occur could occur."[6]

These stories show that experts get things wrong all the time. The effects of such errors range from mild embarrassment to wasted time and money; in rarer cases, they can result in death and even lead to international catastrophe. And yet experts regularly ask citizens to trust their judgment and to have confidence not only that mistakes will be rare, but that the experts will identify those mistakes and learn from them.

Day to day, laypeople have no choice but to trust experts. We live our lives embedded in a web of social and governmental institutions meant to ensure that professionals are in fact who they say they are, and that they can in fact do what they say they can do. Universities, accreditation organizations, licensing boards, certification authorities, state inspectors, and other institutions exist to maintain those standards. In general, these safeguards work well. We are shocked, for example, when we read a story about an incompetent doctor who kills a patient exactly because such stories, in a country where more than a million physicians practice medicine safely every day, are so unusual.

This daily trust in professionals, however, is a prosaic matter of necessity. It is much the same way we trust everyone else in our daily lives, including the bus driver we assume isn't drunk or the restaurant worker we assume has washed her hands. This is not the same thing as trusting professionals when it comes to matters of public policy: to say that we trust our doctors to write us the correct prescription is not the same thing as saying we trust all medical professionals about whether America should have a system of national health care. To say that we trust a college professor to teach our sons and daughters the history of World War II is not the same thing as saying that we therefore trust all academic historians to advise the president of the United States on matters of war and peace.

For these larger decisions, there are no licenses or certificates. There are no fines or suspensions if things go wrong. Indeed, there is very little direct accountability at all, which is why laypeople understandably fear the influence of experts. In a democracy, elected officials who may have accepted—or rejected—expert advice provide accountability. But accountability is something that happens after the fact. It might be morally satisfying to hold someone responsible, but assigning blame doesn't heal the injured or restore the peace.

In general, how do experts go wrong? We will for the moment leave the efforts to stop COVID for the next chapter. In general, however, what can citizens do when they are confronted with expert failure, and how can they maintain their trust in expert communities? Likewise, what responsibilities do experts incur when they make mistakes, and how can they repair their relationship with their client, society?

THE MANY FACES OF FAILURE

There are several kinds of expert failure. The most innocent and most common are what we might think of as the ordinary failures of science. Individuals, or even entire professions, get important questions wrong because of error or because of the limitations of a field itself. They observe a phenomenon or examine a problem, come up with theories and solutions, and then test them. Sometimes they're right, and sometimes they're wrong. The process usually includes a lot of blind alleys and failed experiments along the way. Sometimes errors are undiscovered or even compounded by other experts.

This is how a generation of Americans got fat avoiding eggs. It's why the first US attempt to launch a satellite ended in a gigantic explosion on the launch pad. It's why top experts in foreign policy assumed for decades that the peaceful reunification of Germany was unlikely but then had to reconsider their views as celebratory fireworks filled the skies over a free Berlin.

Science is also learning by doing. The United States invented the nuclear bomb in 1945, but it took another decade of exploding test devices before scientists and researchers around the world gained a better understanding of "electromagnetic pulse," or EMP, an invisible effect of nuclear detonations that plays havoc with electrical systems. The public, for their part, became more aware of EMP when a US nuclear test in the Pacific in 1962 blew out streetlights and shut down telephones hundreds of miles away in Hawaii, an effect the scientists had suspected but whose scale they had underestimated.

There isn't much anyone, including experts, can do about this kind of failure, because it is not so much a failure as it is an integral part of science and scholarship. Laypeople are uncomfortable with ambiguity, and they prefer answers rather than caveats. But science is a process, not a conclusion. Science subjects itself to constant testing by a set of careful rules under which theories can only be displaced by better theories. Laypeople cannot expect experts never to be wrong; if they were capable of such accuracy, they wouldn't need to do research and run experiments in the first place. If policy experts were clairvoyant or omniscient, governments would never run deficits and wars would only break out at the instigation of madmen.

Sometimes, too, expert error comes with *beneficial* effects, but these are rarely treated the same way as mistakes that cost lives or money. When scientists invented oral contraceptives, for example, they were trying to figure out how to help women prevent unwanted pregnancies. They were not directly trying to lower the risk of ovarian cancer—but apparently some kinds of birth control pills do exactly that, and by significant rates. For some women, oral contraceptives have risks; for others, the same pills might extend their lives. Of course, if birth control pills only *increased* cancer risks, we'd be lamenting yet another failure of science, but this positive side effect was just as unknown as many others a half century ago.

Likewise, experts who predicted an all-out international arms race in nuclear weapons at the end of the 1950s were wrong. But they were wrong at least in part because they underestimated the efficacy of their own efforts to limit the spread of nuclear weapons. President John F. Kennedy feared a world of as many as twenty-five nuclear armed powers by the 1970s. (As of 2024, only ten nations have crossed this threshold, including one—South Africa—that has renounced its arsenal.) Kennedy's prediction, based on the best expert advice, was not impossible or even unreasonable; rather, the number of future nuclear powers was lowered with the assistance of policies advocated by those same experts.

In the end, experts cannot guarantee outcomes. They cannot promise that they will never make mistakes or that they will not fall prey to the same shortcomings that govern all human deliberations. They can only promise to institute rules and methods that reduce the chance of such mistakes and to make those errors far less often than a layperson might. If we are to accept the benefits of a profession's work, we must accept something less than perfection, perhaps even a certain amount of risk.

Other forms of expert failure, however, are more worrisome. Experts can go wrong, for example, when they try to stretch their expertise from one area to another. In 2019, for example, writer Naomi Wolf claimed to have found evidence of executions of homosexual men in nineteenth-century Britain. Her claim, however, rested on a misunderstanding of archival materials she incorporated into a book about the history of the criminalization of homosexuality in the United Kingdom. Although Wolf stood by her interpretation, her American publishers canceled the book's publication. The affair prompted looks at Wolf's doctoral thesis—in English language and literature, not history—at Oxford University. The thesis contained multiple errors, which in turn prompted questions about the quality and supervision of such theses at the venerable British university.[7] Wolf, apparently humiliated, now peddles conspiracy theories—she has referred to COVID vaccinations as "bioweapons" that caused "mass murder"—in the swamps of the extreme right-wing media.[8]

Expert trespass is not only a recipe for error; it is maddening to other experts as well. In some cases, the cross-expertise poaching is obvious, as when entertainers—experts in their own fields, to be sure—confuse art with life and start issuing explanations of complicated matters, or when scientists and engineers come to believe that their narrow but deep expertise confers upon them superior skills of social and political organization. In some cases of expert overextension, however, the boundaries are less clear, and the issue is not expertise but *relative* expertise. A biologist is not a medical doctor, but in general terms, a biologist is likely to be relatively better able to understand medical issues than a layperson. Still, this does not mean that anyone in the life sciences is always better informed than anyone else on any issue in that area. A diligent person who has taken the time to read up on, say, diabetes could very well be more conversant in that subject than a botanist. Professionals with extensive expertise in a particular subject might not be any better informed than anyone else on matters outside their own field. Education and credentials in one area do not guarantee expertise in *all* areas.

In the natural sciences, prediction and explanation go hand in hand: once a physical phenomenon is understood, its behavior should be predictable, and can even sometimes be expressed as a law. Social scientists, historians, and other observers of human behavior, by contrast, tend to favor explanation over raw prediction. In many fields outside the hard sciences, conclusions are probabilistic rather than absolute. And yet, society as a client tends to demand, from all experts, far more prediction than explanation. Worse, laypeople tend to regard failures of prediction as indications of the worthlessness of expertise.

Experts face a difficult task in this respect, because no matter how many times scholars might emphasize that their goal is to explain the world rather than to predict discrete events, laypeople and policymakers prefer prediction. (And experts, even when they know better, often gladly oblige.) This is a natural but irresolvable tension between experts and their clients; most people would prefer to anticipate problems and avoid them, instead of explaining them in retrospect. The promises of a prognosis, even if speculative, are always more welcome than the absolute certainties of an autopsy.

Finally, there is outright deception and malfeasance. This is the rarest but most dangerous category. Here, experts for their own reasons (usually careerist defenses of their own shoddy work) intentionally falsify their results. They hope on the one hand that laypeople will not be capable of catching them, and on the other that their colleagues will not notice or will attribute their fraud to honest error.

This most extreme category is the easiest to deal with, so we will start there.

WHEN EXPERTS GO BAD

In 2023, Marc Tessier-Lavigne, the president of Stanford University, resigned. A noted neuroscientist, Tessier-Lavigne stepped down after months of investigations revealed that his earlier work on Alzheimer's disease had "multiple problems" and "fell below customary standards of scientific rigor." He was cleared of possible charges of fraud and misconduct, but a Stanford panel nonetheless concluded that "members of Dr. Tessier-Lavigne's labs engaged in inappropriate manipulation of research data or deficient scientific practices," that "Tessier-Lavigne took insufficient steps to correct mistakes," and that at least a dozen papers (seven of which listed Tessier-Lavigne as a coauthor) had serious problems, including one that was not corrected when "follow-up studies revealed that its key finding was wrong."[9]

In a further blow to the reliability of expertise, the problems in Tessier-Lavigne's record were investigated and publicized not by his peers, but by a student journalist at the Stanford campus newspaper—a freshman, no less—named Theo Baker, who won the prestigious Polk Award for his work on the story. Baker is no stranger to the world of journalism; his parents are two of the most respected reporters in New York and Washington, Susan Glasser and Peter Baker. (When asked about his pedigree as a writer, young Mr. Baker had the perfect response, noting that while his parents were well-known writers, neither of them had won a Polk.)[10]

The Tessier-Lavigne case is one of the most public examples of why the early twenty-first century has been a rough time for scientists, even before the arrival of a global pandemic. Retractions from scientific journals have reached record proportions. Cases of fraud or misconduct now seem almost routine. Attempts to replicate many studies across multiple fields have produced inconclusive results or even failed outright, and at least some of these cases are due to misconduct ranging from minor errors to actual fraud.

Expert deception is not hard to define, but it can be hard to identify. Obvious misconduct occurs when researchers or scholars falsify their results or when would-be experts lie about being credentialed or licensed to practice in their field. (Scientists describe this using the catch-all shorthand "FFP," meaning "fabrication, falsification, or plagiarism.") Such misconduct can be hard to detect specifically because it requires other experts to ferret it out. The Tessier-Lavigne case, for example, was only about flawed rather than falsified work, but the investigation nonetheless took many months, dozens of interviews, a review of more than 50,000 documents, and an 89-page report. Laypeople do not have the time, and are not equipped, to take apart scientific studies, and they have no more inclination to do so than they do to look closely at a credential hanging on a wall to see if it is real.

Sometimes, in the very worst cases, experts aren't experts. People lie, and lie brazenly, about their credentials. This is the kind of bravura fakery that the real-life "Great Pretender," Frank Abagnale, claimed he pulled off in the 1960s (exploits later popularized in the movie *Catch Me If You Can*), including impersonating an airline pilot and a medical doctor. (Ironically, skeptics have since suggested that Abagnale was not nearly as successful in these impersonations as he claimed, and that his claims of expert fakery are themselves fake.)[11] A more common but subtler kind of deception occurs when people who are actual experts augment their credentials with false honors or exaggerations. They might claim to be members of professional associations, or to have attended panels or symposia, or to be honorees or prizewinners, or other embellishments that are in fact fraudulent. Usually, such people are only caught when something happens that causes others to scrutinize their records.

When actual experts lie, they endanger not only their own profession but also the well-being of their client: society. Their threat to expertise comes in both the immediate outcome of their chicanery and the erosion of social trust such misconduct creates when it is discovered. This is why (aside from any legal sanctions that may exist for lying and fraud) professional organizations, scholarly foundations, think tanks, journals, and universities reserve some of their harshest punishments for willful misconduct.

Such punishments, contrary to the popular imagination, do exist. There is a myth among many Americans that it is impossible to fire researchers and university teachers. This is not entirely a baseless belief, because firing a tenured professor is in fact quite difficult. While many professors have "moral turpitude" clauses in their contracts, the social norms of the twenty-first century have lowered that bar to the point that almost nothing a professor does in his or her classroom or personal life can move a school to the point of revoking tenure. Obvious firing offenses like physically threatening a student or outright refusing to show up for work can still trigger a dismissal, but almost anything else in the category of personal conduct is usually overlooked.

Academic misconduct, however, is still a red line for many schools. Academic freedom guarantees the right to express unpopular or unconventional ideas, but it is not a license to produce sloppy or intentionally misleading research. When the University of Colorado, for example, fired Ward Churchill—an instructor who compared the victims of the 9/11 attacks in New York to Nazis—they fired him not for being an insensitive jerk, but because his comments generated new attention to his scholarship, sections of which turned out to be plagiarized. Churchill, of course, claimed that he was a victim of political bias. He appealed his dismissal as a Colorado state employee all the way up to the Colorado Supreme Court and lost.

There can be no doubt that Churchill's record got a close look only because of his political views. Churchill appealed his dismissal on those very grounds, arguing that his plagiarism consisted of innocent mistakes that were only discovered when he took a controversial view. But this in itself is a disturbing position: does it take calling the people who died in the Twin Towers "little [Adolf] Eichmanns," as Churchill did, before anyone takes a close look at a professor's scholarly work? To claim that plagiarism was discovered only because the professor managed to draw enough attention to himself with his odious comments is not much of a defense.

The Churchill case was in some ways unique, not least because of the publicity it attracted. Most cases of professional misconduct in academia go unnoticed by the public. The 2014 gay-marriage study, which represented wholesale falsification of data, was an exception, and gained significant attention largely because of the potential political impact of the conclusion. Most academic studies are not nearly as interesting as one that claims people can be talked out of homophobia, and so they do not generate the same level of interest.

Less publicized cases, however, are no less serious. In 2011, a postdoctoral researcher working on a US government grant at Columbia University was found to have falsified cell biology research related to Alzheimer's disease. The researcher agreed not to accept any federal grants for three years, but by the time the misconduct was discovered, his article had been cited by other scientists at least 150 times. In 2016, a Spanish researcher was dismissed from her institution as well for alleged fraud related to her work on cardiovascular disease.

In a more dramatic case, Andrew Wakefield, a doctor who published a controversial study linking vaccines and autism, had his medical license revoked in the United Kingdom in 2010. British medical authorities claimed that they pulled his license not because he argued for a controversial thesis, but because he broke a lot of basic rules of scientific conduct to do it. The UK General Medical Council found that Wakefield "had done invasive research on children without ethical approval, acted against the clinical interests of each child, failed to disclose financial conflicts of interest, and misappropriated funds."[12]

Like Ward Churchill, Wakefield's supporters argued that he was the victim of a witch-hunt. But discredited research is not the same as misconduct. For example, Peter Duesberg, one of the leading AIDS denialists, remains at Berkeley despite accusations from critics that he engaged in academic misconduct, charges against him that his university investigated and dismissed in 2010.

Still, there is no way around it: a non-negligible amount of published scientific research is shaky at best and falsified at worse. It might be a small consolation to laypeople, but the reason we know any of this misconduct is happening at all is because scientists across all fields admit it. When a 2005 study asked scientists if they personally had committed questionable research practices, about 2 percent of scientists self-reported fabrication, falsification, or "modifying" data at least once; 14 percent said they witnessed this behavior in colleagues. When asked about serious misconduct that falls short of hanging offenses like outright falsification, a third of the respondents admitted they had engaged in less obvious but still shady practices, such as ignoring findings that contradicted their own. More than 70 percent claimed to have witnessed these same behaviors in their colleagues.[13] A 2012 report from the National Academy of Sciences looked back over years of published articles in the biomedical field, and found that overall, the research was solid and retractions were rare. That's the good news; the NAS also found that the bulk of the retractions (some two-thirds, in fact) were because of misconduct of some kind.[14]

Most of this misconduct is invisible to laypeople because it is so dull. Unlike the dramatic stories of massive fraud people see in well-known movies such as *Erin Brockovich* or *The Insider,* most of the retractions in scientific journals are over small-bore mistakes or misrepresentations in studies on narrow topics. The natural sciences seem to be more trouble-prone, but that is likely because their studies are easier to test.

Indeed, natural scientists could point out that retractions in themselves are signs of professional responsibility and oversight. The scientific and medical journals with the highest impact on their fields—the *New England Journal of Medicine,* for example—tend to have higher rates of retractions. No one, however, is quite sure why.[15] Theories abound, some of them reassuring, others less so. Perhaps better journals just have better editors, and they catch more mistakes or misconduct.[16] Perhaps scholars, under pressure or lacking talent, try to cut corners to get into top journals. Or perhaps, with more readers, articles in prestigious journals are more likely to inspire others to try to use the research in their own work and thus encounter the flaws (or lies) further down the line.

The gold standard of any scientific study is whether it can be replicated or at least reconstructed. This is why scientists and scholars use footnotes: not as insurance against plagiarism—although there's that, too—but so that their peers can follow in their footsteps to see if they would reach the same conclusions. If scientists are cooking the books, then this would make their conclusions difficult to replicate, thus undermining or even falsifying their studies.

This kind of verification assumes, however, that anyone is bothering to replicate the work in the first place. Ordinary peer review does not include re-running experiments; rather, the referees read the paper with an assumption that basic standards of research and procedure were met. They decide mostly if the subject is important, whether the data are of sufficient quality, and whether the evidence presented supports the conclusions.

Of course, the replicability requirement seems to recommend greater confidence in the hard sciences like chemistry or physics. The social sciences, like sociology and psychology, rely on studies that often depend on human subjects and thus are therefore more difficult to reproduce. The natural scientists can claim to have clearer standards: if someone asserts that a certain plastic melts at 100 degrees, then everyone else with a sample of the same material and a Bunsen burner can check the finding. When one hundred student volunteers are asked to participate in a survey or exercise, however, things get a lot more difficult. The results might be a snapshot in time, or of a particular region, or skewed in some other way. The research design is supposed to account for these issues, but the only way to know is to try to replicate the experiments.

This is exactly what a team of researchers set out to do in the field of psychology. The results were surprising, to say the least.

As the *New York Times* reported in 2015, a "painstaking" effort to reproduce 100 studies published in three leading psychology journals found that more than half of the findings did not hold up when retested.

> The analysis was done by research psychologists, many of whom volunteered their time to double-check what they considered important work. . . . The vetted studies were considered part of the core knowledge by which scientists understand the dynamics of personality, relationships, learning and memory. Therapists and educators rely on such findings to help guide decisions, and the fact that so many of the studies were called into question could sow doubt in the scientific underpinnings of their work.[17]

This outcome is cause for concern, but is it fraud? Lousy research isn't the same thing as misconduct. In many of these cases, the problem is not that the replication of the study produced a different result but that the studies themselves were inherently "irreproducible," meaning that their conclusions may be useful but that other researchers cannot re-run those human investigations in the same way over and over.

As it turns out, those psychology studies might not even be poor research. Another group of scholars subsequently examined the investigation itself—this is how science works, after all—and concluded that it was, in the words of the Harvard scholar Gary King, "completely unfair—and even irresponsible." King noted that while reproducibility is an "incredibly important" question that should "obsess" scholars, "it isn't true that all social psychologists are making stuff up."[18] The whole business, including yet more rebuttals as well as calls for systematic reform, is now where it belongs: in the pages of the scholarly journals, where experts continue to evaluate all of these arguments and subject them to further analysis.

Are the social sciences, then, just more prone to shoddy or faked work than the natural sciences? Or are the natural sciences just better at policing their scholars? Perhaps not. When cancer researchers tried to replicate studies in their field, they ran into the same problems as the psychologists and others. Daniel Engber, a writer for Slate.com, reported in 2016 on a group of biomedical studies that suggested a "replication crisis" much like the one in psychology, and he noted that by some estimates "fully half of all results rest on shaky ground, and might not be replicable in other labs. These cancer studies don't merely fail to find a cure; they might not offer any useful data whatsoever."[19] The obstacles to replication were much the same as those that bedeviled the social scientists: sloppiness, the passage of time, the inability to reproduce exact conditions from the first trials, and so on.

Here, we move from work that is fraudulent to work that might merely be slipshod. This is too complicated a subject to engage here, but the "replication crisis" in the scholarly community is not based on pure fraudulence. In addition to the physical and temporal constraints on perfect replicability, other problems include poor oversight of grants, intense pressure from academic institutions to come up with publishable results (no matter how trivial), and the tendency among scholars to box up their previous work and throw it away once the paper or study is published. As one young scholar said of the Tessier-Lavigne case, prominent scholars sometimes get too much benefit of the doubt about their work, but he had "mixed feelings about the heat" directed at Tessier-Lavigne. "I think he had a responsibility to do more probably than he did," the younger colleague said, "but that also doesn't mean he wasn't trying to do the right thing."[20]

Research in the social sciences and humanities is especially difficult to replicate because it is based not on experimental procedure but rather on expert interpretation of discrete works or events. A book of literary criticism is exactly what it sounds like: criticism. It is not science. It is, however, an expert judgment that requires a deep knowledge of the subject. Likewise, a study of the Cuban missile crisis is not the same as an experiment in the natural sciences. We cannot re-run October 1962 over and over again, and so an author examining the outcome of the crisis is presenting an expert analysis of one historical case. Such a study might be full of flawed conclusions, but it is the raw material for further discussion rather than a case of professional malfeasance.

Still, there have been some important cases of outright fraud in the social sciences and humanities. In 2000, a historian at Emory University named Michael Bellesiles won Columbia University's prestigious Bancroft Prize in history for a book called *Arming America*, in which Bellesiles claimed to debunk the idea that American ideas about gun ownership were rooted not in the early colonial experience but in other influences nearly a century later. The study was instantly polarizing, because it argued that private gun ownership was uncommon in early America.

A study that might have gone unnoticed attracted closer scrutiny because of its subject matter, with gun control advocates and gun ownership groups immediately taking sides on the Bellesiles argument. As other scholars tried to find the sources on which Bellesiles relied, however, they concluded that he had either misused them or invented them. Columbia withdrew the Bancroft Prize. Emory conducted its own investigation and found that while some of Bellesiles's errors might be ascribed to incompetence, there were unavoidable questions about his scholarly integrity. Bellesiles resigned his post shortly thereafter. His book was dropped by its original publisher, although it was later reissued by a small commercial press.

In 2012, a writer named David Barton published a book on Thomas Jefferson. Barton had no background as a professional historian; his public prominence was largely due to his stature in the evangelical movement. (In 2005, *TIME* called him one of the twenty-five most influential evangelicals in America.) His book attracted kudos and endorsements from leading conservatives, including 2012 presidential contenders Mike Huckabee and the historian-turned-politician Newt Gingrich.

Like the Bellesiles gun study, Barton's work attracted considerable attention because of its political implications as well as the prominence of its author. The book minced no words even in its title, *The Jefferson Lies: Exposing the Myths You've Always Believed about Thomas Jefferson*. Barton's book argued that modern historians not only had smeared Jefferson's private life but also had ignored how many of his beliefs were supportive of modern conservative views. Considering Jefferson's admiration of revolutionary France and his later association with liberalism (in contrast to his conservative nemesis John Adams), this was a bold claim.

Most professional scholars ignored the book, coming as it did from an amateur historian and a non-academic religious publishing house. The book was not, in any case, aimed at scholars, but at an audience already eager to read it. Barton hit the mark: *The Jefferson Lies* quickly made the *New York Times* best-seller list.

The accuracy of the book was soon called into question not by godless liberals at a research university but by two scholars at Grove City College, a small Christian school in Pennsylvania. Under closer scrutiny, many of Barton's claims collapsed. The readers of the *History News Network* later voted it "the least credible book in print," but even more damning, the book's publishers agreed that the book was so flawed that they withdrew it from circulation. The *Atlantic* writer and law professor Garret Epps, in a scathing review of the matter, said, "Most of [Barton's] books are self-published and will never be withdrawn. But the rebuke from Christian scholars and a Christian publishing house is a mark of shame he will carry from now on."[21]

In all of these cases, the fraud and misconduct were found out. To a layperson, however, the eventual reckoning over such work is understandably irrelevant. The bedrock issue is whether studies, in any field, can be trusted.

In a way, this is the wrong question. Rarely does a single study make or break a subject. The average person is not going to have to rely on the outcome of any particular project, say, in cell research. When a group of studies is aggregated into a drug or a treatment of which that one study might be a part, this itself triggers successive studies looking at safety and efficacy. It is possible to fake one study. To fake hundreds and thus produce a completely fraudulent or dangerous result is another matter entirely.

Likewise, no single study in public policy establishes an expert's credentials. Even when a scholar comes to the attention of the policy community because of a book or an article, his or her influence does not rest on the scientific replicability of the work but on the ideas it puts forward. In the social sciences, as in the hard sciences, it is rare that any single study can influence the life of the average citizen without at least some reconsideration by other experts.

What fraud does in any field, however, is to waste time and to delay progress. Much in the same way an error buried early in a complex set of equations can bog down later calculations, fraud or misconduct can delay an entire project until someone figures out who screwed up—or intentionally fudged—the facts. When such cases are revealed to the public, of course, they have legitimate questions about the scope and impact of misconduct, especially if they're paying for it with public money.

I THOUGHT YOU WERE PRE-MED?

There are other sources of expert failure beyond willful fraud or staggering incompetence. One of the most common errors experts make is to assume that because they are smarter than most people about certain things, they are smarter than everyone about everything. They see their expert knowledge as a license to hold court about anything. (Again, I cannot cast the first stone here.) Their advanced education and experience serve as a kind of blanket assurance that they are competent to comment in almost any field.

These experts are like Eric Stratton in the classic comedy *Animal House*. When he rises to defend his unruly college fraternity in student court, his friends ask him if he knows what he's doing. "Take it easy, I'm pre-law," he assures his brothers. "I thought you were premed?" one of them asks. "What's the difference?" Stratton answers.

This overconfidence leads experts not only to get out of their own lane and make pronouncements on matters far afield of their expertise, but also to "over-claim" wider expertise even within their own general area of competence. Experts and professionals, just as people in other endeavors, assume that their previous successes and achievements are evidence of their superior knowledge, and they push their boundaries rather than say the three words every expert hates to say: "I don't know." No one wants to appear to be uninformed or to be caught out on some ellipsis in their personal knowledge. Laypeople and experts alike will issue confident statements on things about which they know nothing, but experts are supposed to know better.

Cross-expertise violations happen for a number of reasons, from innocent error to intellectual vanity. Sometimes, however, the motivation is as simple as the opportunity provided by fame. Entertainers are the worst offenders here. (And, yes, in their field, they are experts. Acting schools are not run by chemical engineers.) Their celebrity affords them easy access to issues and controversies, and to actual experts or policymakers who will work with them because of the natural proclivity to answer the phone when someone famous calls.

Talking with celebrities, however, is not the same thing as educating them. This creates bizarre situations in which experts in one field—entertainment—end up giving disquisitions on important questions in other fields. This bizarre phenomenon has a relatively recent history in the United States, but it began well before celebrities could bloviate at will on Twitter or on their own websites.

In 1985, for example, a California congressman, Tony Coelho, invited the actresses Jane Fonda, Sissy Spacek, and Jessica Lange to testify before the House Agriculture Committee on farm problems. Their qualification? They had played farmers' wives in three popular movies of the decade. The whole business was a stunt, of course, and when asked why he did it, Democrat Coelho took a shot at Republican President Ronald Reagan: "They probably have a better understanding of the problems of agriculture than the actor in the White House," he said at the time.[22]

This was not, however, an isolated incident. Over the years, celebrities have steeped themselves in disputes about which they have very little knowledge. They push fads, create false alarms, and change the daily habits of millions of gullible fans.

Timothy Caulfield, a Canadian health policy specialist, is one of many experts who has had enough. He wrote a book criticizing assaults on established knowledge from celebrities, and by one celebrity in particular: *Is Gwyneth Paltrow Wrong about Everything? When Celebrity Culture and Science Clash.* (I discussed some of Paltrow's feminine-care recommendations—reluctantly—in chapter 4.) As Caulfield put it in a 2016 interview,

> If you ask someone, is Gwyneth Paltrow a credible source of information about breast cancer risk? Most people are going to say no. The science of nutrition? Most people will be skeptical. But because she has such a huge cultural footprint, and because she has made this brand for herself, people will identify with it.
>
> There's the availability bias, too: Celebrities are just everywhere. And the mere fact that they're everywhere, that influences in the impact they have. It's easy to call up a picture of [Paltrow]

on *People* magazine talking about gluten-free as opposed to what the data actually says. And that allows celebrities to have a huge impact on our lives.[23]

This is not harmless. People for a time were reluctant to vaccinate their children because of advice given by the actress Jenny McCarthy, a Playboy pinup who says she studied it all deeply at the "University of Google."

Wealth and pedigree can produce similar expertise problems, not least because Americans in particular tend to see wealthy people as celebrities in their own right, especially when they conduct themselves in public as something like entertainers. Elon Musk, for example, did not become famous because he says things that are silly, often incomprehensible, and at times reprehensible. Rather, he gained multiple platforms to air those views—long before he bought Twitter—because he was already famous for being a rich entrepreneur. (Indeed, he and his business interests might have been better off guarding his other image, that of a maverick entrepreneur, more carefully.) Robert F. Kennedy, Jr., would be just another conspiracy-obsessed podcaster were he not the wealthy son of a notable family. Women would be far less likely to follow health advice from Gwyneth Paltrow if she were not a glamorous actress. More people will see Paltrow, McCarthy, Musk, and Kennedy, and be exposed to their inane ideas, than will ever see—or have the patience to listen to—an ordinary oncologist or epidemiologist.

Activism is the right of every person in an open and democratic society. There is a fundamental difference, however, between activism and celebrities abusing their fame and relying on their names. Activism among laypeople requires taking sides among experts and advocating for preferred policies. When celebrity dilettantes demand to be trusted merely by the fact of their fame, their wealth, or their last name—they are no better than a microbiologist weighing in on modern art, or an economist arguing about pharmacology.

In some cases, experts overextend themselves because their trespass is into an area of expertise close enough to their own that a stretch of professional judgment seems reasonable. This is especially likely among experts who have already been lauded for achievements in their own field. As society has become more complex, however, the idea of geniuses who can hit to any and all fields makes less sense: "Benjamin Franklin," the humorist Alexandra Petri once wrote, "was one of the last men up to whom you could go and say, 'You invented a stove. What do you think we should do about these taxes?' and get a coherent answer."[24]

The Nobel Prize–winning chemist Linus Pauling, for example, became convinced in the 1970s that Vitamin C was a wonder drug. He advocated taking mega-doses of the supplement to ward off the common cold and any number of other ailments. There was no actual evidence for Pauling's claims, but Pauling had a Nobel in chemistry, and so his conclusions about the effect of vitamins seemed to many people to be a reasonable extension of his expertise.

In fact, Pauling failed to apply the scientific standards of his own profession at the very start of his advocacy for vitamins. He began taking Vitamin C in the late 1960s on the advice of a self-proclaimed doctor named Irwin Stone, who told Pauling that if he took three thousand milligrams of C a day—fifty times the recommended daily amount—that he would live twenty-five years longer. "Doctor" Stone's only degrees, however, were two honorary awards from a nonaccredited correspondence school and a college of chiropractic medicine.[25]

Pauling wanted to believe in the concept, and he started gobbling the vitamin. Immediately, he felt its miraculous effects. A more impartial observer might suspect a "placebo effect," in which telling someone a pill will make them feel better makes them think they feel better, but because of Pauling's illustrious contributions to science, his colleagues took him seriously and tested his claims.

None of these examinations of Vitamin C panned out, but Pauling would not hear of it. As Dr. Paul Offit, a pediatrician and a specialist in infectious diseases at the University of Pennsylvania, later wrote, "Although study after study showed that he was wrong, Pauling refused to believe it, continuing to promote vitamin C in speeches, popular articles, and books. When he occasionally appeared before the media with obvious cold symptoms, he said he was suffering from allergies."

Throughout the 1970s Pauling expanded his claims. He argued that vitamins could treat everything, including cancer, heart disease, leprosy, and mental illness, among other maladies. He later went on to suggest looking into the uses of Vitamin C in the fight against AIDS. Vitamin manufacturers, of course, were happy to have a Nobel Laureate as their patron saint. Soon, vitamin supplements (including "antioxidants," a term that became the "gluten-free" and "non-GMO" of its day) were big business.

Except, as it turns out, big doses of vitamins can be dangerous, including increasing the chance of certain kinds of cancers and strokes. Pauling, in the end, hurt not only his own reputation but also the health of potentially millions of people. As Offit put it, a "man who was so spectacularly right that he won two Nobel Prizes" was "so spectacularly wrong that he was arguably the world's greatest quack." To this day, there are people who still think a vitamin-laden horse pill can ward off illness, despite the fact that science worked exactly the way it's supposed to work by testing and falsifying Pauling's claims.

Pauling himself died of cancer at age ninety-three. Whether he got the extra twenty-five years "Doctor" Stone promised him, we'll never know.

Sometimes, experts use the luster of a particular credential or achievement to go even further afield of their area to influence important public policy debates. In the fall of 1983, a New York City radio station broadcast a program about the nuclear arms race. The early 1980s were tense years in the Cold War, and 1983 was one of the worst. The Soviet Union shot down a civilian Korean airliner, talks between the United States and the USSR about nuclear arms broke down in Geneva, and ABC's docudrama on a possible nuclear war, *The Day After*, debuted as one of the most-watched television programs up until that time. It was also soon to be an election year.

I was one of the listeners, as a young graduate student in New York at the time studying the Soviet Union and looking ahead to a career in public policy. "If Ronald Reagan is re-elected," the voice on my radio said in a sharp Australian accent, "nuclear war is a mathematical certainty." The declaration that nuclear war was inescapable got my attention, especially as Reagan was on track to win in a landslide in 1984. Who was this person who was so definite—to the point of *mathematical certainty*—that we were therefore headed for Armageddon?

The speaker was a woman named Dr. Helen Caldicott. She was not a doctor of physics or government or international affairs, but a pediatrician from Australia. Her concern about nuclear weapons, by her own recollection, stemmed from reading Nevil Shute's 1956 postapocalyptic novel *On the Beach* (which was set in her native country). As she later put it, she saw no point in treating children for their illnesses when the world around them could be reduced to ashes at any moment. In short order, she became a prominent voice in debates on arms control and nuclear policy, despite her almost complete lack of credentials or experience with the subject matter.

Caldicott was prone to making definitive statements about highly technical matters. She would discourse confidently on things like the resilience of US missile silos, civil defense measures, and the internal workings of the Soviet foreign policy apparatus. She resided in the

United States for almost a decade, and she became a regular presence in the media representing the antinuclear activist community.

She reached the apex of her cross-expertise influence when she published her 1985 book *Missile Envy*, a book replete with medical terminology as a "diagnosis" of the arms race. (The chapters include "Etiology," "Physical Examination," "Case Study," and so on.) The title of the book is a spoiler: the pediatrician found a psychological grounding for the Cold War in the psyches of old Soviet and American men. She noted that American women, having won the right to vote, "have done virtually nothing with it"; women in government like then–British prime minister Margaret Thatcher, Caldicott said, did not "represent the true attributes of the large majority of sensible, wise women."[26] (When I heard Caldicott on New York radio, she was even more blunt: "Margaret Thatcher," the doctor declared, "is not a woman.") Caldicott went back to Australia in the late 1980s to run for political office. She was defeated.

The expert community is full of such examples. The most famous, at least if measured by impact on the global public, is the MIT professor Noam Chomsky, a figure revered by millions of readers around the world. Chomsky, by some counts, is the most widely cited living American intellectual, having written a stack of books on politics and foreign policy. His post at MIT, however, was as a professor of linguistics. Chomsky is regarded as a pioneer, even a giant, in his own field, but he is no more an expert in foreign policy than, say, the late George Kennan was on the origins of human language. Nonetheless, he is more famous among the general public for his writings on politics than in his area of expertise; indeed, I often encountered college students over the years who were quite familiar with Chomsky but who had no idea his actual field of expertise was linguistics, rather than politics or international affairs.

Like Pauling and Caldicott, however, Chomsky answered a need in the public square. Laypeople often feel at a disadvantage challenging traditional science or socially dominant ideas, and they will rally to outspoken figures whose views carry a patina of expert assurance. It may well be that doctors should look closely at the role of vitamins in the human diet. It is certain that the public should be involved in an ongoing reconsideration of the role of nuclear weapons. But a degree in chemistry or a residency in pediatrics does not make advocates of those positions more credible than any other autodidact in those esoteric subjects.

The public is remarkably tolerant of such trespasses, and this itself is a paradox: while some laypeople do not respect an expert's actual area of knowledge, others assume that expertise and achievement are so generic that experts and intellectuals can weigh in with some authority on almost anything. The same people who might doubt their family physician about the safety of vaccines will buy a book on nuclear weapons because the author's title includes the magic letters "MD."

Unfortunately, when experts are asked for views outside their competence, few are humble enough to remember their responsibility to demur. I have made this mistake, and I have ended up regretting it. In a strange twist, I have also actually argued with people who have insisted that I am fully capable of commenting on a subject when I have made plain that I have no particular knowledge in the matter at hand. It is an odd feeling indeed to assure a reporter, or especially a student, that despite their faith in me, it would be irresponsible of me to answer their question with any pretense of authority. It is an uncomfortable admission, but one we can only wish linguistics professors, pediatricians, and so many others would make as well.

I PREDICT!

In the early 1960s, an entertainer known as "The Amazing Criswell" was a regular guest on television and radio shows. Criswell's act was to make outrageous predictions, delivered with a dramatic flourish of "I predict!" Among his many pronouncements, Criswell warned that New York would sink into the sea by 1980, Vermont would suffer a nuclear attack in 1981, and Denver would be destroyed in a natural disaster in 1989. Criswell's act was pure camp, but the public enjoyed it. What Criswell did not predict, however, was that his own career would fizzle out in the late 1960s and end with a few small roles in low-budget sexploitation films made by his friend, the legendarily awful director Edward D. Wood, Jr.[27]

Prediction is a problem for experts. It's what the public wants, but experts usually aren't very good at it. This is because they're not supposed to be good at it; the purpose of science is to explain, not to predict. And yet predictions, like cross-expertise transgressions, are catnip to experts.

Experts and laypeople alike believe that because experts have a better handle on a subject than others, they will have a better track record of prediction. For experts in the hard sciences, this is always a stronger claim, because they use experimental methods to determine the conditions under which the physical world will behave as they would expect. When unpredictable things happen, scientists have a new starting point for investigation. As the late science-fiction writer (and professor of biochemistry) Isaac Asimov said, the words that have spurred the greatest scientific breakthroughs are probably not "Eureka," but "Gee, that's funny."

Some experts, however, embrace prediction and even charge a handsome fee for it. Pollsters, for example, sell their services to political candidates and to media subscribers, while marketing experts test the waters for new services and products. Polling has come a long way since 1936, when *Literary Digest* predicted that Alf Landon would defeat Franklin Roosevelt (mostly by surveying its own readers). Today, research on public opinion is a science, with its own experts and journals. Some pollsters are partisans who slant their results toward a preferred outcome, but most have an academic background in statistics and methods that allows them, in the main, to make reasonably accurate calls.

When polls and market research get something wrong, however, they can get it very wrong. The Coca-Cola Corporation's introduction of "New Coke" in the mid-1980s was such a disaster that the term "New Coke" itself has become a meme for a failure to read public opinion accurately. Political pollsters and experts also missed several important calls in the early twenty-first century, including the results of various elections in the United States and the United Kingdom.

In fact, a survey of pollsters in 2015 found that they believed their reputations had been tarnished by this string of misses. Some felt that this was a result of media bias (which favors covering failure more than success), while others admitted that technological and demographic changes were making accurate polling a more challenging endeavor. "Polls are wrong is a more interesting story than when the polls do well," the polling expert Barbara Carvalho told FiveThirtyEight (itself a site dedicated to polling). But the pollster Matthew Towery admitted in 2015 that, "obviously, there were several high-profile calamities in the past three years."[28]

The problem here is not so much with polling—whose accuracy is better than the public realizes, but whose results are limited by the involvement of actual human beings—as it is with what people expect from polling. Polls are not a written guarantee of future results. Many things, from unforeseeable events to advertising, can change minds. As in every other expert endeavor, the measure of competence is in the overall trend and in whether the experts examine their own failures carefully. Indeed, pollsters examined their errors from the 2010s—as experts should—and made changes that resulted in far more accurate predictions, especially in the 2022 US midterm elections.[29] For every New Coke, there are thousands of successful product launches and accurate campaign forecasts. As is always the case, however, people tend to remember the bad calls—especially if they didn't like the results—while ignoring the more numerous successes.

In general, the public expects too much from expert prediction, but at least some experts encourage these expectations, to the point where they are willing to stand on their clairvoyance strongly enough to sell it. For decades, the political science professor Bruce Bueno de Mesquita used his own "proprietary software" to make predictions about world events for both public and private customers. His firm's clients over some thirty years have included the US Central Intelligence Agency, which in a 1993 study said that in hundreds of predictions he "hit the bullseye" twice as often as its own analysts did.

Other experts have not been able to test Bueno de Mesquita's claims, since his methods and models are protected as business property rather than presented in published studies. As a *New York Times* profile noted in 2009,

> While Bueno de Mesquita has published many predictions in academic journals, the vast majority of his forecasts have been done in secret for corporate or government clients, where no independent academics can verify them. "We have no idea if he's right 9 times out of 10, or 9 times out of a hundred, or 9 times out of a thousand," [Harvard professor Stephen] Walt says.
>
> Walt also isn't impressed by [the] C.I.A. study showing Bueno de Mesquita's 90 percent hit rate. "It's one midlevel C.I.A. bureaucrat saying, 'This was a useful tool,'" Walt says. "It's not like he's got Brent Scowcroft saying, 'Back in the Bush administration, we didn't make a decision without consulting Bueno de Mesquita.'"[30]

While Bueno de Mesquita's accuracy is unknowable, the more important point is that there has long been a healthy market for his predictions. Organizations with a great deal at stake—lives, money, or both—inevitably embark on voracious searches for information before taking risks. An expert who says he or she can peek into the future will always be more in demand than one who offers more limited advice.

Pollsters and consultants like Bueno de Mesquita are paid to predict things, and the value of their work is up to their clients. But other experts and public intellectuals make predictions, too, and the many failures of expert predictions have done much to undermine public confidence in scholars and professionals. When people who didn't foresee the end of the Soviet Union—or who promised that a major war with Iraq would be an easy win—return to provide yet more advice on life-and-death decisions, the public's skepticism is understandable.

If we leave aside the issue of whether experts *ought* to predict, we're still left with the problem that they *do* predict, and their predictions often are startlingly bad. In a widely read study on "black swan" events—the unforeseeable moments that can change history—Nassim Nicholas Taleb decried the "epistemic arrogance" of the whole enterprise of prediction.

> But we act as though we are able to predict historical events, or, even worse, as if we are able to change the course of history. We produce 30-year projections of social security deficits and oil prices without realizing that we cannot even predict these for next summer—our cumulative prediction errors for political and economic events are so monstrous that every time I look at the empirical record I have to pinch myself to verify that I am not dreaming.[31]

Taleb's warning about the permanence of uncertainty is an important observation, but his insistence on accepting the futility of prediction is impractical. Human beings will not throw their hands up and abandon any possibility of applying expertise as an anticipatory hedge.

The question is not whether experts should engage in prediction. They will. The society they live in and the leaders who govern it will ask them to do so. Rather, the issue is when and how experts should make predictions, and what to do about it when they're wrong.

In a landmark 2005 study, the scholar Philip Tetlock gathered data on expert predictions in social science, and he found what many people suspected: "When we pit experts against minimalist performance benchmarks—dilettantes, dart-throwing chimps, and assorted extrapolation algorithms—we find few signs that expertise translates into greater ability to make either 'well-calibrated' or 'discriminating' forecasts."[32] Experts, it seemed, were no better at predicting the future than spinning a roulette wheel. Tetlock's initial findings confirmed for many laypeople a suspicion that experts don't really know what they're doing.

But this reaction to Tetlock's work was a classic case of laypeople misunderstanding expertise. Tetlock, in fact, did not measure experts against everyone in the world, but against basic benchmarks, especially the predictions of other experts. The question wasn't whether experts were no better than anyone else at prediction, but why *some* experts seemed better at prediction than *others*, which is a very different question. As Tetlock himself noted, "radical skeptics welcomed these results, but they start squirming when we start finding patterns of consistency in who got what right. Radical skepticism tells us to expect nothing. . . . But the data revealed more consistency in forecasters' track records than could be ascribed to chance."[33]

Likewise, James Surowiecki (the "wisdom of crowds" writer) pointed out that although "cognitive diversity" is important— meaning that many views can be better than one—it does *not* mean that if "you assemble a group of diverse but thoroughly uninformed people, their collective wisdom will be smarter than an expert's."[34]

What Tetlock actually found was not that experts were no better than random guessers, but that *certain kinds of experts* seemed better at applying knowledge to hypotheticals than their colleagues. Tetlock used the British thinker Isaiah Berlin's distinction between "hedgehogs" and "foxes" to distinguish between experts whose knowledge was wide and inclusive ("the fox knows many things") from those whose expertise is narrow and deep ("the hedgehog knows but one"). Tetlock's study is one of the most important works ever written on how experts think, and it deserves a full reading. In general, however, one of his more intriguing findings can be summarized by noting that while experts ran into trouble when trying to move from explanation to prediction, the "foxes" generally outperformed the "hedgehogs," for many reasons.

Hedgehogs, for example, tended to be overly focused on generalizing their specific knowledge to situations that were outside of their competence, while foxes were better able to integrate more information and to change their minds when presented with new or better data. "The foxes' self-critical, point-counterpoint style of thinking," Tetlock found, "prevented them from building up the sorts of excessive enthusiasm for their predictions that hedgehogs, especially well-informed ones, displayed for theirs."[35]

Technical experts, the very embodiment of the hedgehogs, had considerable trouble not only with prediction but with broadening their ability to process information outside their area in general. People with a very well-defined area of knowledge do not have many tools beyond their specialization, so their instinct is to take what they know and generalize it outward, no matter how poorly the fit between their own area and the subject at hand.[36] This results in predictions that are made with more confidence but that tend to be more often wrong, mostly because the scientists, as classic hedgehogs, have difficulty accepting and processing information from outside their very small but highly complicated lane of expertise.

There are some lessons in all this, not just for experts, but for lay-people who judge—and even challenge—expert predictions.

The most important point is that failed predictions do not mean very much in terms of judging expertise. Experts usually cover their predictions (and an important part of their anatomy) with caveats because the world is full of unforeseeable accidents that can have major ripple effects down the line. History can be changed by contingent events as simple as a heart attack or a hurricane. Laypeople tend to ignore these caveats, despite their importance, much as they ignore their local weather forecaster when told there is a 70 percent chance of rain. If the three in ten possibility of a sunny day arrives, they think the forecaster was wrong.

None of this lets experts, especially expert communities, off the hook for massive failures of insight. No single Soviet expert in the 1970s could predict the fall of the USSR by 1991; some did, but none of them foresaw the *way* it happened, and often such predictions were more like wishes. But hardening of expert opinion around the opposite view—that the collapse of the Soviet state was practically impossible—was a huge error in judgment that should haunt that field. (Unfortunately, it does not; for thirty years, most Russia specialists have shied away from examining each other's mistakes about the Soviet Union and the end of the Cold War.)

Predictive failure, however, does not retroactively strip experts of their claim to know more than laypeople. Laypeople should not jump to the assumption that a missed call by the experts therefore means all opinions are equally valid (or equally worthless). The polling expert Nate Silver, who made his reputation with remarkably accurate forecasts in the 2008 and 2012 presidential elections, has since admitted that his predictions about Republican presidential nominee Donald Trump in 2016 were based on flawed assumptions.[37] But Silver's insights into the other races remain solid, even if the Trump phenomenon surprised him and others. As the columnist

Noah Rothman later wrote, "Trump has demonstrated that so many of the rules that political professionals spent their careers studying were not predictive this year. But 'everything we knew about politics [this year] was wrong' does not yield to 'we know nothing about politics.'"[38]

Calling experts to account for making worse predictions than other experts is a different matter. But to phrase questions as raw yes-or-no predictions, and then to note that laypeople can be right as often as experts, is fundamentally to misunderstand the role of expertise itself. Indeed, to ask such undifferentiated questions is also to let experts off the hook. There's an old joke about a British civil servant who retired after a long career in the Foreign Office spanning most of the twentieth century. "Every morning," the experienced diplomatic hand said, "I went to the Prime Minister and assured him there would be no world war today. And I am pleased to note that in a career of 40 years, I was only wrong twice." Judged purely on the number of hits and misses, the old man had a pretty good record.

The goal of expert advice and prediction is not to win a coin toss, it is to help guide decisions about possible futures. To ask in 1980 whether the Soviet Union would fall before the year 2000 is a yes-or-no question. To ask during the previous decades how best to bring about a peaceful Soviet collapse and to alter the probability of that event (and to lessen the chances of others) is an entirely different matter.

Given my own background in Russian studies, an alert reader at this point might be wondering if I was part of the community of Soviet experts who got it wrong, and whether I am just throwing spitballs from the back of the classroom. It's a fair question.

I did not get the Soviet collapse wrong—but only because I never had the chance to be wrong in the first place. I finished graduate school in late 1988, when it was already clear that the fissioning of the USSR was under way. Instead, I waited another ten years before making my own howlingly wrong prediction about Russian politics. I know the dangers of making bad predictions, because I have my own for which I must answer.

In early 2000 I wrote that the emergence of a new Russian leader, an unknown bureaucrat named Vladimir Putin, might be a step along the way toward further democracy in Russia. I could not have been more wrong, of course; Putin turned out to be a dictator. He remains a continuing threat to global peace. *Why* I was wrong is still a question that absorbs my own work and my discussions with my colleagues, especially those who shared my view. Were we fooled by Putin in 2000? Or were we right to be optimists, but Putin himself changed along the way and we missed it? Or did something happen inside the Kremlin, so far invisible to outsiders, that took the entire Russian leadership down the path of autocracy and international aggression?

There are elements of truth in all these explanations. Putin's background was cause for worry even in 1999. His views did seem to change after his first two terms in office. Contingency and chance may also have played a role, at least where the Ukraine war is concerned: Putin seems to have cooked up his military adventure while in COVID isolation with few advisers able to reach him—literally and figuratively.

To a layperson, none of these theories matters much—nor should they. When pressed to reach a judgment about Putin (as many of us in Russian affairs were), I rendered a definite opinion rather than taking the more patient, but less interesting, view that it was too early to tell. In trying to unravel today's Russia, however, does my trainwreck of a prediction nearly twenty years ago now invalidate my analysis and advice? Am I no more capable of discussing Putin's motivations than a well-read layperson? For some readers, the answer might be a resounding yes, but the fact remains that the average person would be in over his or her head trying to explain the complexity of Russian politics, or even to teach an introductory course on the subject. (And

I would immodestly suggest that the track record of my work on Russia, including a few predictions, has been pretty good over the years, despite my missed call on Putin.)

Why I and others were wrong in 1999 is an important question, not least because it forces us to revisit our assumptions and engage in the debate and self-correction that is the duty of an expert community. A great many people were pessimistic about Putin, but some of that was no more than reflexive Russophobia or a mere guess, neither of which is useful in policymaking. An uninformed judgment, even when right, is often less useful than a reasoned view, even when wrong, that can then be dissected, examined, and corrected.

REPAIRING THE RELATIONSHIP

Both experts and laypeople have responsibilities when it comes to expert failure. Professionals must own their mistakes, air them publicly, and show the steps they are taking to correct them. Laypeople, for their part, must exercise more caution in asking experts to prognosticate, and they must educate themselves about the difference between failure and fraud.

In general, experts do examine their mistakes but not in places the public is likely to look. The average person is not going to read a medical journal or a statistical analysis of an article in sociology. To be honest, I suspect that most experts and scholars would probably prefer that laypeople avoid doing so, because they would not understand most of what they were reading and their attempt to follow the professional debate would likely produce more public confusion than enlightenment.

This is where public intellectuals—the "foxes," the people who can bridge the gap between experts and laypeople—might shoulder more responsibility. The public is poorly served if the only people talking about a new medical treatment are doctors who have a hard time translating their knowledge into basic English (and who may be invested in a position), or journalists who have no scientific background and cannot evaluate complicated scientific claims. This leaves a wide open space—usually on the Internet—for amateurs, hucksters, charlatans, and conspiracy theorists.

Public intellectuals are often derided within their own fields as mere "popularizers," and there's some truth to the charge. The world probably does not need yet another Bill Nye ("The Science Guy") weighing in on global climate change; Nye is doing the job well enough already. Nor does the foreign policy community need one more former bureaucrat or relatively junior retired military officer crowding the airwaves with deep thoughts merely because there is now too much time and bandwidth to fill. But if the gulf between the public and the experts gets too wide, the experts will talk only to each other, and the public will end up excluded from decisions that will later affect their lives.

Citizens, however, have the most important role here. They must educate themselves not only about issues that matter to them but about the people to whom they're listening. Tetlock, for one, has advocated looking closely at the records of pundits and experts as a way of forcing them to get better at giving advice, so that they will have "incentives to compete by improving the epistemic (truth) value of their products, not just by pandering to communities of co-believers."[39]

Outing the track records of bad pundits, however, will only matter if people bother to pay attention. If they remain passive recipients of information on a television screen, or if they actively search only for information they want to believe, nothing else will matter very much. Instead, laypeople should ask themselves some important questions, including how much they want to learn about a subject, and whether they're really willing to encounter facts that undermine their own beliefs. They must learn to ask better questions about the sources of their information, and they must consider the background of the experts to whom they listen.

If a layperson really wants to believe that Vitamin C can cure cancer, experts with sterling records of research and prediction will have less effect than a website with a picture of a pill on it. If an uninformed citizen really believes that invading a foreign country (or building a wall with one) will solve America's problems, reams of expert writings will not matter to them. Laypeople must take more responsibility for their own knowledge, or lack of it: it is no excuse to claim that the world is too complicated and there are too many sources of information, and then to lament that policy is in the hands of faceless experts who disdain the public's views.

The public also needs to approach expert advice with a certain combination of skepticism and humility. As the philosopher Bertrand Russell wrote in a 1928 essay, laypeople must evaluate expert claims by exercising their own careful logic as well.

> The skepticism that I advocate amounts only to this: (1) that when the experts are agreed, the opposite opinion cannot be held to be certain; (2) that when they are not agreed, no opinion can be regarded as certain by a non-expert; and (3) that when they all hold that no sufficient grounds for a positive opinion exist, the ordinary man would do well to suspend his judgment.

It is not enough to know what the experts agree upon. It is equally important to accept the limits of that agreement and not to draw more conclusions than the weight of expert views can support.

Moreover, laypeople must accept that experts are not policymakers. Experts advise national leaders and their voices carry more impact than those of laypeople, but they do not make the final decisions. In a democracy, even a highly regulated and bureaucratized republic like the United States, few experts are sole policymakers. Politicians, from city councils up through the White House, have the final say on many of the most important decisions in our lives, from drugs to deterrence. If laypeople refuse to take their duties as citizens seriously, and do not educate themselves about issues important to them, democracy will mutate into technocracy. The rule of experts, so feared by laypeople, will grow by default.

Finally, laypeople must make peace with the reality that experts will always get some things wrong as a normal part of their profession, but that these errors are not a reason to throw away the accumulated knowledge of experts in favor of sullen know-nothingism. "I have a confession to make," the Johns Hopkins professor Francis Gavin wrote in an important essay in 2022. "I have been wrong quite a lot lately."

> I believed Vladimir Putin was pursuing a coercive bluff and would not invade Ukraine. I did not think Xi Jinping's China would be so foolish as to crack down on Hong Kong. Donald Trump serving out his full four-year term shocked me as much as his election did. Uber struck me as an impractical fad that would never work out, and, in 2010, when a friend excitedly showed me an iPad he had purchased, I thought he had wasted his money. I also believed the Philadelphia Eagles' 2018 Super Bowl victory was the start of a decades-long football dynasty.[40]

But as Gavin notes: "Few individuals, organizations, or nations get things 100 percent right at first," and the ensuing arguments and debates are signs not of disarray and incompetence, but of healthy self-examination. "It can be messy, feelings can get hurt, and sometimes the incentives cause us to listen to the wrong people for too long while ignoring quieter but wiser voices. These are the costs and burdens of an open society, which we all know too well. This system of unrelenting and sharp debate and disagreement is better than any alternative."

For laypeople to use expert advice and to place professionals in their proper roles as servants, rather than masters, they should not only embrace Gavin's understanding of the meaning of debate, but they must accept their own limitations as well. Democracy cannot function when every citizen is an expert. Yes, it is unbridled ego for experts to believe they can run a democracy while ignoring its voters; it is also, however, ignorant narcissism for laypeople to believe that they can maintain a large and advanced nation without listening to the voices of those more educated and experienced than themselves.

How to find that balance, and thus to mitigate the increasingly worrisome collisions between experts and their clients in society, is the subject of this book's final chapter, but first, we must examine one of the greatest modern crises of expertise in nearly a century: the COVID pandemic.

Chapter 7

The Experts, the Public, and the Pandemic

We didn't know what we didn't know. We're experts in hindsight. We're all geniuses now.

California Governor Gavin Newsom, 2023

What drives me nuts is when I'm challenged by medical experts, okay?

Wisconsin Senator Ron Johnson, 2023

THE PERFECT STORM

Beginning in 2019, the world suffered a once-in-a-century pandemic, one that arrived almost exactly on schedule one hundred years after the great influenza pandemic of 1918. A new coronavirus—one of many types of viruses that cause respiratory disease—emerged in Wuhan, China, and rapidly spread around the planet. The virus was SARS-CoV-2; the disease it caused was officially designed by the World Health Organization as COVID-19, for "Coronavirus disease 2019." Various nations handled the pandemic differently and not always wisely (which is how regional epidemics sometimes become pandemics). In the United States, despite the heroic efforts of front-line medical professionals, the pandemic became an ongoing disaster, with wave after wave of infections rolling in from a perfect storm of paranoia, panic, and polarization.

Many of the problems we've explored in this book, from "doing your own research" to the obstacles impeding rational discussion, were already trends corroding public life and undermining American democracy before 2020. The pandemic turned those trends into mortal dangers, and people died because of them. The COVID death toll around the world was immense, but in the United States it was much larger than it should have been. With only 4 percent of the world's population, the United States had nearly a quarter of the world's reported COVID cases, and by the end of 2023, Americans were more than a fifth of the seven million people who died of the disease, making the United States the only G-7 country among the top five nations with the most pandemic deaths. The COVID Crisis Group, a nonpartisan group of policy and health experts who issued a comprehensive report on the US response to COVID in 2023, estimated that the American flailing over COVID measures resulted in at least a *half million* additional deaths than otherwise might have been expected from the disease.[1]

When I first started writing about the death of expertise in the early 2010s, I was convinced that a disaster of some kind would overcome some of our attachment to our own ignorance. I was not hoping for a catastrophe; indeed, I dreaded such an eventuality. But I believed that shared adversity might defeat irrational narcissism and willful ignorance. Obviously, I was too optimistic.

I also made a fundamental error by including a pandemic among general "disasters." A pandemic, as I should have realized and as events later showed, is the kind of catastrophe almost perfectly suited to weaken a society already distrustful of established knowledge. Most types of disasters engender, at least for a time, a sense of cooperation and fellowship. During fires or floods or earthquakes, we take shelter, but we also think of our neighbors. We search for them, rescue them, and feed them. We pass messages from family to family about the missing and the injured. We donate blood. Even wars, divisive as they can be, also bring us together. We honor the service of the men and women who fight for us. We realize that somewhere, an enemy sees us all as more alike than different, regardless of our petty arguments among ourselves. Yes, there are ugly moments during such crises, including violent protests, hoarding, runs on banks and grocery stores—and suspicions of people who might look like the foreigners attacking us. In general, however, visible threats often encourage people to cooperate.

Pandemics defeat these instincts. A pandemic instead takes our cooperative impulses and reclassifies them as dangers. We do not reach out to our neighbors; we push them away from us and slam our doors. We do not congregate in public for support; we empty the streets. We do not see strangers as fellow citizens in the great struggle to rebuild a city or defeat a foreign enemy; they are sources of possible illness and death and must be shunned. Government authorities, in such a crisis, are not the organizers of public action or the defenders of the nation. Instead, they are authoritarians who are locking us out of our workplaces and into our homes because of their insistence that we are under siege from invisible pathogens.

The measures required to cope with a pandemic, many of which rest on the temporary restriction of personal liberties, test even the most cohesive society. The United States, however, has always prided itself on its individualism and the consequent suspicion of overbearing government authority, and these cultural foundations, combined with the death of expertise, helped make COVID especially lethal among Americans. Other nations had their own vulnerabilities to deal with, but the United States was among the few countries that turned COVID from a natural disaster into a self-inflicted catastrophe whose social, political, and physical damage continues to this day.

And yet, as I write in late 2023, COVID has been tamed—mostly through vaccination—and life in the United States and most other nations has returned to something like normal, with COVID now taking a permanent place on the roster of infectious diseases that require regular monitoring. The US economy, against gloomy pandemic-era expectations, has mostly recovered: unemployment is low and post-pandemic inflation is cooling. Supply-chain bottlenecks have eased. Schools and universities, malls and restaurants, theaters, and sports events are all full again. COVID marches on, of course, with thousands more infected each month and the sufferers of "long COVID" still unsure how their battle with the disease will shape the rest of their lives, but the virus is now part of an ongoing public health challenge rather than an existential crisis. In May 2023, the World Health Organization declared the pandemic state of emergency over. The United States government followed suit the same month.

This chapter is not a full recounting of the COVID pandemic. Rather, I want to point out three ways in which responses to the pandemic, especially in the United States, worsened the crisis of expertise. First, the social and cultural environment heading into 2020 was already infused with distrust and even paranoia about science and expert knowledge, and among many people, the pandemic deepened those feelings. Second, the polarized condition of American politics and the failure of leadership in the national government virtually ensured that a natural disaster would become a political weapon in the hands of charlatans and opportunists. And third, the experts made both honest mistakes and unarguably poor decisions. The history of COVID around the world includes inspiring stories of wise decisions, medical gallantry, public sacrifice, and scientific triumph. Unfortunately, that history is also marred by panic, ignorance, cowardice, venality, and political mendacity that cost lives, damaged democratic institutions, and accelerated the declining respect for knowledge.

PRIMED FOR PARANOIA

A significant number of Americans were already primed by the media, their political leaders, and their own stubborn narcissism to reject expert advice during a crisis. I've discussed that environment in this book and in other venues. The collapse of gatekeeping in the media, the explosion of worthless Internet sources, the emergence of celebrity pseudo-experts, and the insistence by millions of people that they can "do their own research" all combined to make a brutal pandemic even more deadly.

When COVID arrived in North America, the United States was already well on the way to becoming a "post-truth" society, in which knowledge was under attack from all directions. Today, anti-science paranoia in the United States is mostly a characteristic of the far right, and it has been institutionalized in the Republican Party. But much of the madness that blanketed the world during the pandemic defied categorization along the traditional lines of "right" or "left." The sudden onset of disease and the dramatic measures taken to combat the spread of the virus drew together multiple movements devoted to various delusions, uniting people who follow the QAnon cult, who believe that vaccines have cellular signal receptors in them, or who think a secret cabal was using biological warfare to institute a single planetary government.

Such ideas were not the exclusive province of right-wing flacks on cable and radio and ghoulish trolls on social media. As a group of health activists wrote in 2023, the pandemic was also exploited by what they call the "conspirituality" movement, made up of "influencers who have curdled New Age spirituality and wellness with the politics of paranoia—peddling vaccine misinformation, tales of child trafficking, and wild conspiracy theories."[2]

The term itself has been around since at least 2011, when an article published in the *Journal of Contemporary Religion* defined it as a "hybrid" belief system based on political disillusionment and the popularity of alternative worldviews.

> It has international celebrities, bestsellers, radio and TV stations.
>
> It offers a broad politico-spiritual philosophy based on two core convictions, the first traditional to conspiracy theory, the second rooted in the New Age: 1) a secret group covertly controls, or is trying to control, the political and social order, and 2) humanity is undergoing a "paradigm shift" in consciousness. Proponents believe that the best strategy for dealing with the threat of a totalitarian "new world order" is to act in accordance with an awakened "new paradigm" worldview.[3]

Conspirituality, already rooted in hostility to science and expertise, was a perfect accelerant for the irrationality and paranoia that overtook millions of people during the pandemic. Worse, as a 2021 profile of a conspirituality believer showed, while "left-wing, magazine-friendly wellness and far-right conspiracy theories" always shared a culture of distrust, the pandemic accelerated the way "the former is becoming a mainstream entry point into the latter."[4] People who began an online search for health information quickly fell down rabbit holes into bizarre conspiracy materials of every imaginable sort.

Unhinged theories were already seducing people before the pandemic because of the mutually reinforcing effects of decades of attacks on established knowledge and a growing partisan divide in which people lost trust not only in institutions, but in each other. As the body count grew, a nation already prone to narcissism and grievance-mongering turned on itself in the scramble to fix blame. As the conservative writer David French pointed out, many citizens embraced "a simple conviction, an unstated premise that lends credibility to any claim, however outlandish: 'they' are so evil and so loathsome that they'd happily unleash an epidemic on the world or crush the livelihoods of millions merely to obtain a political advantage."[5] Americans not only traded insults about the pandemic, they literally delighted in other's deaths, trolling people online about the illness and deaths of their relatives—including children.[6] "These are not the convictions of a healthy society," French rightly observed. "These are the convictions of people consumed by rage and fear."

Appeals to paranoia and ignorance have long been part of the American political environment, but they were especially destructive at a time when the nation was riven in every direction by partisan hostility. The pandemic consequently made everything worse by plunging millions of people into fear and loneliness. Confined to their home with few companions, ordinary citizens took comfort from the warm light of computer and phone screens that offered to explain—in terrifying detail—why all of these bewildering problems were falling on innocent people who only weeks earlier had been living otherwise normal lives.

Both as a disease and a political issue, COVID-19 struck at multiple weak points in the edifice of American life. A mysterious disease (from China, no less, a nation that often serves as a source of American anxiety) forced citizens to rely on the media for information from white-jacketed experts and government officials. Those same officials, grasping at solutions in a time of public panic, instituted deeply unpopular measures. National emergencies are always fertile ground for fear and misinformation, but the tragic reality is that when COVID blew across America's shores, it found a country already ripe for disaster.

THE FAILURE OF ELECTED GOVERNMENT

The road to America's COVID meltdown did not begin with President Donald Trump, but much of the ensuing disaster was directly a result of the chaos and cowardice that overtook Trump's White House in 2020. Instead of calm and reassuring leadership, Trump (who took office in 2017) provided millions of people with a role model of denial, ignorance, and petulance.

Some of Trump's most loyal advisers tried to warn him that the pandemic was an immense danger. Trade adviser Peter Navarro—at this writing under indictment in Georgia for his part in Trump's attempts to overturn the 2020 election—predicted to his White House colleagues in January 2020 that the death toll in the United States could run into the millions. As the journalist Maggie Haberman recounted, his warnings were an extension of his "natural paranoia" about China and thus were easily dismissed by senior staff because of his own credibility issues.[7] (The fact that the somewhat eccentric trade adviser was weighing in on a health crisis illustrated how disorganized the lines of communication were in the Trump White House.) National Security Adviser Robert O'Brien, however, told Trump that same month that COVID would be "the biggest national security threat you face in your presidency," but almost anyone in the Trump administration who wanted to battle the pandemic first had to battle a resolutely ignorant president.[8]

Before discussing other failures of elected government during the pandemic, it is important to acknowledge that the Trump administration collectively made one especially vital and correct decision. In April 2020, the White House launched "Operation Warp Speed," the crash program to work with private industry to develop a vaccine in record time. The result was an amazing feat of science, in which government, industry, and scientific establishments spanning multiple countries joined forces to produce highly effective vaccines. Most people, especially those too young to remember earlier scourges such as polio, cannot comprehend how remarkable it was to create a safe and effective vaccine in the space of only a year or so. The Trump administration has much to answer for—including creating a hesitancy among Americans to take the very vaccines developed by Operation Warp Speed—but the concept itself, proposed and funded on a bipartisan basis, saved lives.[9]

If only the rest of the Trump administration's response had been so effective. The dysfunction of the Trump White House, on COVID and on so many other issues, has been amply documented in multiple books and articles. The common thread, and a lesson for the ages in the study of leadership, is that Trump's personality—his insecurities, his unwillingness to listen to almost anyone around him, his deeply narcissistic reactions to every difficulty—hobbled effective policy-making on COVID, as it did on so many issues. Trump treated the virus the same way he treated many other moments of adversity during his administration: as a personal affront and a threat to his political fortunes that had to be defused. All other decisions flowed from this one imperative.

In early 2020, for example, an official of the Centers for Disease Control, Dr. Nancy Messonnier, said at a White House press briefing that the virus would likely spread to the United States and that "disruption to everyday life might be severe." Trump was "furious," according to a report in the *Wall Street Journal*, and wanted her fired.[10] The journalist Jonathan Chait later detailed the chronology of Trump's subsequent positions in the spring of 2020:

> Trump insisted that month that China was "getting it under control more and more, that the United States had just 15 people [with COVID], and the 15 within a couple of days is going to be down to close to zero." He repeated over and over: "Just stay calm. It will go away." (March 10). "It's going to go away, hopefully at the end of the month. And, if not, hopefully it will be soon after that." (March 31). "It is going to go away. It is going away." (April 3). "I always say, even without it [a vaccine], it goes away." (June 16).[11]

Trump was spouting dangerous nonsense, and as he later admitted to journalist Bob Woodward, he knew it was nonsense. "This is deadly stuff," Trump told Woodward in March 2020, only a month after he blew his stack about Messonnier. He wanted to "play it down," he said to Woodward, to avoid a panic.[12]

But panic was already engulfing the country—and the White House. The day after the Messonnier briefing, Trump announced that Vice President Mike Pence would lead the administration's pandemic efforts. (Alex Azar, the Secretary of Health and Human Services, found out about this decision only a few hours before Trump announced it.)[13] The decision itself made a certain amount of sense; presidents often toss vice presidents or other senior officials into thankless jobs, in part to show government engagement but also to insulate the president himself from missteps or setbacks. Pence, however, was at the time the ultimate Trump loyalist, and when the president put him in charge, it was a clear signal from the administration that the president viewed COVID as a political problem more than a public health issue. Meanwhile, Trump's son-in-law, Jared Kushner, set up shop with a kind of parallel crisis team, with direct (and better) access to the president.[14] The White House's efforts to rely on family and political cronies, and its insistence on downplaying the pandemic, created what the COVID Study Group called "a unique environment" in which "beleaguered public health authorities"—the experts—had to carry out their duties; worse, by May 2020, "President Trump and some of his key advisers were effectively at war with their own government."[15]

As the crisis deepened and the pandemic death toll increased, the president grew more frustrated. Trump, who has always believed that he is his own best messenger, soon decided that he could basically argue his way out of the pandemic. He began holding very long press conferences in the late afternoon that were less about COVID than they were an indulging of his tendency to talk, off the cuff and at great length, about whatever was bothering him at any given moment. Trump argued with reporters, slammed Democratic governors, and gave medically unsound advice. (For a time, he touted hydroxychloroquine, an anti-malarial drug that is useless against COVID, based on a "feeling" that it might prevent infection.)[16]

In April 2020, Trump's belief that he should be speaking to the nation almost every day (or perhaps that the nation should be *listening to him* every day) led to his now-infamous comments about possible cures. Speaking to his subordinates in the room with him, he said:

> So, supposing we hit the body with a tremendous—whether it's ultraviolet or just very powerful light—and I think you said that that hasn't been checked, but you're going to test it. And then I said, supposing you brought the light inside the body, which you can do either through the skin or in some other way, and I think you said you're going to test that, too. It sounds interesting. And then I see the disinfectant, where it knocks it out in a minute. One minute. And is there a way we can do something like that, by injection inside or almost a cleaning. Because you see it gets in the lungs, and it does a tremendous number on the lungs. So it would be interesting to check that.[17]

Sitting nearby, Dr. Deborah Birx, a physician, career military officer, and ambassador who was at the time serving on Trump's COVID task force, was visibly uncomfortable. ("I didn't know how to handle that episode," she said months later. "I still think about it every day.")[18] Some of Trump's aides, worried that he did not understand the briefing he'd been given just before going onstage, were worried about what the president might say in public. "A few of us tried to stop it in the West Wing hallway," said one former senior official. "But I lost, and it went how it did."[19]

Shortly after this cringe-inducing moment, Trump soon ceased doing such briefings, reportedly because aides finally made him understand that they had become politically damaging. The president, for his part, blamed "the Lamestream Media" for asking only "hostile questions" and stomping on his efforts to communicate with the American people.[20]

Trump was not alone in politicizing the pandemic and damaging faith in government. The New York City area, as a densely populated international hub, was hit early and hard by COVID, and New York Governor Andrew Cuomo generated a great deal of praise (including, at the time, from me) early in the pandemic when he appeared regularly on television to give briefings in exactly the calm, assured, and empathetic tone that Trump lacked. Cuomo, however, made the lethal mistake of requiring nursing homes to accept COVID patients from hospitals in order to clear beds for incoming cases. The result was a wave of fatalities among the elderly—among the most vulnerable to the disease—in those facilities. Cuomo and his aides then tried to cover up this disastrous policy choice by fudging the numbers and underreporting the elderly deaths, according a later New York State audit, by some 50 percent. "The public," according to the audit, "was misled by those at the highest level of state government through distortion and suppression of the facts when New Yorkers deserved the truth."[21]

The nursing home disaster did not stop Cuomo from trying to turn the pandemic to his personal and political advantage. In March 2020, when Cuomo's response to the crisis was already generating presidential nomination buzz, a publisher reached out to the governor about a book project. Cuomo signed a deal for a book to be delivered before the 2020 election (of course) worth more than five million dollars—and then set his aides to work on writing it. Not only was the book project a distraction during a time of crisis, but a report later commissioned by the New York legislature found that the deal likely influenced the underreporting of elderly deaths.[22]

Cuomo's attempts to hide his early mistakes were disgraceful and especially damaging from a leader who purported to be a fearless advocate for science but who mostly seemed to be a fearless advocate for Andrew Cuomo. In the end, the governor got to keep the money, but not his office. He resigned in 2021 over a scandal not about COVID, but about sexual harassment.

Back in Washington, Trump and his team multiplied and compounded their errors. As part of their effort to change the national dialogue away from the administration's response, the president and his supporters soon turned to scapegoating, blaming China for the pandemic, and turning a scientific question into a political debate that continued long after Trump left office. Initially, the president praised China's cooperation—itself an odd position, because Beijing was hardly forthcoming about the crisis that began in the city of Wuhan. Trump, however, soon turned on the Chinese, referring to COVID as "the China virus"; by June 2020 he was calling it "the Kung Flu." The authoritarian Chinese regime deserved (and still deserves) plenty of criticism for its secretiveness about the origins of the pandemic, but Trump and his supporters were trying to deflect blame for the poor American response onto the Chinese, including the use of racially offensive jokes.

Arguing over Chinese culpability early in 2020 was like arguing about who was responsible for a plane crash while the wreckage was still burning and injured people were still trapped in the fuselage, but Trump's fellow Republicans were eager to get the president out from under responsibility for the pandemic's growing toll. Trump's allies used the well-worn tactic of "just asking questions" to spread a narrative meant to take the heat off Trump and move it to China.

As early as February 2020, for example, Republican Senator Tom Cotton of Arkansas, in a conversation with Fox Business anchor Maria Bartiromo, said that he was certain that the virus did not originate from meat sold in a Wuhan "wet market." He then mentioned a nearby laboratory, the Wuhan Institute of Virology; Bartiromo called it a "superlab," but Cotton said it's "unclear" what the institute does, while asserting that the United States has similar labs "run by our military."[23] The implication was clear: COVID was possibly a biological weapon that somehow got away from Chinese government researchers. When Bartiromo noted the protests of China's ambassador to the United States that Cotton was making accusations about "biological warfare," Cotton said: "The burden of proof right now is on the Chinese Communist Party, the ambassador of China, and his fellow communists."

That's not how burdens of proof work, either in logic or in law, but Cotton was using a classic "motte and bailey" form of rhetoric when discussing COVID's origins. (A "motte and bailey" method, drawn from a metaphor about how castles were once constructed, places an extreme accusation next to a more reasonable position, allowing the debater later to express disingenuous dismay that anyone could have confused the two.) The senator, after leaving the implication of a bioweapon metaphorically hanging in the air, quickly took to Twitter to list various other possibilities for the origins of the pandemic, including "deliberate release," which he said was "very unlikely" but shouldn't be ruled out.[24] Democrats—and some experts—took the bait, making their own extreme case in which any notion of a lab leak was pure conspiracy theorizing. Not only was the lab-leak theory wrong, they argued, but it was racist and off-limits politically, socially, and scientifically.[25]

The current scientific consensus still supports the "zoonotic" theory of the pandemic's origins (meaning they believe that COVID somehow jumped from animals to humans). But because of politics and distrust of the scientific community—some of it, as we will see, justly earned—most people around the world have now embraced the lab-leak theory. As science writer David Quammen noted in 2023, "various factors" influenced the public, but "a preponderance of empirical evidence is not one of them"; instead, the lab-leak story gained traction based on "cynicism and narrative appeal."[26]

On October 2, 2020, Trump announced that he and the First Lady had tested positive for COVID. The president, in respiratory distress, was admitted to Walter Reed Medical Center later that day. Rather than use his illness to impress the seriousness of the disease on his followers, Trump stage-managed his hospital stay; according to one report, once Trump was stable enough to leave the hospital, he wanted to appear on the steps and open his shirt to reveal a Superman emblem.[27] (Trump apparently got the idea from watching entertainer James Brown. Aides, for once, prevailed and squelched this inane idea.) Instead, Trump returned the White House, climbed the stairs to the South Portico balcony, and immediately took off his mask, despite visibly struggling to breathe.

Trump and the right-wing media made pandemic measures into political symbols; Trump, especially, treated standard pandemic responses as a sign of weakness. Trump's allies on Fox News assisted in this politicization, railing against masks and lockdowns and pushing dubious treatments like hydroxychloroquine. (Fox chairman Rupert Murdoch, however, took every precaution. "He was scared for himself and was very careful," according to a person who spoke to Murdoch during the pandemic.)[28]

Trump's most fervent supporters in politics and in the media remain hostile to such measures, not least because Trump continued his crude pandering in his second bid to regain the American presidency. When new variants of the virus began to spread in the summer of 2023, Trump released a video decrying "tyrants" who were going to impose new pandemic mandates. "We will not comply," he said, defying measures that did not actually exist. Fortunately, most people in the United States are vaccinated, and governments at all levels have learned a great deal about monitoring and treating the disease. Nonetheless, as the COVID Crisis Group noted in 2023, "one key predictor of infections and total COVID deaths" in each state during the pandemic "was the share of people that voted for President Trump in the 2020 presidential election."

Or, as a member of the group noted simply about the course of the pandemic and the American lives lost: "Trump was a comorbidity."[29]

THE EXPERTS BECOME POLITICIANS

The history of the fight to stop COVID is replete with stories of medical heroism from medical professionals at every level. But where the death of expertise is concerned, the scientific community and its allies in the public policy arena made two fundamental mistakes early in the pandemic. One is that they tried to take the place of elected officials as they attempted to fill the vacuum left by poor leadership in the nation's capital and other regions of the United States. The other is that doctors, along with local authorities, made nakedly political calculations about who should be allowed to flout pandemic restrictions—and when.

Masks and Lockdowns

No one likes wearing a mask. They're inconvenient and uncomfortable—especially if they're high-quality and properly fitted. They impede a host of normal human interactions based on the ability to see the faces of other people and hear them clearly when they speak. And no one likes being a prisoner in their own home. But some masks prevent the transmission of certain kinds of disease, and sometimes the only way to stop the spread of a pathogen is to prevent people from being near each other. When the pandemic picked up momentum in the United States, however, inconstancy and conflicting signals from the scientific community helped fuel charges that masks and lockdowns were rooted more in politics and panic than in science.

Part of the problem was that the experts initially misunderstood how the virus was transmitted. Did it travel through the air ("aerosol" transmission), or was it contained in small amounts of moisture ("droplet" transmission) that left the body and then fell, waiting for humans to touch the infected surfaces? The difference matters: If the virus can linger in the air and proximity is the key, then the best measures would involve avoiding indoor group activities and keeping a distance from other people in general. If the virus is trapped in little globs of moisture, however, then strict hygiene is essential. Scientists, including those at the World Health Organization, initially got this wrong—COVID is an airborne threat—which is why the pandemic continued to spread even as hand sanitizers vanished from panic-buying and Americans spent weeks wiping down their groceries.

Worse, the medical experts were slow to change their minds in the face of emerging evidence of airborne COVID transmission. The mistake about "aerosols versus droplets," in the words of writer Zeynep Tufekci, provided "a fascinating sociological window into how science can get it wrong and why," a story worth a book in itself.[30] It was also a mistake that cost precious time, because the scientists, stubbornly stuck on the droplet model, at first did not realize how many asymptomatic but infected people were spreading the virus.

As the medical professionals came to realize the danger of airborne transmission, Anthony Fauci (at the time the director of the National Institute for Allergy and Infectious Diseases) and other prominent experts realized that such news could spark a public run on masks, which in turn could inflict devastating shortages on the health care workers who needed them. And so they tried to manage public anxieties and steer people away from trying to get masks. Neither Fauci nor Birx early on advocated for mask-wearing; in

February 2020, the US Surgeon General, Jerome Adams, tweeted out: "Seriously people—STOP BUYING MASKS!"[31]

The medical community changed course in the spring of 2020, after which they were predictably accused by many in the public of mendacity and flip-flopping (especially in the binary world of social media).[32] The more basic problem, however, is that preventing panic and averting a mask shortage isn't the job of expert advisers. Asked in May 2020 why he wore a mask in public, Fauci answered that he did it "to protect myself and protect others," but also "because I want to make it be a symbol for people to see that that's the kind of thing you should be doing."[33] Admirable, perhaps, but such statements should have come from elected leaders after they have conferred with experts; they should, in tandem with their advisers, explain the risks and requirements of such problems to the public and then lead the nation in modeling the behavior they'd like to see in others.

The problem for the medical experts, of course, is that Trump wanted no part of any of that. He continued to resist any mask-wearing of any kind, despite polls eventually showing that even a majority of Republicans soon accepted the necessity of at least some sort of mask requirement. In a July 2020 White House meeting, Kushner advised Trump to support mask mandates. Chief of Staff Mark Meadows objected. "We can't do the masks," he told the president. "The base will just turn on you." Trump agreed, thus undermining Republican state and local officials who could not afford to be seen as bucking their own leader on this issue.[34]

The scientists unwisely stepped into this breach with predictable results. The American public has little tolerance for complexity, but the recommendations on mask-wearing were difficult to parse even for the most well-intentioned citizens. What kind of mask would work best? (An N-95 respirator, properly and consistently worn—if you could find one and knew how to put it on.) What about surgical or cloth masks, or even a bandanna? Would they work? (Probably not very much, but they were better than nothing.) When and where should masks be worn? Everywhere, all the time? Indoors—even at home? The public wanted clear and unambiguous answers that the scientists could not give them: yes or no, safe or unsafe, masks on or masks off. The experts, still wrong-footed by their mistakes about "droplets" and woefully unaccustomed to explaining complicated issues to ordinary citizens, made a hash of the messaging and simply tried to push for "masks" as a generic measure until many Americans—even those who wanted to be cooperative—simply gave up.[35]

The same inconsistency and mixed messaging plagued the lockdown mandates. If the virus was more likely to spread indoors, then it made perfect sense in those early days to shut down everything until we knew more—especially places full of children sitting all day in close quarters. If two hours in a movie theater with strangers was a hazard, how much more of a threat was it to put kids inches away from each other for six or eight hours and then send them back and forth from their homes on crowded buses? The same logic applied to the shutdown of air travel and the consequent mask mandates on airplanes—measures that persisted despite the eventual lack of evidence that schools and airplanes were significant areas for transmission.

Once again, the problem wasn't that scientists couldn't figure this out, but rather that they were reluctant to face down both public anxieties and public anger in an atmosphere rife with bad faith and paranoia.[36] In the already polarized political environment, each side hoisted their flags and charged into battle over public health measures. Trump and his movement had coalesced around masks and lockdowns as symbols of government autocracy, but many of Trump's opponents soon adopted a blind insistence on such mandates as their own version of political signaling.

When public places began to reopen in 2021, for example, many liberals objected to removing pandemic restrictions. As the writer Emma Green observed at the time, these were the "liberals who can't quit lockdown," for whom "diligence against COVID-19 remains an expression of political identity—even when that means overestimating the disease's risks or setting limits far more strict than what public-health guidelines permit."

> For many progressives, extreme vigilance was in part about opposing Donald Trump. Some of this reaction was born of deeply felt frustration with how he handled the pandemic. It could also be knee-jerk. "If he said, 'Keep schools open,' then, well, we're going to do everything in our power to keep schools closed," Monica Gandhi, a professor of medicine at UC San Francisco, told me. Gandhi describes herself as "left of left," but has alienated some of her ideological peers because she has advocated for policies such as reopening schools and establishing a clear timeline for the end of mask mandates.[37]

Some of these measures persist in small pockets of the United States; the strangest case might be the upstate New York school whose marching band, as of 2023, is *still* playing instruments through holes in their masks—outdoors—and whose young students still observe masked "silent lunches."[38]

The mask and lockdown advocates argued that they had the stronger point in a time of great uncertainty. Prophylactic measures, they contended, even if ragged and inconsistent, were less dangerous than flatly ignoring visible public health dangers. But "following the science" means following *all* of the science, and these rigid, dogmatic responses downplayed the fact that science was also showing that some COVID policies did, in fact, carry a destructive price. The lockdowns, as the COVID Study Group wrote later, were not a solution, but a "blunt sledgehammer" that took the place of better preparation; they were instituted as the result of an inability to agree on almost anything else. Trump was infuriatingly ignorant, but many of his opponents, too, were soon adopting positions based on their political preferences and tribal alliances rather than on a dispassionate assessment of risk.

Overall, the American public tends to be unwilling to accept nuance in public policy—not that there was much to be had in the guidance coming from Washington or from various states and localities. The federal structure of the United States, a bulwark against excessive national power, is also an obstacle to the short-term implementation of cooperative national solutions. In more cohesive societies such as Germany and South Korea, more cohesive cultures and different government structures helped to mitigate the impact of pandemic measures; American experts and public officials, however, were (in the words of the COVID Crisis Group) trapped in a debate that posited a "false choice between public health and economic health."[39]

The extended closure of public spaces in the United States produced deep social and economic wounds, especially in large cities, but the greatest damage may have been done in public schools. The controversy over when to reopen schools was a particularly important area of expert failure in the United States. (Many nations made the decision to close schools; most reopened sooner than in America.) People can weather slowdowns and recessions and bankruptcies, especially if the government is willing to step in with aid, but they will draw a much harder line on damage to their children. The closures of educational institutions went on too long in many parts of the United States, resulting in emotional and intellectual damage to American students.

On this issue, too, liberals and many local public health officials dug in, partly as a matter of sheer obstinacy. "Getting liberals to reverse their position on school closures was not easy," as Jonathan Chait wrote later.

> Economist Emily Oster, one of the first figures to publish data showing schools were not a major vector for COVID transmission, became a hate figure on the left. Many progressive activists bitterly contested growing evidence both that in-person schooling was relatively safe and that school closures had created catastrophic learning loss.[40]

Again, this was in many cases a stubborn reaction, a kind of reflexive opposition to people who doubted the need for any pandemic measures at all. "But the evidence," as Chait noted, "did eventually win out," while the Republicans descended into an "epistemic disaster" that persists to this day.

Unfortunately, the evidence did not win out in time. "In the chaotic early months of the pandemic, teachers were celebrated as essential workers, heroically continuing to serve America's children from their homes, often with limited resources and inadequate technology," a *New York Times* profile of Randi Weingarten, the president of the American Federation of Teachers (AFT), observed in 2023.

> But during the summer of 2020, things started to shift. There was already early research showing that students were suffering academically from remote learning. Schools across Europe had begun reopening without any major outbreaks, and many of America's private and parochial schools were making plans to resume in-person learning at the start of the new school year. A lot of public-school parents wanted their children to be back in the classroom, too. But many teachers seemed resistant to the idea.[41]

Their unions were even more resistant to the idea, to the point of militancy. In 2020, Weingarten's AFT proposed a reopening plan that included "adequate personal protective equipment, a temporary suspension of formal teacher performance evaluations, a limit on student testing, a cancellation of student-loan debt and a $750 billion federal aid package to help schools prepare to reopen safely." This wasn't even close to a realistic plan to reopen schools, and yet Weingarten warned in July 2020 that the AFT might support strikes if teachers were forced back to the classroom.

The pressure from the AFT had a clear effect on national policy. Within weeks of taking office in 2021, President Joe Biden called Weingarten and told her: "I am not abandoning you on schools. I want you to know that." He then backpedaled on his campaign promises to get the schools open. "Biden," according to the writer Franklin Foer, "wanted to ease the unions into accepting his goals, avoiding that sort of confrontation that might explode in a strike."

> For the sake of avoiding conflict, especially conflict with an ally, the Biden administration trimmed its goal of returning kids to school to a fraction of what had been promised on the campaign trail. The announcement came as an aside in a press conference. [Press Secretary] Jen Psaki explained that Biden had really meant that he wanted more than half of the pre-K-to-8 schools to attend at least one in-person session a week by the end of his first hundred days. He was, in effect, conceding that for thousands of students, the rest of the school year would be lost to the pandemic.[42]

Biden, in this account, saw his job as restoring calm after Trump had turned the pandemic into a national conflict, a mission that included avoiding a possible strike by the teachers. But that meant effectively writing off the rest of academic year 2021. As Foer noted simply about Biden's eventual acquiescence: "It was the price of peace."

The furious reactions among heavily Democratic teacher unions to plans for reopening American schools were difficult to separate from antipathy to Trump, but partisanship is no excuse for malpractice. As the Weingarten profile pointed out, a Brown University study found that Democratic school districts, "with correspondingly strong teachers' unions, returned to in-person learning more slowly and gradually than Republican districts with weaker unions." In the spring of 2021, Weingarten changed course and affirmed that the AFT was committed to school openings in 2022—thus publicly ratifying Biden's surrender—but too late to avert the damage done to students, or to the reputation of their teachers.

The concerns of the teachers were, in many cases, understandable fears about safety, but the earlier intransigence of some of their union leaders did significant harm, at least in the short term, to their already battered standing as educators. In the summer of 2020, however, another expert community—this time the medical professionals—embraced one of the greatest self-inflicted wounds to the cause of expertise of the entire pandemic.

The Summer of George Floyd

On May 25, 2020, a White police officer murdered a Black man named George Floyd during an arrest in Minneapolis. The incident was captured on video and protests soon broke out all over the United States, as Americans of every race and heritage reacted with rage and horror against the brutality in the images from Minnesota.

Doctors and scientists had a problem on their hands. The killing of George Floyd produced an outpouring of grief and anger that would not be denied. Americans wanted to gather, they wanted to support each other, they wanted to vent their fury, and they wanted to shout their demands for justice into the face of their government. And yet because of COVID restrictions, most Americans could not congregate in public. They could not go to church or sing in a choir. They could not celebrate their marriages, bury their dead, or gather for a picnic. They were whipsawed by various ordinances, including some that required masks even outdoors. American schoolchildren were still trapped in their homes, trying to learn through glowing screens.

America's cities were beginning to boil, and public safety officials faced a no-win situation because there were no good answers: If states and localities tried to suppress the demonstrations, their directions would be ignored. But if they allowed the protests, they were admitting that restrictions were capricious rules that could bend in the political wind. How could one cause be important enough to allow thousands upon thousands of people to gather in close proximity, while all other citizens were told that *their* rights—including their freedom to worship and to engage in peaceful assembly—were secondary to the needs of public health and that they must stay home?

Fauci, who would later enter right-wing demonology caricatured as a leftist authoritarian, gave one of the most diplomatic and sensible answers to be found among the scientists:

> It's a difficult situation. We have the right to peacefully demonstrate and the demonstrators are exercising that right. . . . It's a delicate balance because the reasons for demonstrating are valid and yet the demonstration itself puts oneself at an additional risk. The only thing we can do as public health officials is to keep warning people to be careful. And if you are going out to please make sure you wear a mask and you keep the mask on at all times.[43]

Wisely, Fauci refused to be drawn into the political issue of Floyd's death, despite repeated baiting by Republican Representative Jim

Jordan of Ohio during a congressional hearing in the summer of 2020: "I'm not favoring anybody over anybody," Fauci told Jordan, who repeatedly interrupted him. "I'm just making a statement that is a broad statement, [to] avoid crowds of any type, no matter where you are, because that leads to the acquisition and transmission."[44]

Other doctors, however, were eager to show solidarity with the protests. Almost 1,300 medical professionals signed an open letter supporting the demonstrations, casting Floyd's death as a health crisis itself, on the same level as the pandemic. "Infectious disease and public health narratives," they wrote, "adjacent to demonstrations against racism must be consciously anti-racist, and infectious disease experts must be clear and consistent in prioritizing an anti-racist message. White supremacy is a lethal public health issue that predates and contributes to COVID-19." As one of the letter's signatories said later, "the way forward is not to suppress protests in the name of public health but to respond to protesters [sic] demands in the name of public health, thereby addressing multiple public health crises."[45]

Noble (and stilted) rhetoric, but even people who empathized with the protesters had to notice that the previous strict prohibitions on gathering were now, for the sake of an important political cause, apparently negotiable. Ranu S. Dhillon, an infectious-disease expert at Harvard Medical School, told the *Washington Post* that he viewed the protests "as risky but necessary—just like working in a nursing home or grocery store," a comment that showed how utterly out of touch many professionals were with ordinary people who were afraid to visit elderly relatives or go to the market.[46] Jeffrey Flier, the former dean of Harvard Medical School, made a pointed observation to *Politico* in June 2020: "Many public health experts have already severely undermined the power and influence of their prior message . . . Covid death counts, and infections [and] deaths were presented as preeminent concerns compared to all other considerations—until nine days ago."[47]

The available evidence does not so far suggest that the protests created a major surge in COVID infections, but to argue that the demonstrations did not result in more infections is a post-hoc rationalization—and, for experts, a trap. At the time, medical guidance was clear that people should not gather in large groups or be in close proximity, and certainly not while singing and shouting. Thus, if the doctors believed that the risks of such gatherings could be mitigated with masks or by being outdoors, they should have already been pressing for the lifting of the strictest measures everywhere with the same advice they gave the protesters. If, however, they were still holding to the theories that underpinned the lockdowns—and especially the school closures—then their approval of the demonstrations meant they were consciously setting aside those concerns in the name of a cause with which they agreed. Either way, they were acting as political advocates rather than scientists, and in the words of retired environmental scientist Peter Sandman, they "clearly damaged the credibility of public health as a scientific enterprise that struggles to be politically neutral."[48]

THE NEEDLES AND THE DAMAGE DONE

The global pandemic emergency is formally over, but in the United States the political damage from the COVID wars remains. The most intrusive measures, including lockdowns and masking, are long gone. The experts, as they should, are assessing what they did right and wrong. In 2022, the director of the Centers for Disease Control, Rochelle Walensky, ordered a full review of the CDC's performance. "To be frank," Walensky said at the time, "we are responsible for some pretty dramatic, pretty public mistakes, from testing to data to communications," and she called for a major reorganization of the agency.[49] The report was not yet released as of mid-2023, when Walensky left government service.

The larger problem, as the COVID Study Group noted, is that the CDC functions as it does because it was set up that way by the American legislature.

> Even if CDC tried to reform, so much of what it did was administer programs and processes mandated by Congress, with little discretion to make policy. . . . The deep issue is that the CDC's culture *reasonably reflects the role and missions Congress has granted to it.*[50] [emphasis added]

The CDC may well be poorly organized but for the CDC—or any other government agency—to change, they need to receive a new charge from the people, as expressed through their elected representatives.

Unfortunately, many American citizens are still fighting over everything from Chinese labs to vaccines. For most Americans, especially the elderly and other vulnerable groups, avoiding the most serious consequences of COVID is a matter of getting vaccinated and staying current on booster shots—in other words, taking the same measures they take against the flu, pneumonia, and other health hazards. And yet, the United States still lags the rest of the developed world in protection against COVID. As of late 2023, some 70 percent of Americans have had an initial vaccination, but fewer than 20 percent have had any kind of booster. The rates are much better among people over sixty-five, who for various reasons (including the increased danger of death in their age group) are more attentive to getting vaccinated.[51] In neighboring Canada, however, the vaccination and booster rate for everyone five years and older are both more than 80 percent, while in South Korea, vaccination is now almost universal, with initial shot and booster rates among adults at more than 95 percent.

The overall numbers, however, obscure the deep political divisions in the United States over vaccination and general COVID preventive measures. As a study by the Global Health Program of the Council on Foreign Relations put it, in the United States "COVID-19 exploited and compounded existing local racial inequities, health disparities, and partisan politics."[52] New England approaches Canadian levels of vaccination; rates along the route from Boston to my small county in Rhode Island hover near 80 percent (although boosters, once again, are lagging). Move to the American South and West, however, and the numbers tell the story of continuing antipathy to vaccinations. At the end of 2022, the states with the worst levels of vaccination—all well below 60 percent even for the first shot— were Wyoming, Alabama, Mississippi, Louisiana, and Tennessee. The death rate (that is, deaths adjusted for population size) were the worst in Arizona, Washington, D.C., and New Mexico, followed by Mississippi, Colorado, and Idaho. Put another way, the pandemic in the states of Vermont, Utah, and Washington resulted in death rates similar to those of Denmark, Switzerland, and Germany, while Mississippi, Arizona, and West Virginia were similar to three nations with the highest death rates in the world during the same period: Russia, Bulgaria, and Peru.[53]

Unfortunately, much of the American right for the foreseeable future seems likely to remain firmly in the grip of an anti-science and anti-expertise mindset that predates COVID but that found in the pandemic a cause to turn ignorance into generic anti-establishment radicalism.[54] A *New York Times/Siena* poll of Republicans in 2023 found that nearly 70 percent of likely GOP voters would trust "the common sense of ordinary people" over "the knowledge of trained experts."[55] (In 2022, 52 percent of Americans said that public health officials had done an excellent or good job at managing the pandemic, but that number was anchored by the 72 percent of Democrats who felt that way; only 29 percent of Republicans agreed.)[56] Likewise,

Robert F. Kennedy, Jr., initially ran for president as a Democrat, but he was far more popular among Republican voters—and donors.[57] Nonetheless, his brief political ascendance is a warning of hard times ahead for science and established knowledge.

During the 2024 presidential election, even candidates challenging Trump, such as Florida Governor Ron DeSantis, emulated his attacks on science. DeSantis, like many Republicans who adopted the protective coloration of populism, is a highly educated man, and he was an early advocate of stringent pandemic measures. He supported restrictions on public gatherings (for which the Trump campaign later nicknamed him "Lockdown Ron"), praised Fauci, and pushed Floridians to get vaccinated.[58] But as his presidential aspirations grew in 2021, he reversed course, attacking Fauci and denying that he ever supported such measures. "Tapping into suspicion of public health authorities, which the Republican right was fanning," a 2023 *New York Times* analysis noted, "he effectively stopped preaching the virtues of Covid vaccines. Instead, he emphasized his opposition to requiring anyone to get shots, from hospital workers to cruise ship guests."[59]

DeSantis's about-face showed the power of public messaging. Florida's lead in vaccinations soon evaporated, and when the Delta variant of the virus swept the country in the summer of 2021, Florida suffered a disproportionate number of COVID deaths.[60] DeSantis then fired his state's surgeon general (who was critical of the governor's new policies) and replaced him with the politically more convenient Dr. Joseph Ladapo, a well-known COVID vaccine skeptic. Ladapo was the perfect appointee for the new era of the death of expertise; an early advocate for hydroxychloroquine, he was later accused of personally cherry-picking data to make COVID vaccines seem dangerous to young men.[61] In September 2023, Ladapo advised all Floridians under sixty-five years of age to avoid the new booster shots recommended by the US government. DeSantis supported his surgeon general, saying: "I will not stand by and let the FDA and CDC use healthy Floridians as guinea pigs for new booster shots that have not been proven to be safe or effective."[62]

COVID was tailor-made for an era of declining faith in expertise. It came from uncertain origins inside an authoritarian nation, its effects varied across populations, and its transmission was initially not well understood. Each uncertainty produced understandable fear in ordinary people. But for others—particularly those who could turn the pandemic into a partisan hammer, or who found new fame as self-appointed oracles to a terrified public—these uncertainties were a godsend. When the experts were wrong about something, angry ignoramuses could bellow that such failures were proof that doctors and public health officials knew nothing and were a symptom of a cosseted elite who should be overthrown. When the experts were proven right about anything, overbearing busybodies demanded that the public must unfailingly obey every rule, no matter how poorly conceived, and endure any costs, economic or otherwise, in the name of "science."

The experts failed at some important points during the COVID crisis. But much of what the public believed to be "failure" was *science*, as experts worked through a new problem with limited data. They argued and tested competing explanations and solutions. Such debates and discussions, along with the inevitable costs of trial and error during a time of emergency, are the normal processes of scientific investigation. But the political environment in the United States in early 2020 virtually guaranteed that almost all aspects of the pandemic response—both failures and successes—would become divisive and partisan issues.

Conclusion

Experts and Democracy

A people who mean to be their own Governors must arm themselves with the power which knowledge gives.

James Madison

I reserve the right to be ignorant. That's the Western way of life.

The Spy Who Came In from the Cold

"THE EXPERTS ARE TERRIBLE"

During the 2016 "Brexit" debate over whether the United Kingdom
should leave the European Union, advocates of leaving the EU specifically identified experts—most of whom were warning that Brexit
was a terrible idea—as enemies of the ordinary voter. A leader in
the Brexit movement, Michael Gove, argued that facts were not as
important as the feelings of the British voter. "I think people in this
country," he sniffed, "have had enough of experts." Interrupted mid-
sentence, Gove tried to clarify, adding that he was referring to experts
from "organizations with acronyms, saying that they know what is
best and getting it consistently wrong."

But as an American writer and foreign policy expert, James Traub,
later noted about Gove's sniping,

The word "expert" is, of course, the pejorative term for someone who knows what he or she is talking about—like Gove, I imagine, who graduated from Oxford and spent years as a minister in Conservative Party governments. What Gove was actually saying was that people should be free to build gratifying fantasies free from unpleasant facts.[1]

Nigel Farage, the leader of the nativist United Kingdom Independence Party, even suggested that the "experts" were on the take, working for the British government or in the pay of the European Union itself.[2] In June 2016, the "leave" vote won with just under 52 percent of the vote in a national referendum.

The attack on the experts was part of a strategy meant to capitalize on the political illiteracy of a fair number of British voters and their instinctive mistrust of the educated and urban elites who overwhelmingly opposed Brexit. The strategy worked, and the United Kingdom finally left the EU in 2020. But the results of Brexit itself validated the warnings of the experts; within two years, Britain's economy was one of the poorest performers in the G-20. In June 2023, the *Guardian* columnist Jonathan Freeland wrote: "We don't need to rehearse on this seventh anniversary all the ways in which Brexit has disappointed even those who voted for it." The "Leavers," he noted,

> promised increased prosperity, cheaper food, flourishing trade and a flush NHS. They said we'd be free of all that tedious European red tape and would take back control of our borders, encouraging anyone agitated by immigration to believe that fewer people would come in. There would be no downside, only upsides....
>
> Look around to see how all that turned out.[3]

That same month, *The Economist* reported that multiple polls all showed that "sizeable majorities of Britons now regret the decision to leave the European Union," with this "Bregret" reaching margins as high as 60–40 against the original decision.[4]

The resentfulness of the uneducated against the ostensible "elites" has likewise become a mainstay of American politics. The rise of Donald Trump firmly embedded anti-intellectualism and the consequent distrust of expertise in a broad swath of American voters. During his first campaign, Trump explicitly campaigned against experts. "They say, 'Oh, Trump doesn't have experts,'" Trump told a 2016 rally crowd. "You know, I've always wanted to say this. . . . The experts are terrible. They say, 'Donald Trump needs a foreign policy adviser.' . . . But supposing I didn't have one. Would it be worse than what we're doing now?"[5]

As the next four years showed, it was in fact worse. With few exceptions (the Abraham Accords normalizing relations between Israel, the United Arab Emirates, and Bahrain, along with Operation Warp Speed would be among them), Trump and his advisers bungled a series of major policy challenges, from North Korean nuclear weapons to immigration. Americans might have lost trust in experts, but they soon tired of Trump's relentless drama and narcissism, and he lost the 2020 election by seven million votes and 74 electoral votes. Nonetheless, Trump's sneering at experts outlasted him; the former president tapped into a long-standing American belief that experts and intellectuals are not only running the lives of ordinary people, but also doing a lousy job of it. Representative Jim Jordan of Ohio, a Republican Trump ally, sounded like a Midwestern Michael Gove when he said in 2023: "You know what Americans can't stand? You know what they can't stand about this town? So-called experts. The unelected experts who try to run our lives."[6] Win or lose in 2024, Trump made this message stick, and it is now a part of American life.

When I first wrote about Trump in the 2017 edition of *The Death of Expertise*, I was willing to believe that Trump's political base did not hold him accountable for his ignorance and errors because they lacked the ability to see his errors as actual mistakes. At the time, I quoted psychologist David Dunning—who along with his colleague Justin Kruger discovered the Dunning-Kruger Effect—when he noted that "some voters, especially those facing significant distress in their life, might like some of what they hear from Trump, but they do not know enough to hold him accountable for the serious gaffes he makes."[7]

Today, we have to reconsider that view. Just as many of Brexit's "Leavers" remain strongly in favor of their vote, many Americans who support Trump have doubled down on their loyalty, at levels that now suggest a cult-like following rather than political support.

In Trump (and other celebrities, such as Elon Musk and Robert F. Kennedy, Jr.), the American public has found public figures who indulge their paranoia about shadowy forces ruining their lives. Citizens feel they *know* these celebrities and can trust them. Social scientists call such attachments "parasocial relationships," in which people feel a deep personal connection to famous people who, in the main, have no idea who they are. Parasocial relationships are not new; the term was first coined in the 1950s and can describe any kind of fandom, from Beatlemania to adoration of political leaders, in which ordinary people come to believe they know and are connected to celebrities.[8] Extreme cases can turn to stalking, but for most people, some sense of "knowing" famous people is a normal part of public media and entertainment. A good example is the famous mid-twentieth-century news anchor Walter Cronkite, a man so trusted in public life that his nickname in much of America was "Uncle Walter."

In the twenty-first century, however, people can gorge on endless hours of videos and podcasts and other media, and literally spend entire days immersed in these parasocial relationships. Trump, among others, exploited this by presenting himself as a friend, a protector, and the only source of facts and truth against the "fake news," but other celebrities have followed the same formula. Experts, meanwhile, are faceless and forbidding. They do not live their lives and conduct their work in public. They are not flashy or interesting, and they cannot compete with well-known public figures (such as a president) who insist that intellectual ability is itself a suspicious characteristic in a national leader. When it comes to science and health advice, why listen to some white-jacketed nerd when you can hear from Gwyneth Paltrow, Joe Rogan, or even President Donald J. Trump?

As I noted in 2017, American political elites and their intellectual allies are distrusted because their own actions encourage many voters to think the worst of them. At the time, I discussed (and remain appalled by) an interview that Barack Obama's Deputy National Security Adviser, Ben Rhodes, gave to David Samuels of the *New York Times Magazine* about the administration's controversial plan to make a nuclear deal with Iran. Rhodes proudly identified think tanks, experts, and journalists who he claimed were part of the administration's press for the deal:

> "We created an echo chamber," he admitted, when I asked him to explain the onslaught of freshly minted experts cheerleading for the deal. "They were saying things that validated what we had given them to say."
>
> When I asked whether the prospect of this same kind of far-reaching spin campaign being run by a different administration is something that scares him, he admitted that it does. "I mean, I'd prefer a sober, reasoned public debate, after which members of Congress reflect and take a vote," he said, shrugging. "But that's impossible."[9]

Rhodes, in effect, bragged that the deal with Iran was sold by warping the debate among the experts themselves, and by taking advantage of the fact that the new media, and especially the younger journalists now taking over national reporting, wouldn't know any better. "The average reporter we talk to is 27 years old, and their only reporting experience consists of being around political campaigns," Rhodes said. "That's a sea change. They literally know nothing."

I was especially concerned that Samuels had a good point about how policymakers like Rhodes weren't thinking ahead to the dangers of *other* elites (who replace each other in power in a democracy) simply deciding to short-circuit any public debate for things they, too, wanted to do. A few years later, the warning Samuels gave to Rhodes became a reality on the very same issue of Iran. Trump campaigned against the Iran deal—with plenty of shallow rhetoric and no real interest in a policy debate—and once he was in office, he simply pulled America out of it, with a consequent increase in tensions with Iran, a hit to American diplomatic credibility, and far less ability to influence the course of the Iranian nuclear program.[10] Trump likewise pulled out of the Intermediate-Range Nuclear Forces Treaty with virtually no discussion, destroying a longstanding cornerstone of nuclear stability between the United States and Russia.[11]

There is plenty of blame to go around for the parlous state of the role of expertise in American life, and this book has apportioned much of it. Experts themselves, as well as educators, journalists, corporate entertainment media, and others, have all played their part. In the end, however, there is only one group of people who must bear the ultimate responsibility for this current state of affairs, and only they can change any of it: the citizens of the United States of America.

EXPERTISE AND DEMOCRACY: THE DEATH SPIRAL

Expertise and government rely upon each other, especially in a democracy. The technological and economic progress that ensures the well-being of a population requires the division of labor, which in turn leads to the creation of professions. Professionalism encourages experts to do their best in serving their clients, to respect their own boundaries, and to demand their boundaries be respected by others, as part of an overall service to the ultimate client: society itself.

Dictatorships, too, demand this same service of experts, but they extract it by threat and direct its use by command. This is why dictatorships are less efficient and less productive than democracies, despite the historical myths many Americans continue to believe about the putative efficiency of Nazi Germany and other such regimes.[12] In a democracy, the expert's service to the public is part of the social contract. Citizens delegate the power of decision on myriad issues to elected representatives and their expert advisers, while experts, for their part, ask that their efforts be received in good faith by a public that has informed itself enough to make reasoned judgments.

The relationship between experts and citizens, like almost all relationships in a democracy, is built on trust. When that trust collapses, experts and laypeople become warring factions. And when that happens, democracy itself can enter a death spiral that presents an immediate danger of decay either into rule by the mob or toward elitist technocracy. Both are authoritarian outcomes, and both threaten the United States today.

This is why the collapse of the relationship between experts and citizens is a dysfunction of democracy itself. The abysmal literacy, both political and general, of the American public is the foundation for all of these problems. It is the soil in which the other dysfunctions have taken root and prospered.

As the writer Susan Jacoby put it in 2008, the most disturbing aspect of the American march toward ignorance is "not lack of knowledge per se but arrogance about that lack of knowledge."

The problem is not just the things we do not know (consider the one in five American adults who, according to the National Science Foundation, thinks the sun revolves around the Earth); it's the alarming number of Americans who have smugly concluded that they do not need to know such things in the first place. . . . The toxic brew of anti-rationalism and ignorance hurts discussions of U.S. public policy on topics from health care to taxation.[13]

Ordinary Americans might never have liked the educated or professional classes very much, but until recently they did not widely disdain actual learning as a bad thing in itself. It might even be too kind to call this merely "anti-rational"; it is almost reverse evolution, away from tested knowledge and backward toward folk wisdom and myths passed by word of mouth—except with all of it now sent along at the speed of electrons.

This plummeting literacy and growth of willful ignorance are part of a vicious circle of disengagement between citizens and public policy. People know little and care less about how they are governed, or how their economic, scientific, or political structures function. Yet, as these processes thus become more incomprehensible, citizens feel more alienated. Overwhelmed, they turn away from education and civic involvement, and withdraw into other pursuits. This, in turn, makes them into less capable citizens, and the cycle continues and strengthens, especially when the public appetite for escape is easily fed by any number of leisure industries.

Awash in gadgets and conveniences that were once unimaginable even within their own lifetimes, Americans (and many other Westerners, if we are to be fair about it) have become almost childlike in their refusal to learn enough to govern themselves or to guide the policies that affect their lives. This is a collapse of functional citizenship, and it enables a cascade of other baleful consequences. And when these citizens must pull together—such as during the COVID pandemic—they find that they have neither the basic knowledge nor the civic reflexes to cope with a disaster that cannot be wished away or ignored.

The irony is that the same citizens who are too impatient to learn very much and who resent "the state" and its growing power are have in fact *themselves become the enablers of expert rule.*

In the absence of informed citizens, more knowledgeable administrative and intellectual elites will take over the daily direction of the state and society. In a passage often cited by Western conservatives and especially loved by American libertarians, the Austrian economist F. A. Hayek wrote in 1960: "The greatest danger to liberty today comes from the men who are most needed and most powerful in modern government, namely, the efficient expert administrators exclusively concerned with what they regard as the public good."[14]

Even the most intellectually minded thinkers across the American spectrum would agree with Hayek. Unelected bureaucrats and policy specialists in many spheres exert tremendous influence on the daily lives of Americans. Today, however, this situation is by default rather than by design. Populism reinforces this elitism because the celebration of ignorance cannot launch communications satellites, negotiate the rights of US citizens overseas, or provide for effective medications, all of which are daunting tasks even the dimmest citizens now demand and take for granted. Faced with a public that has no idea how most things work, experts likewise disengage, choosing to speak mostly to each other rather than to laypeople.

Meanwhile, Americans have increasingly unrealistic expectations of what their political and economic system can provide. This sense of entitlement is one reason they are continually angry at "experts" and especially at "elitists," a word that many people around the world use interchangeably, but that in American usage often means almost anyone with any education who refuses to coddle the public's mistaken beliefs. When told that ending poverty or preventing terrorism—or recovering from a pandemic—is a lot harder than it looks, Americans roll their eyes. Unable to comprehend the complexity around them, they choose instead to comprehend almost none of it and then sullenly blame experts, politicians, and bureaucrats for seizing control of their lives.

THE KNOWERS AND THE DECIDERS

This underscores another problem motivating the death spiral in which democracy and expertise are caught: citizens do not understand, or choose not to understand, the difference between experts and elected policymakers. For many Americans, all elites are now just an undifferentiated mass of educated, rich, and powerful people. This is patent silliness. Not all rich people are powerful, and not all powerful people are rich. Intellectuals and policy experts are seldom rich *or* powerful. (Trust me on that one.) Indeed, the super-wealthy are sometimes the worst enemies of expertise, because they find it intolerable that there are still areas of endeavor where no amount of their money can buy entry into fields that require years of acquired knowledge and experience. The continued efforts of men such as Elon Musk and his erstwhile adviser David Sacks to inject themselves into the diplomacy of the Russo-Ukraine war while knowing virtually nothing about the issue are particularly wince-inducing examples, among many.

The COVID pandemic reinforced this confusion, in part because of the mistakes of experts who tried to assume the role of policymakers, but also because of disingenuous and pusillanimous political leaders who directed the public's anger away from themselves and toward the scientists. When experienced members of Congress accused doctors such as Anthony Fauci of "running our lives" during the pandemic, they knew they were pushing risible nonsense: Fauci had no such power, and political leaders could have ignored him at will (as they eventually did). But to take responsibility is to court the consequences of leadership, and why bother taking such a risk when unelected civil servants are so easily blamed? Florida Governor Ron DeSantis was one of many who used this tactic. He praised Fauci for "doing a really good job" in early 2020, and then two years later, he said: "Someone needs to grab that little elf and chuck him across the Potomac," an especially irresponsible outburst considering that Fauci, an elderly scientist, has had to have armed security guards protecting him from unhinged threats to his safety since 2020.[15]

Whatever else George W. Bush may have gotten wrong during his presidency, he was right when he reminded Americans that when it came to the actions of his administration, he was "the decider." Experts can only propose; elected leaders dispose. In fact, policy-making experts and elected leaders are almost never the same group, and it cannot be otherwise: there are simply not enough hours in the day for a legislator, even in a city council or a small US state (and much less for a president) to master the many issues required to make policy. This is why policymakers engage experts—the knowers—to advise them.

Sometimes, this partnership between advisers and policymakers fails. Experts get things wrong, and they counsel political leaders to take courses of action that can result in disaster. Critics of the role of expertise point to national traumas like the Vietnam War as one such example. With the benefit of hindsight, these criticisms are often made as though such painful choices could have been avoided by consulting the wisdom of the common citizen.

This call to fall back on the knowledge and virtue of laypeople, however, is irresponsible romanticism. Evan Thomas, a journalist and biographer of Richard Nixon, admitted that the "best and the brightest," among them academics like Henry Kissinger and "corporate titans" like Secretary of Defense Robert S. McNamara, "were far from perfect" and that they "bear the blame for Vietnam and the 58,000 American soldiers who died there, not to mention the millions of Vietnamese."[16] But as Thomas points out, those same experts and elites "strengthened a world order balanced precariously on the edge of nuclear war. They expanded trade, deepened alliances and underwrote billions in foreign aid."

None of these policies would have been popular in and of themselves, but they helped the United States and the West to survive the Cold War and to reach its peaceful end. More important, what kinds of policies would nonexperts or populists have chosen? Thomas challenged readers to "contrast the mistakes of the 1960s to times when Washington allowed foreign policy to be set by public consensus."

> In the 1930s, Congress closed off free trade to protect American industry and listened to voters who wanted a smaller, less costly military with no entangling alliances. The results? The Smoot-Hawley tariff contributed to the Great Depression, and the failure of the League of Nations allowed the rise of fascism and global war.

This illustrates an important point: then as now, Americans tend to think about issues like macroeconomic policy or foreign affairs only when things go wrong. The rest of the time, they remain happily unaware of the policies and processes that function well every day while the nation goes about its business.

The question nonetheless remains whether America really needs all these experts, especially when their advice becomes so spread out over so many people that no one seems responsible when disaster strikes. Andrew Bacevich, for one, has called for vanquishing the modern expert class, at least in public policy:

Policy intellectuals—eggheads presuming to instruct the mere mortals who actually run for office—are a blight on the republic. Like some invasive species, they infest present-day Washington, where their presence strangles common sense and has brought to the verge of extinction the simple ability to perceive reality. A benign appearance—well-dressed types testifying before Congress, pontificating in print and on TV, or even filling key positions in the executive branch—belies a malign impact. They are like Asian carp let loose in the Great Lakes.[17]

The irony here is that Bacevich himself is a prolific author, a former senior military officer, and a retired professor who regularly proposes very specific instructions for the same group of mortals. Still, he has a point: in addition to the five or six hundred visible policymakers at the top levels of the US government, there are thousands of experts behind them who may, in fact, not be very good at what they do.

Experts cannot dodge their own responsibilities here. The Knowers cannot merely hide behind elected officials every time something goes wrong, telling the public to leave them alone and instead to go and punish the Deciders. When the experts screw up, the leaders who trusted their advice on behalf of the public need to adjudicate their failures and to decide what kind of correction is needed.

Sometimes, the remedy for expert failure is the time-honored blue-ribbon panel and its recommendations. Sometimes the answer is just to fire somebody. In his seminal work on expertise, however, Philip Tetlock suggests other ways in which experts might be held more accountable without merely trashing the entire relationship between experts and the public. There are many possibilities, including more transparency and competition, including institutions requiring experts in any field not only to maintain a complete record of their work, but to come clean about how often they were right or wrong. Journals, universities, and other gatekeepers can and should hold their peers responsible more often for mistakes. Whether this would work is another matter—for one thing, "right" and "wrong" are often more complicated conclusions than a straight yes-or-no determination—and Tetlock acknowledges the many barriers to such solutions.

The most daunting barrier, however, is the public's own laziness. None of these efforts to track and grade experts will matter very much if ordinary citizens do not care enough to develop even a basic interest in such matters. Tetlock points out that laypeople, unfortunately, are not usually interested in finding experts with excellent track records: they are mostly interested in experts who are accessible without much effort and who already agree with their views. In the era of growing parasocial attachments, this problem has become even more severe, as people come to rely more heavily on celebrities for expert judgments. As Tetlock rightly notes, it is not enough to encourage accountability among the "providers of intellectual products" if the "consumers are unmotivated to be discriminating judges of competing claims and counterclaims." These consumers may well be less interested in "the dispassionate pursuit of truth than they are in buttressing their prejudices," and when this happens, laypeople approach the role of expertise with "the psychology of the sports arena, not the seminar room."[18]

Experts need to own their advice and to hold each other accountable. For any number of reasons—the glut of academic degrees, the lack of interest on the part of the public, the inability to keep up with the production of knowledge in the Information Age—they have not lived up to this duty as conscientiously as their privileged position in society requires. They can do better, even if those efforts might, in the main, go unnoticed.

Experts can take at least some measures to improve their accountability. There are other issues in the relationship with the public, however, that are beyond their control. Laypeople need to think about the ways in which they misunderstand the role of expert advice in a democratic republic. Among the many misconceptions the public has about experts and policymakers, five are especially worth considering.

First, experts are not puppeteers. They cannot control when leaders take their advice. Even in the closest relationships between an elected politician and an expert adviser, there is not a complete fusing of beliefs. Whether Nixon and Kissinger—or Obama and Rhodes—no leader is merely the vessel by which experts implement ideas. Perhaps no American president illustrated this problem better than Trump, who was, by many accounts, virtually unbriefable; he would not read reports or listen to his own advisers. But experts being shown the door for offering their views is hardly a new problem.

Any expert worth his or her salt has stories of defeat in the policy game. I was many years ago an aide to a senior US senator who treated me as a trusted adviser but who also once threw me out of his office in a fusillade of curses after a briefing I gave him during the tense days leading up to the 1991 Gulf War. While there is usually a close identity of interests and views between a political leader and the expert staff, the policymaker or elected official has pressures and responsibilities the expert will never feel, and conflict is inevitable.

Second, experts cannot control how leaders implement their advice. There is a kind of "monkey's paw" problem here for experts. ("The Monkey's Paw," readers might recall, is a famous early twentieth-century story about a magic talisman that granted wishes in the worst way: when the main character in the tale wishes for money, it comes in the form of compensation for the death of his son.) Experts can advise policymakers on what to do, but they may find their advice taken in ways that were never intended. An economist who is also an environmentalist might believe that lowering taxes is a good idea, for example, only to find later that her advice was indeed taken—by a Congress wanting to lower taxes on coal or gasoline.

Third, no single expert guides a policy from conception through execution, a reality that the public often finds bewildering and frustrating. This is why policy analysis is an entire scholarly discipline in itself, especially in the study of large organizations such as governments and businesses. The Knowers and the Deciders may have settled on what they want, but the institutions below them, like players in a huge game of "telephone," can mangle intended policies and turn them into something else, with perverse effects, by the time the whole project comes to fruition.

Fourth, experts cannot control how *much* of their advice leaders will take. Experts can offer advice, but often political leaders hear only the parts they *want* to hear—specifically, the parts that will be popular with their respective constituencies. They will then mobilize experts that emphasize the message they prefer. Some experts might, for example, advocate cutting taxes; others might call for increased spending on pet projects ranging from the social safety net to national defense. Both positions—cutting taxes and increasing spending— may have a logical foundation, but they cannot usually be adopted at the same time. The experts, however, cannot control the fact that politicians might well choose all of the options anyway, even if they conflict with each other. (The next set of experts called in will then be asked to help solve the mystery of a massive budget deficit.)

The public, unfortunately, is much the same way. When nutritional scientists took eggs off the list of dietary culprits, they did not intend for people to order fast-food egg sandwiches every morning as part of a healthy breakfast. People hear what they want to hear and then stop listening. And when their incomplete adoption of an expert's advice produces poor results, they blame the experts for being incompetent, because everybody needs to blame somebody.

Finally, experts can only offer alternatives. They cannot, however, make choices about *values*. They can describe problems, but they cannot tell people what they should want to do about those problems, even when there is wide agreement on the nature of those challenges.

Is the earth's climate changing? The experts know it is, and they believe they know why. Whether their models, extrapolated out for decades and centuries, are accurate is a legitimate area for debate. What experts cannot answer is what to *do* about climate change. It might well be that Boston or Shanghai or London will be underwater in fifty years, but it might well also be that voters—who have the right to be wrong—will choose to shift that problem to later generations rather than to risk jobs (or comfort) now.

Experts can tell the voters what is likely to happen, but voters must engage those issues and decide what they value most, and therefore what they want done. Letting Boston slide into the harbor is not my preferred outcome, but it is not a failure of expertise if people ignore the experts and let it happen anyway: it is instead a failure of civic engagement. If Boston is to become Venice, it should be by choice, not by accident. When voters remain utterly unwilling to understand important issues because they are too difficult or discomfiting, it is unsurprising that experts will give up talking to them and instead rely on their positions in the policy world to advocate for their own solutions.

Experts sometimes give poor advice or make mistakes, but an advanced society and its government cannot do without them, no matter what an increasing number of Americans seem to believe. To ignore expert advice is simply not a realistic option, not only due to the complexity of policymaking, but because to do so is to absolve citizens of their responsibilities to learn about issues that matter directly to their own well-being. Moreover, when the public no longer makes a distinction between experts and policymakers and merely wants to blame everyone in the policy world for outcomes that distress them, the eventual result will not be *better policy* but more *politicization of expertise*. Politicians will never stop relying on experts; they will, however, move to relying on experts who will tell them—and the angry laypeople banging on their office doors—whatever it is they want to hear.

This is the worst of all worlds, in which both democracy and expertise are corrupted because neither democratic leaders nor their expert advisers want to tangle with an ignorant electorate. At that point, expertise no longer serves the public interest, but the interest of whatever political clique is taking the temperature of the public at any given moment. We are already perilously close to this outcome in modern America.

A REPUBLIC, IF YOU KNOW WHAT ONE IS

The challenges of expert accountability are compounded by the fact that most Americans do not seem to understand their own system of government. The United States is a *republic*, not a *democracy*. One hardly ever hears the word "republic" anymore, which reveals, in a small way, the degree to which modern Americans confuse "democracy" as a general political philosophy with a "republic" as its expression in a form of government. In 1787, Benjamin Franklin was supposedly asked what would emerge from the Constitutional Convention being held in Philadelphia. "A republic," Franklin answered, "if you can keep it." Today, the bigger challenge is to find anyone who knows what a republic actually is.

This is crucial because laypeople too easily forget that the republican form of government under which they live was not designed for mass decisions about complicated issues. Indeed, it is specifically engineered to prevent such plebiscites; there is no mechanism in the United States for a Brexit-like, single national vote on major issues.

Neither, of course, was the American republic designed for rule by a tiny group of technocrats or experts. Rather, it was meant to be the vehicle by which an informed electorate—*informed* being the key word here—could choose other people to represent them and to make decisions on their behalf.

Classical American thought might be rooted in the glory that was Athens, but the United States is not, nor was it ever meant to be, anything like the Athenian marketplace. And for that, Americans should be grateful. As the writer Malcolm Gladwell pointed out in 2010, large organizations do not make decisions by polling everyone in them, no matter how "democratic" it might seem.

> Car companies sensibly use a network to organize their hundreds of suppliers, but not to design their cars. No one believes that the articulation of a coherent design philosophy is best handled by a sprawling, leaderless organizational system. Because networks don't have a centralized leadership structure and clear lines of authority, they have real difficulty reaching consensus and setting goals. They can't think strategically; they are chronically prone to conflict and error.
>
> How do you make difficult choices about tactics or strategy or philosophical direction when everyone has an equal say?[19]

This is one of many challenges modern republican government was designed to overcome. Even when most people know what they're doing in their own area of competence, they cannot agglomerate their decisions into coherent public policy the same way as if they are guessing the weight of a bull or trying to pin down the target price of a stock. The republican solution allows a smaller group of people to aggregate the public's often irresolvable demands while leavening them with expert knowledge.

Determining what the public really wants, however, is exponentially more difficult when the electorate is not competent in any of the matters at hand. Laypeople complain about the rule of experts and they demand greater involvement in complicated national questions, but many of them abdicate their own important role in the process: namely, to stay informed and politically literate enough to choose representatives who can act on their behalf. In the words of Ilya Somin, "When we elect government officials based on ignorance, they rule over not only those who voted for them but all of society. When we exercise power over other people, we have a moral obligation to do so in at least a reasonably informed way."[20]

This is not the place for a meditation on the American form of representative democracy, especially since there are already plenty of copies of *The Federalist Papers* still available. But the death of expertise and its associated attacks on knowledge fundamentally undermine the stability of any republican system of government. Worse, these attacks are campaigns conducted by those least capable of supplanting that system; tearing down is easier than building up. The most poorly informed people among us, the citizens most loudly dismissive of experts, are too often those who will demand the greatest say in matters about which they have exerted almost no effort to educate themselves.

Consider how quickly people change their preferences based on who they think is advocating a position. The comedian Jimmy Kimmel was once again the prankster here: he stopped people on the street in late 2015, and asked them which of the tax plans offered by Hillary Clinton and Donald Trump they preferred. The interviewees, however, did not know that Kimmel had switched the details of each plan. As *The Hill* newspaper later reported, the answers depended on whom people thought they were supporting: "Sure enough, one by one, the Clinton voters were stunned to discover that they were vouching for the proposal of her archrival." One man, when told he was supporting Trump's plan rather than Clinton's, decided to go for broke: "Well, I support Donald Trump, then."[21]

As it turns out, Kimmel's hijinks illustrated a truth long known to pollsters and campaign experts: voters are often more interested in candidates and their personalities than in their ideas or policies. The *Huffington Post*'s polling director, Ariel Edwards-Levy, put it this way:

> Americans, regardless of their political views, don't have a solid opinion about every single issue of the day, particularly when it concerns a complicated or obscure topic. People tend, reasonably, to rely on partisan cues—if a politician they support is in favor of a bill, they're likely to think it's a good idea, or vice versa.[22]

When Levy and her colleagues conducted a more formal version of the Kimmel ambush, they found the same thing: Republicans who strongly disagree with Democratic Party positions on health care, Iran, and affirmative action objected far less if they thought the same policies were those of the Republican candidate. Democrats, for their part, went in the other direction: they were less supportive of their own party's policies if they thought they were Republican positions.

At least tax policy and health care are real issues with real positions attached to them. In 2015, Public Policy Polling, a liberal polling group, asked both Republicans and Democrats whether they would support bombing the country of Agrabah. Nearly a third of Republican respondents said they would support such action. Only 13 percent were opposed, and the rest were unsure. Democrats were less inclined to military action: only 19 percent of self-identified Democrats supported bombing while 36 percent decisively voiced their opposition.

Agrabah doesn't exist. It's the fictional country in the 1992 animated Disney film *Aladdin*. Liberals crowed that this poll was evidence of the ignorance and aggressiveness of Republicans, while conservatives countered that it only showed how Democrats were reflexively against military action no matter how little they knew about the situation. For experts, however, there was no way around the overall reality captured in the poll, even if only accidentally: 43 percent of Republicans and 55 percent of Democrats had an actual, defined view on bombing a place in a cartoon.[23]

Some of these games are unfair to the public. Ordinary people are busy living their lives, not trying to figure out if they're being manipulated by pollsters or pranked by comedians like Kimmel. This is especially true when voters are presented with "all sides" of the issues in the media without any indication of which views are more authoritative than another. As the psychologist Derek Kohler put it,

> Government action is guided in part by public opinion. Public opinion is guided in part by perceptions of what experts think. But public opinion may—and often does—deviate from expert opinion, not simply, it seems, because the public refuses to acknowledge the legitimacy of experts, but also because the public may not be able to tell where the majority of expert opinion lies.[24]

A talk show, for example, with one scientist who says genetically modified organisms (GMOs) are safe and one activist who says they are dangerous looks "balanced," but in reality that is ridiculously skewed, because nearly nine out of ten scientists think GMOs are safe for consumption. At some point, amid all the bickering, the public simply gives up and goes back to relying on simpler sources of information, even if it is a half-baked tweet or a meme on Facebook.

This is no excuse, however, for citizen ignorance and disengagement—and especially for hyper-partisan attachments that make people change their minds about policy only because of who advocated them. If the public has no idea about the substance of an issue, and will vote based on who they *like* rather than what they *want*, it is difficult to put too much blame on policymakers and their expert advisers for being confused themselves. How can a republic function if the people who have sent their representatives to decide questions of war and peace cannot tell the difference between Agrabah, Ukraine, or Syria?

Put another way, when the public claims it has been misled or kept in the dark, experts and policymakers cannot help but ask, "How would you know?"

When laypeople disregard expertise and declare themselves fed up with everything and everyone, they forget that the people they elected still have to make decisions, every day, about an ongoing blizzard of issues. These officials do not have the luxury of casting a pox upon the experts and the polls and then retreating to their televisions and computer screens and phones. They have to make commitments, sometimes of lives and always of money, on everything from navigation rights to child care. These decisions, and how they are implemented, will affect the lives of all citizens, the informed as well as the ignorant, the involved and the detached.

The breakdown of trust between the public, experts, and elected officials in a republic goes in all directions. The public, especially, needs to be able to trust leaders and their expert advisers. This relationship becomes impossible to sustain, however, when laypeople have no idea what they're talking about or what they want.

When that trust breaks down, public ignorance can be turned by cynical manipulation into a political weapon. Anti-intellectualism is itself a means of short-circuiting democracy, because a stable democracy in any culture relies on the public genuinely understanding the implications of its own choices. Most laypeople, already suspicious of the educated classes, need little prodding to rebel against experts—even when such rebellions are cynically led by other intellectuals.

In 1942, President Franklin D. Roosevelt asked radio listeners to go and purchase maps so they could follow along as he narrated the progress of World War II. Maps quickly sold out across the country. In 2006, fewer than sixty-five years later, a national study found that nearly half of Americans between the ages of eighteen and twenty-four—that is, those most likely to have to fight in a war—did not think it was necessary to know the location of other countries in which important news was being made.[25] A decade later, during the 2016 election, Donald Trump raised cheers when he summed up his approach to terrorists in the Middle East: "I would bomb the shit out of them. I'd blow up the pipes, I'd blow up the refineries, I'd blow up every single inch, there would be nothing left." Trump's challengers for the 2024 Republican nomination have veered away from talk of war far from American shores; instead, some of them have been keen to begin military operations against Mexico.[26]

A republic, if you can keep it. Or if you can find it on a map.

I'M AS GOOD AS YOU

Finally, and most disturbing, citizens of the Western democracies, and Americans in particular, no longer understand the concept of democracy itself. This, perhaps more than anything, has corroded the relationship between experts and citizens. The relationship between experts and citizens is not "democratic." All people are not, and can never be, equally talented or intelligent. Democratic societies, however, are always tempted to this resentful insistence on equality, which becomes oppressive ignorance if given its head.

And this, sadly, is the state of modern America. Citizens no longer understand democracy to mean a condition of political equality, in which one person gets one vote, and every individual is no more and no less equal in the eyes of the law. Rather, Americans now think of democracy as a state of actual equality, in which every opinion is as good as any other on almost any subject under the sun. Feelings are more important than facts: if people *think* vaccines are harmful, or if they *believe* that half of the US budget is going to foreign aid, then it is "undemocratic" and "elitist" to contradict them.

This problem is not new, nor is it unique to the United States. The British writer C. S. Lewis warned long ago of the danger to democracy when people no longer recognize any difference between political equality and actual equality, in a vivid 1959 essay featuring one of his most famous literary creations, a brilliant and evil demon named Screwtape.

As one of the Inferno's most senior bureaucrats, Screwtape is invited to give the commencement address at Hell's training college for new tempters. During his speech, Screwtape leaves aside what, for him, is the dull business of individual temptation and instead surveys the global landscape. While he is repulsed by human progress (including the French and American revolutions, and the abolition of slavery, among other moments), he sees great hope—for Hell, not for human beings—in capturing the concept of democracy and wresting it away from its noble meaning.

"*Democracy* is the word with which you must lead them by the nose," Screwtape gleefully advises the graduates, and he then promises that by use of the word "purely as an incantation," human beings can be fooled not only into believing an obvious lie, but led to nurture that lie as a cherished feeling:

> The feeling I mean is of course that which prompts a man to say *I'm as good as you.*

No man who says *I'm as good as you* believes it. He would not say it if he did. The St. Bernard never says it to the toy dog, nor the scholar to the dunce, nor the employable to the bum, nor the pretty woman to the plain. The claim to equality, outside the strictly political field, is made only by those who feel themselves to be in some way inferior. What it expresses is precisely the itching, smarting, writhing awareness of an inferiority which [a human being] refuses to accept.

And therefore resents. Yes, and therefore resents every kind of superiority in others; denigrates it; wishes its annihilation.[27]

This was the same warning José Ortega y Gasset gave when he wrote *Revolt of the Masses* in 1930: "The mass crushes beneath it everything that is different, everything that is excellent, individual, qualified and select. Anybody who is not like everybody, who does not think like everybody, runs the risk of being eliminated."[28]

"*I'm as good as you,*" Screwtape chortles at the end of his address, "is a useful means for the destruction of democratic societies."

And so it is. When resentful laypeople demand that all marks of achievement, including expertise, be leveled and equalized in the name of "democracy" and "fairness," there is no hope for either democracy or fairness. Everything becomes a matter of opinion, with all views dragged to the lowest common denominator in the name of equality. An outbreak of whooping cough because an ignoramus would not vaccinate a child is a sign of tolerance; the collapse of a foreign alliance because a provincial isolationist can't find other nations on an atlas is a triumph of egalitarianism.

Democracy, as practiced in the United States in the early twenty-first century, has become a resentful, angry business. Fragile, narcissistic college students jostle against outraged, wounded talk-radio addicts, all of whom demand to be taken with equal seriousness by everyone else, regardless of how extreme or uninformed their views are. Experts are derided as elitists, one of many groups putatively oppressing "we the people," a term now used by voters indiscriminately and mostly to mean "me." Expert advice or any kind of informed deliberation by anyone whom laypeople perceive as an elite—which is to say almost everyone but themselves—is rejected as a matter of first principles. No democracy can go on this way.

THE REVOLT OF THE EXPERTS

I did not intend in 2017 to end this book on such a note of pessimism, but the intervening years have not provided much cause for hope. Ignorance can be overcome if people are willing to learn. Nothing, however, can overcome the toxic confluence of arrogance, narcissism, and cynicism that Americans now wear like a full suit of armor against the efforts of experts and professionals.

Traditional solutions no longer work. Expert outreach is dismissed as condescension. Education, instead of breaking down barriers to continued learning, is teaching young people that their feelings are more important than anything else. The media, mired in competition at every level, now asks consumers what they'd like to know instead of telling them what's important. The Internet is a mixed blessing, a well of information poisoned by the equivalent of intellectual sabotage.

Faced with the public's resolute ignorance, experts are defeated. "Many of us feel powerless against it," said David Autor, a labor economist at MIT. "We feel we can train our students, but our students aren't the public and we don't know how to school the public." A Yale professor, Dan Kahan, was more pessimistic: "Bombarding people with knowledge doesn't help," he said in 2015. "It doesn't do anything to explain things to people, but here I am just explaining the facts over and over again. Maybe the joke's on me."[29]

One hopeful sign is that experts seem to be rebelling against attacks on their expertise. In decrying the Brexit outcome, for example, James Traub bluntly said that it was time for the defenders of classical Western liberalism "to rise up against the ignorant masses."[30] Of course, to do so is to risk the dread accusation of "elitism," a charge that has always had more impact in egalitarian America than in more stratified cultures in Europe and elsewhere, as Traub himself recognized: "It is necessary to say that people are deluded and that the task of leadership is to un-delude them. Is that 'elitist'? Maybe it is; maybe we have become so inclined to celebrate the authenticity of all personal conviction that it is now elitist to believe in reason, expertise, and the lessons of history."

Nonetheless, professionals across a spectrum of fields in several countries seem fed up. Anecdotally, I was struck that after my original article on the "death of expertise" appeared, I was contacted by scientists, doctors, lawyers, teachers, and many other professionals in America and around the world. They told me not only of their frustration, but of their anger and sadness over ruptured relationships with patients, clients, and students, and even the cooling of close personal friendships, all because they are finally demanding an end to ill-informed lectures about their own area of competence.

Medical doctors, especially, seem to have had enough. To take a humorous recent example, in 2015, Kimmel—yet again—ran a satirical public service announcement in which actual doctors engaged in expletive-filled rants against recalcitrant patients who feared vaccinations. "Remember that time you got polio?" asked one of the physicians. "No, you don't. Because your parents got you [expletive] vaccinated." Another said, "I have to use my only day off to talk to you idiots about vaccines?" as another chimed in: "Because you listened to some moron who read a forwarded email?"

The Kimmel spot went viral, reported in major media and replayed (as of this writing) more than nine million times on YouTube alone.

The reaction, of course, was swift. Sites such as Infowars.com and a host of anti-vaccination bloggers (of course) called the doctors ignorant, tools of a corrupt system, and the other usual insults. These kinds of efforts in the media probably saved lives at the time, but such messages were lost in the typhoon of anti-vaccine madness that swept over America during the COVID pandemic, and they were not enough to dent the campaign against established knowledge or to reverse its effects on American democracy.

In the end, experts cannot demand that citizens pay attention to the world around them. They cannot insist people eat healthy meals or exercise more. They cannot drag citizens by the neck away from the latest memes on social media and make them look at a map instead. They cannot cure narcissism by fiat.

When I first wrote *The Death of Expertise*, this was the moment when I predicted that a tragedy might snap us out of our delusions. Experts should confront their bad calls, and this was mine:

> I suspect that a possible resolution will lie in a disaster as yet unforeseen. It may be a war or an economic collapse. (Here, I mean a major war that touches America even more deeply than the far-away conflicts fought by brave volunteers, or a real depression, rather than the recession of the early twenty-first century.) It may be in the emergence of an ignorant demagoguery, a process already underway in the United States and Europe, or the rise to power of a technocracy that finally runs out of patience and thus dispenses with voting as anything other than a formality.

Almost all of these events, as I said at the outset of this book, have come to pass, and those we've avoided were defeated by expert guidance (and a dash of luck). But the demagogues remain with us; turned back here and there by alarmed citizens, they continue to poison the public life of the democracies. And as I wrote in 2021, the technocrats are already making their accommodations to authoritarianism; someone needs to deliver the mail and keep the lights on, and because demagogues care little for actual governing, others will pick up the slack and quietly exercise power while the masses cheer for their chosen reality-show champions.

The creation of a vibrant intellectual and scientific culture in the West and in the United States required democracy, secular tolerance, and trust. Without such virtues, knowledge and progress fall prey to ideological, religious, and populist attacks. Nations that have given in to such temptations have suffered any number of terrible fates, including mass repression, cultural and material poverty, and defeat in war.

I still have faith in the American system, despite the worrisome political and social trends of the past decade. I continue to believe the people of the United States are still capable of shrugging off their self-absorption and isolation and taking up their responsibilities as citizens. They did it in 1941, and again after the trials of Vietnam and Watergate, and yet again after the attacks of 9/11, and in my view, they did it by turning Donald Trump out of the White House. Each time, however, they slid back into complacency, and each time, the hole of ignorance and disaffection they dug for themselves got deeper. At some point, they might no longer see daylight.

We can only hope that before this happens, citizens, experts, and policymakers will engage in a hard debate about the role of experts and educated elites in American democracy. Any such hope, for now, has been thwarted by the partisan combat that erupted after the COVID pandemic. If I thought, however, there was no chance of ever returning to our senses, I would not have bothered with another edition of this book. I still have confidence that we can, at some point, embrace many realities we once accepted as obvious, chief among them that although every single vote in a democracy is equal to every other, every single opinion is not. The sooner American society reestablishes new ground rules for productive engagement between the educated elites and the society they serve, the better, but after the political events and natural disasters of the past decade, it's going to take longer than any of us might have hoped.

We cannot sustain democracy without repairing the relationship between experts and citizens. Experts need to remember, always, that they are the servants and not the masters of a democratic society and a republican government. If citizens, however, are to be the masters, they must equip themselves not just with education, but with the kind of civic virtue that keeps them involved in the running of their own country. Laypeople cannot do without experts, and they must accept this reality without rancor. Experts, likewise, must accept that their advice, which might seem obvious and right to them, will not always be taken in a democracy that may not value the same things they do. Otherwise, when democracy is understood as an unending demand for unearned respect for unfounded opinions, anything and everything become possible, including the end of democracy and republican government itself.

That, at least, is my expert opinion on the matter. I could be wrong.

NOTES

Introduction

1. Pride Chigwedere et al., "Estimating the Lost Benefits of Antiretroviral Drug Use in South Africa," *Journal of Acquired Immune Deficiency Syndromes* 49(4), December 1, 2008.
2. A 2022 poll by Morning Consult found that only 34 percent of Americans could locate Ukraine—the largest nation entirely in Europe—on a map. This finding was an improvement over 2014, when only 1 in 6 could spot Ukraine; those the least likely to know where it was, however, were the most eager to intervene against Russia's seizure of Crimea.
3. Kyle Dropp, Joshua D. Kertzer, and Thomas Zeitzoff, "The Less Americans Know about Ukraine's Location, the More They Want U.S. to Intervene," *Monkey Cage* Blog, *Washington Post* online, April 7, 2014.
4. The story—which urban legend chronicler Jan Brundvant might classify as a "FOAF" tale—meaning something that ostensibly happened to a "Friend Of A Friend"—was debunked, but not before millions saw it online.

Chapter 1

1. José Ortega y Gasset, *The Revolt of the Masses* (New York: W. W. Norton, 1993), 16–18.
2. Richard Hofstadter, *Anti-Intellectualism in American Life* (New York: Vintage, 1963), 34.

3. Ilya Somin, "Political Ignorance in America," in Mark Bauerlein and Adam Bellow, eds., *The State of the American Mind* (West Conshohocken, PA: Templeton, 2015), 163–164.

4. John Hendrickson, "The First MAGA Democrat," *The Atlantic*, June 26, 2023.

5. Dana Goodyear, "Raw Deal: California Cracks Down on an Underground Gourmet Club," *New Yorker*, April 30, 2012.

6. Nidhi Subbaraman, "The Feds Just Asked the Woman Who Started a Facebook Cabbage Juice Cult to Remove False Claims from Her Website," *BuzzFeed News*, October 4, 2018.

7. Olga Khazan, "27% of Surgeons Still Think Obamacare Has Death Panels," *Atlantic* online, December 19, 2013.

8. Kaiser Family Foundation, 2013 Survey of Americans on the US Role in Global Health.

9. Henry Blodget, "Here's What Day Traders Don't Understand," *Business Insider*, March 29, 2010.

Chapter 2

1. See Quoted in David Dunning, "We Are All Confident Idiots," *Pacific Standard* online, October 27, 2014.

2. Justin Kruger and David Dunning, "Unskilled and Unaware of It: How Difficulties in Recognizing One's Own Incompetence Lead to Inflated Self-Assessments," *Journal of Personality and Social Psychology* 77(6), December 1999, 1121–1122.

3. Dunning, "We Are All Confident Idiots."

4. John Allen Paulos, *Innumeracy: Mathematical Illiteracy and Its Consequences* (New York: Hill and Wang, 2001), 9.

5. Michael Crichton, "Panic in the Sheets," *Playboy*, December 1991; archived at MichaelCrichton.com.

6. There's an entire subject in statistics, called "Bayesian analysis," named for an eighteenth-century English mathematician, which deals with this question.

7. Social scientists, no less than any other, are aware of this problem. See Charles O. Jones, "Doing before Knowing: Concept Development in Political Research," *American Journal of Political Science* 18(1), February 1974.

8. Maria Konnikova, "How a Gay-Marriage Study Went Wrong," *New Yorker* online, May 22, 2015.

9. Jonathan Kay, "Has Internet-Fueled Conspiracy Mongering Crested?," in Mark Bauerline and Adam Bellow, eds., *The State of the American Mind* (West Conshohocken, PA: Templeton, 2015), 138–139.

10. Kira Lerner, "'Anger and Radicalization': Rising Number of Americans Say Political Violence Is Justified," *The Guardian* online, July 25, 2023.

11. Indeed, the scholar Ross E. Cheit has argued that the poorly handled cases in the 1980s and 1990s backfired tragically, as the pendulum of public opinion swung from always believing small children to being highly skeptical of any claims of abuse at all. Still, the Satanic element was part of a hysteria, and later studies by academics and law enforcement found no evidence of such networks in day-care centers or anywhere else. See Ross E. Cheit, *The Witch-Hunt Narrative* (New York: Oxford University Press, 2014).

12. For a detailed account of life among the QAnon conspiracy believers, see Will Sommer, *Trust the Plan: The Rise of QAnon and the Conspiracy That Unhinged America* (New York: Harper, 2023).

13. Jef Rouner, "Guide to Arguing with a Snopes-Denier," *Houston Press*, April 2, 2014.

14. Ali Mahmoodi et al., "Equality Bias Impairs Collective Decision-Making across Cultures," *Proceedings of the National Academy of Sciences* 112(12), March 24, 2015, 3835–3840.

15. Chris Mooney, "The Science of Protecting People's Feelings: Why We Pretend All Opinions Are Equal," *Washington Post* online, March 10, 2015.

16. Karl Taro Greenfield, "Faking Cultural Literacy," *New York Times* online, May 24, 2014.

17. Quoted in Chris Mooney, "Liberals Deny Science, Too," *Washington Post* online, October 28, 2014.

18. The one difference was that conservatives reacted more intensely to data that contradicted their beliefs, but the researchers suggest that this is because "issues that challenge conservatives are the issues currently more polarizing in society today." The authors made these and the following comments in a press release from Ohio State University titled "Both Liberals, Conservatives Can Have Science Bias," February 9, 2015.

19. Jonathan Chait, "Democrats Learned from Their Covid Mistakes. Republicans Didn't. Democrats on School Closing, Republicans on Vaccines: A Case Study," *New York* online, July 24, 2023.

Chapter 3

1. Aatish Bhatia, Claire Cain Miller, and Josh Katz, "Study of Elite College Admissions Data Suggests Being Very Rich Is Its Own Qualification," *New York Times* online, July 24, 2023.

2. Daniel W. Drezner, "A Clash between Administrators and Students at Yale Went Viral," *Washington Post* online, November 9, 2015.

3. A study by the Educational Testing Service, the group that administers the Scholastic Aptitude Test, or SAT, to college-bound students, found that there was no associated increase in ability connected to the

explosion of college attendance. See Educational Testing Service, *America's Skills Challenge: Millennials and the Future* (Princeton, NJ: Educational Testing Service, 2015).

4. Ben Casselman, "Shut Up about Harvard," FiveThirtyEight.com, March 30, 2016; see also Jeffrey Seligo, "The College-Admissions Process Is Completely Broken," *The Atlantic*, April 18, 2022.

5. Robert Hughes, *Culture of Complaint* (New York: Time Warner, 1993), 68.

6. Valerie Strauss, "I Would Love to Teach, But . . . ," *Washington Post* online, December 31, 2013.

7. Emma Brown, "Former Stanford Dean Explains Why Helicopter Parenting Is Ruining a Generation of Children," *Washington Post* online, October 16, 2015.

8. Megan McArdle, "Sheltered Students Go to College, Avoid Education," BloombergView.com, August 13, 2015.

9. Jeffrey J. Selingo, "Helicopter Parents Are Not the Only Problem. Colleges Coddle Students, Too," *Washington Post*, October 21, 2015.

10. Robby Soave, "Yale Students Tell English Profs to Stop Teaching English: Too Many White Male Poets," Reason.com, June 1, 2016.

11. Ryan Quinn, "Report: Adjunct Who Showed Images of Prophet Was 'Vilified,'" *Insider Higher Ed*, May 22, 2023.

12. See Tom Nichols, "Academic Freedom Is Not a Matter of Opinion," *The Atlantic* online, January 12, 2023.

13. Vimal Patel, "After Lecturer Sues, Hamline University Walks Back Its 'Islamophobic' Comments," *New York Times* online, January 17, 2023. The instructor's lawsuit, as of late 2023, remains unresolved in U.S. federal court.

14. Jonathan D. Glater, "To: Professor@University.edu Subject: Why It's All about Me," *New York Times* online, February 22, 2006.

15. Over the past decade, I have been told anecdotally by younger colleagues that it is now almost a standard question during a job interview to ask aspiring professors to talk about a moment where they learned more from their students than the students learned from them. It would be unfortunate if it is true that this is now a common part of a job interview, because it is an insipid question that serves mostly as a signal from the institution that the faculty member is expected to enter the classroom already in awe of the wisdom of teenagers.

16. James V. Schall, *Another Sort of Learning* (San Francisco: Ignatius, 1988), 30–37.

17. David Dunning, "We Are All Confident Idiots," *Pacific Standard* online, October 27, 2014.

18. Tiny Castleton State College in Vermont, now a "university," is one of many examples in New England alone. Lisa Rathke, "Switching from a College to a University Could Mean More Money, More Students," *Huffington Post*, July 12, 2015.

19. McArdle, "Sheltered Students Go to College."

20. Catherine Rampell, "The Rise of the 'Gentleman's A' and the GPA Arms Race," *Washington Post* online, March 28, 2016.

21. Jeff Denning, Eric Eide, Kevin Mumford, Rich Patterson, and Merrill Warnick, "The Grade Inflation Conversation We're Not Having," *The Chronicle of Higher Education* online, April 13, 2023.

22. Richar Arum, "College Graduates: Satisfied, but Adrift," in Mark Bauerlein and Adam Bellow, eds., *The State of the American Mind* (West Conshohocken, PA: Templeton, 2015), 68.

23. The 2016 data were an extension of studies previously done by Professors Stuart Rojstaczer and Chris Healy, who continued to gather data on grades after writing papers on the subject in 2010 and 2012. They maintain a database of their work at www.gradeinflation.com.

24. For just two of many reports and reactions from both conservatives and liberals, see Katy Waldman, "Yale Students Erupt in Anger over Administrators Caring More about Free Speech than Safe Spaces," *Slate*, November 7, 2015; and Shoshanna Weismann, "How Babies Are Made," *Weekly Standard*, November 10, 2015.

25. Mará Rose Williams, "Race Protests at Mizzou Could Stunt Freshmen Enrollment," *Kansas City Star* online, January 13, 2016.

26. Anemona Hartocollis, "Long after Protests, Students Shun the University of Missouri," *New York Times* online, July 9, 2017.

27. Conor Friedersdorf, "The New Intolerance of Student Activism," *The Atlantic* online, November 9, 2015.

28. Florida Governor Ron DeSantis made attacks on "Marxism" and "wokeness" in public education a part of his 2024 bid for the American presidency, with predictable results. Other state university systems, however, have had to beat back attacks on tenure, diversity, and academic freedom. See Patricia Mazzei, "DeSantis's Latest Target: A Small College of 'Free Thinkers,'" *New York Times* online, February 14, 2023, and Johanna Alonso, "Chaos at New College of Florida," *InsideHigherEd.com*, August 16, 2023, and Heather Hollingsworth, "Conservatives Take Aim at Tenure for University Professors," AP.com, January 8, 2023.

29. See Paul Tough, "Americans Are Losing Faith in the Value of College. Whose Fault Is That?" *New York Times Magazine* online, September 5, 2020.

Chapter 4

1. Nicholas Carr, "Is Google Making Us Stupid?," *The Atlantic* online, July/August 2008.

2. Caitlin Dewey, "What Was Fake on the Internet This Week: Why Do We Even Bother, Honestly?," *Washington Post* online, October 30, 2015.

3. Caitlin Dewey, "What Was Fake on the Internet This Week: Why This Is the Final Column," *Washington Post* online, December 18, 2015.

4. Damian Thompson, *Counterknowledge* (New York: W. W. Norton, 2008), 11.

5. Allen West, "Obama's America: Look What Our Troops Are Being FORCED to Do for Islam's Holy Month," allenbwest.com, June 29, 2015.

6. West's wife was vaccinated. See Associated Press, "Allen West, Texas Gubernatorial Candidate, Hospitalized with Covid-19," October 11, 2021.

7. Michael Miller, "Gwyneth Paltrow's No Vagina Expert, Doctors Say," *People* online, January 29, 2015. Dr. Gunter's blog is at drjengunter.wordpress.com.

8. Laura Hooper Beck, "I Went to a Spa for My Uterus and This Is My Story," FastCompany.com, January 27, 2015.

9. Arwa Mahdawi, "The Truth about Gwyneth Paltrow's Diet? It Is as Strange as You'd Expect," *The Guardian* online, March 21, 2023.

10. Frank Bruni, "California, Camelot and Vaccines," *New York Times* online, July 4, 2015.

11. Andrew Zhang, "Judge Denies RFK Jr.'s Request for Restraining Order against Google in Censorship Suit," *Politico*, August 23, 2023. The polling data are from *FiveThirtyEight.com*, accessed the day of the court decision.

12. " 'Stop Googling Your Symptoms,' Teenage Cancer Victim Told before Death," *Daily Telegraph*, June 16, 2015.

13. Matthew Fisher et al., "Searching for Explanations: How the Internet Inflates Estimates of Internal Knowledge," *Journal of Experimental Psychology* 144(3), June 2015, 674–687.

14. Tom Jacobs, "Searching the Internet Creates an Illusion of Knowledge," *Pacific Standard* online, April 1, 2015.

15. This and subsequent references are from the University College of London CIBER Briefing Paper, "The Google Generation: The Information Behaviour of the Researcher of the Future," January 11, 2008.

16. "AI Used to Target Kids with Disinformation," *BBC.com*, September 16, 2023.

17. Robert Epstein, "How Google Could Rig the 2016 Election," *Politico*, August 19, 2015.

18. James Surowiecki, *The Wisdom of Crowds* (New York: Anchor, 2005), xii–xiii.

19. Quoted in Tom Simonite, "The Decline of Wikipedia," *MIT Technology Review*, October 22, 2013.

20. Ibid.

21. Andrea Peterson, "Liberals Are More Likely to Unfriend You over Politics— Online and Off," *Washington Post* online, October 21, 2014.

22. Christopher Tokita et al., "Polarized Information Ecosystems Can Reorganize Social Networks via Information Cascades," *PNAS* 118, no. 50, December 6, 2021.

23. For a summary of these studies, see Thomas B. Edsall, "We're Staring at Our Phones, Full of Rage for 'the Other Side,'" *New York Times* online, June 15, 2022.

24. A. O. Scott, "Everybody's a Critic. And That's How It Should Be," *New York Times Sunday Review* online, January 30, 2016.

25. Andrew Sullivan, "Democracies End When They Are Too Democratic," *New York* online, May 1, 2016.

26. David Dunning, "We Are All Confident Idiots," *Pacific Standard* online, October 27, 2014.

27. Megan McArdle, "Your Assessment of the Election Is Way Off," *Forbes* online, April 14, 2016.

28. See Aisha Counts, Tom Maloney, and Bloomberg, "Twitter's Value Has Plunged 66% under Elon Musk's Erratic Leadership, Costing Him Billions of Dollars on Paper," *Fortune* online, May 30, 2023; Camila Domonoske, "Tesla's Stock Lost over $700 Billion in Value. Elon Musk's Twitter Deal Didn't Help," Oregon Public Radio, January 6, 2023; and Derek Saul, "Tesla Stock Hits 4-Month High as Elon Musk's Net Worth Soars," *Forbes* online, June 2, 2023.

Chapter 5

1. Sarah Kaplan, "How, and Why, a Journalist Tricked News Outlets into Thinking Chocolate Makes You Thin," *Washington Post* online, May 28, 2015.

2. Elisabetta Povoledo, "Pope Calls for 'Peace in All the World' in First Easter Message," *New York Times* online, March 31, 2013.

3. Pew Research Center, "The Age of Indifference: A Study of Young Americans and How They View the News," June 28, 1990, 1.

4. Richard Arum, "College Graduates: Satisfied, but Adrift," in Mark Bauerlein and Adam Bellow, eds., *The State of the American Mind* (West Conshohocken, PA: Templeton, 2015), 73.

5. BBC News online, "Teens Shun Traditional News Channels for TikTok and Instagram, Ofcom Says," July 21, 2022.

6. James E. Short, "How Much Media? Report on American Consumers," 2013. Institute for Communication Technology Management, Marshall School of Business, University of Southern California, http://classic.marshall.usc.edu/assets/161/25995.pdf.

7. Jan Zverina, "U.S. Media Consumption to Rise to 15.5 Hours a Day—Per Person—by 2015," UC San Diego News Center, November 6, 2013.

8. Quoted in Benjamin Mullen, "Buyouts Hit the *Dallas Morning News*," Poynter. org, July 7, 2015.

9. Quoted in Jeremy Peters, "Some Newspapers, Tracking Readers Online, Shift Coverage," *New York Times* online, September 5, 2010.

10. Ibid.

11. See Mason Walker, "U.S. Newsroom Employment Has Fallen 26% since 2008," Pew Research Center, July 13, 2021.

12. National Journal Group, *Washington in the Information Age*, 2015, Washington, DC.

13. The station was WREB in Holyoke. Cole was a right-winger, but one of his successors tacked to the left, referring to conservative callers as "Nazis" on the air—all years before Limbaugh ever took to the microphone.

14. Daniel Engber, "Joe Rogan's Show May Be Dumb. But Is It Actually Deadly?" *The Atlantic* online, February 10, 2022.

15. Steven Metz, "As Celebrity Pundits Rise, U.S. National Security Policy Suffers," *World Politics Review*, August 14, 2015.

16. Mindich in Bauerlein and Bellow, *State of the American Mind*, 101.

17. Brian Stelter, "The End of Companion Television," *The Atlantic*, December 2, 2022.

18. Ben Kamisar, "Almost a Third of Americans Still Believe the 2020 Election Result Was Fraudulent," NBC News Meet the Press blog online, June 20, 2023.

19. Anne Pluta, "Trump Supporters Appear to Be Misinformed, Not Uninformed," FiveThirtyEight.com, January 7, 2016.

20. Justin McCarthy, "Trust in Mass Media Returns to All-Time Low," Gallup. com, September 17, 2014;

21. Megan Brenan, "Americans' Trust In Media Remains Near Record Low," Gallup.com, October 18, 2022.

22. Paul Farhi, "How Biased Are the Media, Really?," *Washington Post* online, April 27, 2012.

23. Jeffrey Gottfried, "Republicans Less Likely to Trust Their Main News Source if They See It as 'Mainstream'; Democrats More Likely," Pew Research Center, July 1, 2021.

24. The hatred of Congress and loyalty to one's one member of Congress is sometimes referred to as "Fenno's Paradox," named for the political scientist, Richard Fenno, who pioneered research on the issue in the 1970s.

25. Dale Maharidge, "People's Stories: What Happens When No One Wants to Print Their Words Anymore?," *Nation* online, March 2, 2016.

26. Michael Nunez, "Want to Know What Facebook Really Thinks of Journalists? Here's What Happened When It Hired Some," Gizmodo.com, May 3, 2016.

27. Mary Papenfuss, "Elon Musk's Tweet Traffic Jumped 737% after He Ordered Algorithm Change: Report," *Huffington Post*, February 17, 2023. See also Jack McCordick, "Twitter's Elon Musk Defends Decision to Limit Tweets in Turkey during Tight Presidential Election," *Vanity Fair*, May 14, 2023.

28. Will Saletan, "Unhealthy Fixation," Slate.com, July 15, 2015.

29. John Bohannon, "I Fooled Millions into Thinking Chocolate Helps Weight Loss. Here's How," io9.Gizmodo.com, May 27, 2015.

30. Joshua Foust, "The Birth (and Death) of a Meme: Embedded Reporters Don't Always Get the Story," *Columbia Journalism Review* online, September 10, 2008.

31. Sheila Coronel, Steve Coll, and Derek Kravitz, "*Rolling Stone*'s Investigation: 'A Failure That Was Avoidable,'" *Columbia Journalism Review* online, April 5, 2015.

32. David Marchese, "Jann Wenner Defends His Legacy, and His Generation's," *New York Times* online, September 15, 2023.

33. Emily Yoffe, "The College Rape Overcorrection," Slate.com, December 7, 2014.

34. Quoted in Greg Jaffe, "VA Study Finds More Veterans Committing Suicide," *Washington Post* online, February 1, 2013.

35. Brandon Friedman, "Military Suicides Top Combat Deaths—But Only Because the Wars Are Ending," *TIME* online, January 16, 2013.

Chapter 6

1. Helen Thompson, "Teen Schools Professor on 'No Irish Need Apply' Signs," Smithsonian.com, August 5, 2015.

2. Geoffrey Norman, "Do I Dare to Eat an Egg," *The Weekly Standard* online, March 16, 2015.

3. Peter Whoriskey, "The Science of Skipping Breakfast: How Government Nutritionists May Have Gotten It Wrong," *Washington Post* online, August 10, 2015.

4. Seweryn Bialer and Joan Afferica, "Reagan and Russia," *Foreign Affairs*, Winter 1982–1983, 263.

5. Stephen M. Meyer, "Testimony before the Senate Foreign Relations Committee," in Theodore Karasik, ed., *Russia and Eurasia Armed Forces Review Annual* 15, 1991 (Gulf Breeze, FL: Academic International Press, 1999), 348.

6. Richard Ned Lebow and Thomas Risse Kappen, "Introduction," in Richard Ned Lebow and Thomas Risse Kappen, eds., *International Relations Theory and the End of the Cold War* (New York: Columbia University Press, 1995), 2.

7. See Concepción de León, "Naomi Wolf's Publisher Cancels U.S. Release of 'Outrages,'" *New York Times* online, October 21, 2019, and Jack Grove, "Naomi Wolf's Dissertation—Public at Last," InsiderHigherEd.com, April 28, 2021.

8. The writer Naomi Klein, often mistaken for Wolf, believes that Wolf being caught out, "and then getting shamed, getting mocked and getting pulped," is her "origin story" about her "flip to the pseudopopulist right." See Michelle Goldberg, "Naomi Klein, Naomi Wolf and the Political Upside Down," *New York Times* online, September 4, 2023, and K. J. Yossman, "Naomi Wolf's Claims COVID-19 Vaccine Rollout Was 'Mass Murder' Breached U.K. TV Rules, Sees GB News Network Hauled into Regulatory Meeting," *Variety* online, May 9, 2023.

9. Stephanie Saul, "Stanford President Will Resign after Report Found Flaws in His Research," *New York Times* online, July 19, 2023.

10. Jill Tucker, "Meet the Stanford Student Whose Reporting Led to Resignation of President Marc Tessier-Lavigne," *San Francisco Chronicle* online, July 19, 2023.

11. See, for example, Matt Miller, "Was the Story of *Catch Me If You Can* Frank Abagnale Jr.'s Greatest Con?," *Esquire*, May 5, 2021.

12. W. Ian Lipkin, "Anti-Vaccination Lunacy Won't Stop," *Wall Street Journal* online, April 3, 2016.

13. See Richard Van Noorden, "Political Science's Problem with Research Ethics," *Nature* online, June 29, 2015; Brian C. Martinson, Melissa S. Anderson, and Raymond de Vries, "Scientists Behaving Badly," *Nature* 435, June 9, 2005, 737–738.

14. Ferric C. Fang, R. Grant Steen, and Arturo Casadevall, "Misconduct Accounts for the Majority of Retracted Scientific Publications," *PNAS* 109(42), October 1, 2012.

15. Carl Zimmer, "A Sharp Rise in Retractions Prompts Calls for Reform," *New York Times* online, April 16, 2012.

16. Jeffrey Brainard and Jia You, "What a Massive Database of Retracted Papers Reveals about Science Publishing's 'Death Penalty,'" *Science*, October 25, 2018.

17. Benedict Carey, "Many Psychology Findings Not as Strong as Claimed, Study Says," *New York Times* online, August 27, 2015.

18. Quoted in Rachel Gross, "Psychologists Call Out the Study That Called Out the Field of Psychology," Slate.com, March 3, 2016.

19. Daniel Engber, "Cancer Research Is Broken," Slate.com, April 19, 2016.

20. Quoted in Saul.

21. Garret Epps, "Genuine Christian Scholars Smack Down an Unruly Colleague," *Atlantic* online, August 10, 2012.

22. "Actresses' Role in Farm Issue Stirs Criticism," *Los Angeles Times* online archive, May 3, 1985.

23. Jessica Goldstein, "Is Gwyneth Paltrow Wrong about Everything? This Scientist Thinks So," ThinkProgress.com, April 21, 2016.

24. Alexandra Petri, "Dr. Carson, This Is Not Brain Surgery," *Washington Post* online, November 5, 2015.

25. This account is drawn from Paul Offit, "The Vitamin Myth: Why We Think We Need Supplements," *Atlantic* online, July 19, 2013.

26. Helen Caldicott, *Missile Envy* (New York: Bantam, 1985), 235; Helen Caldicott, *If You Love This Planet* (New York: W. W. Norton, 1992), 156.

27. There is a claim that has circulated in various articles about Criswell over the years that he got one prediction within shouting distance of something like creepy accuracy. He apparently told the television host Jack Paar in March 1963 that President Kennedy would not run for reelection in 1964 because

of something that would happen to him in November 1963. This, however, might yet be an urban legend, at least until someone turns up an old videotape or kinescope (if any exists).

28. Carl Bialik, "Most Pollsters Say Their Reputations Have Worsened," FiveThirtyEight.com, December 28, 2015.

29. Andrew Fischer, "Polls Were Great in 2022. Can They Repeat Their Success in 2024?" *New York Times* online, July 12, 2023.

30. Clive Thompson, "Can Game Theory Predict When Iran Will Get the Bomb?" *New York Times Magazine* online, August 12, 2009.

31. Nassim Nicholas Taleb, *The Black Swan* (New York: Random House, 2010), xxiv–xxv.

32. Philip E. Tetlock, *Expert Political Judgment* (Princeton, NJ: Princeton University Press, 2005), 20.

33. Ibid., 20.

34. James Surowiecki, *The Wisdom of Crowds* (New York: Anchor, 2005), 31.

35. Tetlock, *Expert Political Judgment*, 21.

36. See ibid., 101–103.

37. See, for example, Tina Nguyen, "How Nate Silver Failed to Predict Trump," *Vanity Fair*, February 1, 2016.

38. Noah Rothman, "Why They Think Trump Can Win in Nov?," *Commentary* online, April 27, 2016.

39. Tetlock, *Expert Political Judgment*, 23.

40. Francis Gavin, "Is Being Wrong So Bad?" *Texas National Security Review* 5(3), Fall 2023, 3.

Chapter 7

1. It is possible that the American share was less of the global total due to poor reporting from countries such as Russia, but the COVID Crisis Group, a nonpartisan study group of more than thirty medical and policy experts, used Western Europe as the baseline for comparison to the United States and still found the American case and death rates higher than might have been expected in an advanced nation. See The COVID Crisis Group, *Lessons from the COVID War* (New York: Public Affairs, 2023), 10.

2. Derek Beres, Matthew Remski, and Julian Walker, *Conspirituality: How New Age Conspiracy Theories Became a Health Threat* (New York: Public Affairs, 2023), TK.

3. See Charlotte Ward and David Voas, "The Emergence of Conspirituality," *Journal of Contemporary Religion* 26(1), 2011, 103.

4. Eva Wiseman, "The Dark Side of Wellness: The Overlap between Spiritual Thinking and Far-Right Conspiracies," *The Guardian* online, October 17, 2021.

5. Quoted in Tom Nichols, *Our Own Worst Enemy: The Assault from Within on Modern Democracy* (New York: Oxford University Press, 2021), 103–104.
6. Kaitlyn Tiffany, "How Telling People to Die Became Normal," *The Atlantic* online, September 5, 2023.
7. See Maggie Haberman, "Trade Adviser Warned White House in January of Risks of a Pandemic," *New York Times* online, April 6, 2020, and *Confidence Man* (New York: Penguin, 2023), 414.
8. Quoted in Bob Woodward, *Rage* (New York: Simon & Schuster, 2020), xiii.
9. See COVID Crisis Group, *Lessons from the COVID War*, 244–252.
10. Rebecca Ballhaus and Stephanie Armour, "Health Chief's Early Missteps Set Back Coronavirus Response," *Wall Street Journal* online, April 22, 2020.
11. Jonathan Chait, "Where Is the Republican Soul-Searching for Getting COVID Wrong?," *New York Magazine* online, May 2, 2023.
12. See Bob Woodward, *Rage*. Audio of the Woorward interview is available online; see Robert Costa and Philip Rucker, "Woodward book: Trump says he knew coronavirus was 'deadly' and worse than the flu while intentionally misleading Americans," *The Washington Post* online, September 9, 2020.
13. Ballhaus and Armour, "Health Chief's Early Missteps."
14. The administration took pains to note that Pence and Kushner were in contact and coordinating, but Kushner clearly had the upper hand. See Adam Cancryn and Dan Diamond, "Behind the scenes, Kushner takes charge of coronavirus response," *Politico*, April 1, 2020, and COVID Crisis Group, 123.
15. COVID Crisis Group, 208.
16. The press conferences were, in general, disastrous both from a political and scientific perspective. See Libby Cathey, "9 Controversial Moments That Led Trump to Stop His White House Coronavirus Briefings," *ABC News* online, July 21, 2020.
17. Quoted in Meredith McGraw and Sam Stein, "It's Been Exactly One Year since Trump Suggested Injecting Bleach. We've Never Been the Same," *Politico*, April 23, 2021.
18. Ibid.
19. Ibid.
20. Lauren Aratani, "Trump Says Briefings 'Not Worth the Effort' Amid Fallout from Disinfectant Comments," *The Guardian* online, April 25, 2020.
21. Office of the New York State Comptroller, "DiNapoli: State's Pandemic Response to Nursing Homes Hindered by Ill-Prepared State Agency," March 15, 2022.
22. The full New York State Assembly report is available online. "Read the New York State Assembly Report on Andrew Cuomo's Impeachment Investigation," *New York Times* online, November 22, 2021.

23. See Joe Pompeo, "Inside the Viral Spread of a Coronavirus Origin Theory," *Vanity Fair* online, April 10, 2020; the article contains a link to video of the Cotton segment with Bartiromo.

24. The original tweet is at https://twitter.com/SenTomCotton/status/1229 202134048133126?s=20.

25. See Sheryl Gay Stolberg and Benjamin Mueller, "Lab Leak or Not? How Politics Shaped the Battle over Covid's Origin," *New York Times* online, March 19, 2023. Both sides sloppily used "lab leak" to mean several possibilities; see Daniel Engber, "The Republican Lab-Leak Circus Makes One Important Point: 'Lab Leak' Has Too Many Meanings," *The Atlantic* online, July 12, 2023.

26. David Quammen, "The Ongoing Mystery of Covid's Origin," *New York Times Magazine* online, July 25, 2023.

27. Haberman, *Confidence Man*, 459–460.

28. Quoted in Gabriel Sherman, "Inside Rupert Murdoch's Succession Drama," *Vanity Fair* online, May 2023.

29. COVID Crisis Group, *Lessons from the COVID War*, 7.

30. Zeynep Tufekci, "Why Did It Take So Long to Accept the Facts about Covid?," *New York Times* online, May 7, 2021.

31. COVID Crisis Group, *Lessons from the COVID War*, 174–178.

32. As the authors of *Conspirituality* so aptly put it: "While well-meaning researchers and scientists were constantly working to keep up with the evolving science and offer the best assessments they could with the evidence at hand, social media was working in binaries to punish anything perceived as flip-flopping." Beres, Remski, and Walker, *Conspirituality*, 7.

33. Quoted in Veronica Stracqualursi, "Fauci Says He Wears a Mask to Be a Symbol of What 'You Should Be Doing,'" CNN.com, May 27, 2020.

34. Quoted in COVID Crisis Group, *Lessons from the COVID War*, 177. Arkansas Governor Asa Hutchinson was a notable exception, calling masks "the uniform of a responsible citizen." Hutchinson ran against Trump for the 2024 Republican presidential nomination and never managed to poll beyond single digits.

35. I recall a moment in late 2021 when I knew the mask mandates would collapse and probably never return. I was in a New England college town with a very liberal city government and very strict mask mandates, and I went to a recently reopened restaurant. I had to wear a mask from the door to the host station, after which I was seated at the bar shoulder to shoulder with other patrons— where we were all allowed to take our masks off. As one young college student said to another at the bar: "This is kind of stupid, isn't it?" See Tufekci and Dylan Scott, "The Most Consistently Botched Part of the US Pandemic Response," *Vox*, January 14, 2022.

36. In an infamous (and callous) May 2020 social media eruption, conservative writer Bethany Mandel tweeted: "You can call me a Grandma killer. I'm not

sacrificing my home, food on the table, all of our docs and dentists, every form of pleasure (museums, zoos, restaurants), all my kids' teachers in order to make other people comfortable. If you want to stay locked down, do. I'm not." This was six months before any vaccines were available and the US COVID death toll passed the 100,000 mark. Charlie Nash, "Conservative Commentator Bethany Mandel Trends on Twitter after 'Grandma Killer' Coronavirus Comments," Mediate.com, May 6, 2020.

37. Emma Green, "The Liberals Who Can't Quit Lockdown," *The Atlantic* online, May 4, 2021.

38. David Zweig, "The School That Couldn't Quit Covid," *The Free Press* (thefp. com), April 10, 2023.

39. COVID Crisis Group, *Lessons from the COVID War*, 159.

40. Jonathan Chait, "Democrats Learned from Their Covid Mistakes. Republicans Didn't." *New York Magazine* online, July 24, 2023.

41. Jonathan Mahler, "'The Most Dangerous Person in the World Is Randi Weingarten,'" *New York Times Magazine* online, April 28, 2023.

42. Franklin Foer, *The Last Politician: Inside Joe Biden's White House and the Struggle for America's Future* (New York: Penguin, 2023), 69–70.

43. Quoted in Rashaan Ayesh, "Fauci: 'Very Concerned' about Spread of Coronavirus amid George Floyd Protests," *Axios.com*, June 6, 2020.

44. "Dr. Fauci and Rep. Jordan Have a Tense Exchange over Limiting Protests Because of the Coronavirus," Yahoo News, July 31, 2020.

45. Mallory Simon, "Over 1,000 Health Professionals Sign a Letter Saying, Don't Shut Down Protests Using Coronavirus Concerns as an Excuse," CNN.com, June 5, 2020.

46. Quoted in Rachel Weiner, "Political and Health Leaders' Embrace of Floyd Protests Fuels Debate over Coronavirus Restrictions," *Washington Post* online, June 11, 2020.

47. Dan Diamond, "Suddenly, Public Health Officials Say Social Justice Matters More than Social Distance," *Politico.com*, June 4, 2020.

48. Quoted in Bryan Walsh and Alison Snyder, "Scientists Caught between Pandemic and Protests," *Axios.com*, June 10, 2020.

49. Sharon LaFraniere and Noah Weiland, "Walensky, Citing Botched Pandemic Response, Calls for C.D.C. Reorganization," *New York Times* online, August 17, 2022.

50. COVID Crisis Group, *Lessons from the COVID War*, 64–65.

51. The *New York Times* keeps an online tracker of vaccination rates at "See How Vaccinations Are Going in Your County and State," https://www.nytimes. com/interactive/2020/us/covid-19-vaccine-doses.html; for Canada, see https://health-infobase.canada.ca/covid-19/vaccination-coverage/.

52. Thomas Bollyky et al., "Assessing COVID-19 Pandemic Policies and Behaviours and Their Economic and Educational Trade-offs across US States

from Jan 1, 2020, to July 31, 2022: An Observational Analysis," *The Lancet* 401(10385), April 22, 2023.

53. Ibid. Despite the arguments over mitigation measures, the CFR study found that "only vaccine coverage had a strong association with the state-by-state variation."

54. For example, convicted January 6 rioter Alan Hostetter (a former police officer) "became active in Southern California right-wing politics in 2020 through opposition to coronavirus mitigation measures and Black Lives Matter demonstrations." See Rachel Weiner and Spencer S. Hsu, "Former Police Chief Convicted after Defending Self with False Jan. 6 Claims," *Washington Post* online, July 13, 2023.

55. "Toplines: July 2023 Times/Siena Poll of the Likely Republican Primary Electorate," *New York Times* online, July 31, 2023.

56. Christine Chung and Carly Olson, "The Pandemic Has Eroded Americans' Trust in Experts and Elected Leaders Alike, a Survey Finds," *New York Times* online, July 7, 2022.

57. Kennedy in 2023 said he was "proud" to have Trump's support. See Nicholas Kerr, "Robert Kennedy Jr.'s Presidential Campaign Attracts GOP-Friendly Donors, Few Celebs," July 17, 2023, and Nathaniel Rakich, "If RFK Jr. Wants to Be President, He's Running in the Wrong Primary," *FiveThirtyEight.com*, August 4, 2023.

58. Nicholas Nehamas, "Covid Hero or 'Lockdown Ron'? DeSantis and Trump Renew Pandemic Politics," *New York Times* online, September 10, 2023.

59. See Sharon LaFraniere, Patricia Mazzei. and Albert Sun, "The Steep Cost of Ron DeSantis's Vaccine Turnabout," *New York Times* online, July 22, 2023.

60. Florida, with 7 percent of the nation's population, had 14 percent of COVID deaths from July to October 2021. See ibid.

61. Arek Sarkissian, "Florida Surgeon General Altered Key Findings in Study on Covid-19 Vaccine Safety," *Politico.com*, April 24, 2023.

62. Kendra Nichols, "DeSantis Discourages Latest Covid Boosters, Contradicting Federal Guidance," *Washington Post* online, September 14, 2023.

Conclusion

1. See James Traub, "First, They Came for the Experts," *Foreign Policy*, July 7, 2016.

2. Quoted in Michael Deacon, "Michael Gove's Guide to Britain's Greatest Enemy . . . the Experts," *Telegraph* online, June 10, 2016.

3. Jonathan Freedland, "With Even Leavers Regretting Brexit, There's One Path Back to Rejoining the EU," *The Guardian* online, June 23, 2023.

4. See "As Britons Grow More Unhappy with Brexit, What Happens Next?," *The Economist* online, June 27, 2023, and "'Bregret'? Many Brits Are Suffering from Brexit Regret," CNBC.com, March 3, 2023.

5. Quoted in Nick Gass, "Trump: 'The Experts Are Terrible,'" Politico.com, April 4, 2016.

6. The Republicans posted the Jordan video on the House GOP Judiciary committee's account: https://x.com/JudiciaryGOP/status/1651229152349913 088?s=20.

7. David Dunning, "The Psychological Quirk That Explains Why You Love Donald Trump," Politico.com, May 25, 2016.

8. Arthur Brooks, "Parasocial Relationships Are Just Imaginary Friends for Adults," *The Atlantic* online, April 6, 2023.

9. David Samuels, "The Aspiring Novelist Who Became Obama's Foreign-Policy Guru," *New York Times Sunday Magazine* online, May 5, 2016.

10. I was an opponent of the deal, but once it was in force, I was an opponent of simply wrecking a flawed but workable deal that the United States had pledged to honor. See Jane Darby Menton, "What Most People Get Wrong about the Iran Nuclear Deal," *ForeignPolicy.com*, May 7, 2023.

11. For my reasoning on this issue, see Tom Nichols, "Mourning the INF Treaty," *Foreign Affairs* online, March 4, 2019.

12. A classic episode of the original *Star Trek* series, first aired in 1968, featured a misguided attempt by a well-meaning professor—of course—to base an entire planet on the Nazi experience. It all ends in disaster, but the dying professor still calls Nazi Germany "the most efficient state Earth ever knew," with the show's voice of reason, Mr. Spock, chiming in to say, "Quite true." In reality, Nazi Germany was deeply corrupt and inefficient, and many of its leading scientists and intellectuals fled the country after 1933. Many Americans, however, still believe in the myth of Nazi efficiency.

13. Susan Jacoby, "The Dumbing of America," *Washington Post* online, February 17, 2008.

14. Friedrich Hayek, *The Constitution of Liberty: The Definitive Edition* (Chicago: University of Chicago Press, 2011), 378.

15. See Andrew Kaczynski, "Ron DeSantis Praised Anthony Fauci for Covid Response in Spring 2020 for 'Really Doing a Good Job,'" CNN.com, June 1, 2023, and Dylan Abad, "DeSantis: Fauci a 'Little Elf' That Should Be Chucked 'across the Potomac,'" WFLA.com, August 25, 2022. See also Isaac Stanley-Becker, Yasmeen Abutaleb. and Devlin Barrett, "Anthony Fauci's Security Is Stepped up as Doctor and Face of U.S. Coronavirus Response Receives Threats," *Washington Post* online, April 1, 2020.

16. Evan Thomas, "Why We Need a Foreign Policy Elite," *New York Times* online, May 8, 2016.

17. Andrew Bacevich, "Rationalizing Lunacy: The Intellectual as Servant of the State," *Huffington Post*, May 8, 2015.
18. Philip E. Tetlock, *Expert Political Judgment* (Princeton, NJ: Princeton University Press, 2005), 231–232.
19. Malcolm Gladwell, "Small Change: Why the Revolution Will Not Be Tweeted," *New Yorker*, October 4, 2010.
20. Ilya Somin, "Political Ignorance in America," in Mark Bauerlein and Adam Bellow, eds., *The State of the American Mind* (West Conshohocken, PA: Templeton, 2015), 166.
21. Neetzan Zimmerman, "Kimmel Fools Hillary Supporters into Backing Trump's Tax Plan," *The Hill*, September 30, 2015.
22. Ariel Edwards-Levy, "Republicans Like Obama's Ideas Better When They Think They're Donald Trump's," *Huffpost Politics*, September 1, 2015.
23. Nick Saffran, "Wipe That Grin Off Your Smug Faces, Progressive Pollsters," TheFederalist.com, December 29, 2015.
24. Derek Kohler, "Why People Are Confused about What Experts Really Think," *New York Times* online, February 14, 2016.
25. Jacoby, "Dumbing of America."
26. A 2022 poll by Morning Consult found that only 34 percent of Americans could locate Ukraine—the largest nation entirely in Europe—on a map. This finding was an improvement over 2014, when only 1 in 6 could spot Ukraine; those the least likely to know where it was, however, were the most eager to intervene against Russia's seizure of Crimea. See
27. C. S. Lewis, *The Screwtape Letters with Screwtape Proposes a Toast* (New York: Image, 1981), 136–139 (emphases in the original).
28. José Ortega y Gasset, *The Revolt of the Masses* (New York: W. W. Norton, 1993), 18.
29. See Daniel Libit, "How the Expert Class Got Trumped and Berned," CNBC.com, May 12, 2016; and Julie Beck, "Americans Believe in Science, Just Not Its Findings," *Atlantic* online, January 29, 2015.
30. James Traub, "It's Time for the Elites to Rise Up against the Ignorant Masses," *Foreign Policy*, June 28, 2016.

INDEX

For the benefit of digital users, indexed terms that span two pages (e.g., 52–53) may, on occasion, appear on only one of those pages.